TALES
of the
WEIRD

Tom Slemen

The Tom Slemen Press

Copyright © 2013 Tom Slemen

All rights reserved.

ISBN-10: 1503023044
ISBN-13: **978-1503023048**

DEDICATION

This book is dedicated to a reader I sadly never got to meet - Graham Heyes (1973-2008). Remembered with love by parents Anne and Malcolm, brother Robert, sister Sarah and Gran Marjorie.

CONTENTS

Introduction	1
The Secret Zoo	10
Tardis Reports	16
Lost in a Stockroom	35
Into the Tapestry	44
A Scottish Werewolf	49
Henri	55
The Scarlet Room	59
The House in the Park	65
Spirit Aunts	71
French Toast	76
Blackpool's Phantom Tsunami	82
Grandfather Werewolf	85

The Indestructible Arthur Brown	90
It Happened on Halloween	94
Operation Firestone	123
A Spooky Selection Box	127
Reaper Reports	150
I Never Believed in Ghosts Until…	160
Strange Hallucinations	174
The Soul Mates Phenomenon	195
Alter Egos	205
The Offer	217
Paranormal Postal Mysteries	220
Some Modern Vampires	223
The Orgisher	236
Tales of the Evil Eye	250
A Woman of Many Parts	272
An Evil Royal Rapist	295

INTRODUCTION

For many years I've delved into the fascinating subject of the supernatural, and this book is the result of a fraction of the cases I've either investigated at first hand or researched after some tip-off from the public, many of whom read my books or listen to the occasional radio programmes I have been involved in. The process of researching a story is very rewarding sometimes, especially when pieces of information from different witnesses – who are usually not known to one another – fit together like some paranormal jigsaw puzzle. Take the case of "Mrs Bendy" for example. I was talking about local ghosts on a Merseyside radio programme some years ago and an elderly woman named Mona Williams phoned me on air to tell of a very strange entity which terrorised her and her sister Jane at a house on Liverpool's Queens Drive in Walton in the 1930s. Mona was seven at the time and her sister Jane was five, and one warm summer evening at 11pm, while their father was working the late shift at a factory, Mona's mother went into the back garden to talk to her neighbour, a Mrs Wilson, over the fence. The two women often gossiped like this on such lazy summer nights. On this humid night, little Mona Williams woke up, and, unable to get back to sleep, she shouted for her mother to fetch her a glass of water, but never received an answer because her mother was, of course 'jangling' in the back garden with Mrs Wilson. Mona therefore got up out of her bed and walked onto the landing, headed for the kitchen downstairs to get a glass of water. Her younger sister Jane woke up and asked her where she was going, and Mona told her to stay in the room while she got a glass of water, but Jane said she wanted to go with her, so Mona acted the part of the big sister and held Jane's hand as they went down the stairs. Upon reaching the bottom of the stairs, the flap of the letterbox in the front door opened, and a voice that sounded like that of an old woman said, 'Hello little girls, can you let me in?'

'I can't,' Mona told the stranger, 'I'll have to ask me Mam first.'

'But I live here, little one,' said the old lady, and her voice seemed to increase in pitch, almost to a yelp as she added: 'Let me in?'

'I can't,' Mona told her, and she looked about the darkened hallway, wondering where her mother was. The only illumination was coming from the gaslight in the kitchen. 'Mam! Mam! Where are you?' Mona shouted.

'Let me in,' said the voice, going even higher in pitch.

'I can't! Mam!' Mona backed away from the front door as an oddly-coloured hand slid through the letterbox. It reminded her of the white putty her father had used to mend a pane of glass in the greenhouse.

'Let me in you little rascal,' said the night visitor.

All of a sudden, something resembling (to Mona's childish mind, anyway) an iced bun, made of that same putty-like substance, oozed through the letterbox, and once it emerged a few inches, it seemed to slowly inflate.

'What's that, Mona?' Jane asked, mesmerised by the thing coming through the rectangular hole in the door.

Mona had a bad feeling about the peculiar proceedings and she said, 'Come on Jane!' And backed away all the way to the kitchen door.

That doughy material bulged to form a head – the head of a woman with a heavily wrinkled face and huge black eyeballs.

Jane started to cry at the unearthly sight.

'Let me in, I do live here!' said the eerie pallid head, and then more of the material the entity was made from squeezed through and formed a bare foot, and that foot moved downwards as the shin that it was attached to grew and became elongated in a weird linear motion that reminded Mona of those sausage-shaped balloons when they are inflated. Mona could see two small palms waving about on the other side of the door through the panes of frosted glass, and these palms pressed on the glass as if the 'clay' lady was trying to steady herself.

'Oh, I'm stuck!' said the creepy entity, and began to laugh. 'Will one of you girls help pull me through?'

Mona yanked Jane backwards as she almost fell into

the kitchen. She ran across the chequerboard tiles and out into the back garden where her mum was gabbing away as she smoked a Woodbine cigarette.

'Mam!' Mona screamed, giving Mrs Williams quite a start. Jane ran to her mother and hid under her skirt.

'What in God's name is going on? What are you two doing out of bed, eh?' Mrs Williams was annoyed at the interruption in her gossiping.

'There's an old woman and she's coming through the letterbox!' Mona gasped, short of breath because she was so terrified, and she kept looking at the kitchen door in case the thing followed her into the garden.

'I won't be a minute,' Mrs Williams told her neighbour, 'these two are bleedin' nuisances.'

Mrs Williams grappled with a hysterical Jane under her skirt and picked her up, but the little girl screeched and kicked at her mother and looked in terror at the kitchen, thinking the same as Mona – that the weird 'putty lady' would come and get her.

When Mrs Williams went into the kitchen, she said to Jane, 'See? There's nobody there! Has that Mona been scaring you with silly stories?'

Jane threw up all over her mum's shoulder with fear, and when Mrs Williams turned the air blue with profanities, she noticed Mona had not come into the kitchen with her. The child was hiding in the bushes in the garden, literally wetting herself.

When Mrs Williams went into the hallway, she found the letterbox flap open, and there was a strong sickly sweet smell hanging in the air. For the next three nights, she and her husband had to let the girls sleep with them because they refused to sleep in their room. Something had obviously scared them, but what?

A Mrs Jones, a spinster who lived a few doors down from the Williams family, said that on a number of occasions over the years she had seen something which resembled a ball of white mist moving about outside the house the Williams family lived in. She had not mentioned it to anyone in case they thought she was seeing things. The thing had always put in an appearance after dark.

That case of the 'Putty Woman' was filed away in my vast collection of ghost stories and other tales of the weird passed on to me by members of the public, and then, about three years afterwards, a solider named Ethan who had served in Afghanistan contacted me via email and asked if I had any reports of ghosts on Queens Drive in Walton. He wrote: 'The reason I'm asking is because on November 5 1990, when I was fifteen, I was coming down the stairs with a box of fireworks that I had saved up for weeks to buy, and I was looking forward to letting them off in my best mate's garden, when I noticed something sticking out the letterbox of the front door.' Ethan thought it was a rolled-up evening newspaper [such as the *Liverpool Echo*] at first which had just been delivered, but as he reached the bottom of the steps, he saw that the object was an arm with a small hand at the end of it. This hand started to grow before Ethan's startled eyes as the arm moved about, and for a moment he thought it was his friend Gary playing some late Halloween trick on him, and Ethan was about to open the door to catch him – when a weird-looking face appeared at the semi-circular window in the door. It was the white wrinkled face of an evil-looking old woman. It was not a mask, but a real face, and the mouth was opening and closing and he could hear a faint high-pitched voice on the outside of the door. It sounded as if the woman, or whatever she was, was cussing. The door then rattled violently as if someone was shaking it and a second small hand, the size if a baby's hand, came through the letterbox.

Ethan ran into the living room and found it empty. His mother and father had gone to a neighbour's house a few doors down to see their fireworks being let off for Guy Fawkes Night. Ethan was that scared, he ditched the tin or fireworks, ran into the back garden and climbed over the fence to get away. He told his mother and father and his best mate what had happened but they all said it had just been someone with a mask messing about. Ethan never saw the bizarre entity again but lived in mortal fear of encountering it again for many years.

When I enquired as to the address he had lived at on Queens Drive at the time, Ethan supplied me with the number of the house – and it turned out that it was the very same house where Mona Williams and her sister had encountered the Putty Woman nearly seventy years before. As if this wasn't a vindication of something truly sinister which had gone on at the address on Queens Drive, I subsequently received more matching stories about the Putty Woman – only these newly-discovered witnesses called her Mrs Bendy. In the 1950s, the Williams family had left their house on Queens Drive and moved to the West Derby district, and the Griffiths family took up residency at the house around 1953. Around Halloween that year, a 16-year-old girl named Carol Jones was hired to babysit the two young children of the Griffiths one evening, and around 9pm, there was a number of faint knocks at the door of the house. Carol had just put the children to bed, and went to see who it was. The Griffiths had told the girl not to open the door to anyone who might call, and that they would let themselves in with the key when they returned. Carol came down the stairs and saw someone putting what she thought was a white gloved hand through the letterbox. 'Let me in, I live here!' said a female voice, but Carol could not tell (as the other witnesses such as Ethan and Mona had) if the caller was elderly from her voice.

Recalling the instructions of the Griffiths not to admit anyone into the house in their absence, Carol tried to explain that she was not allowed to open the door.

'But I live here, I *live* here, girl!' she cried, and then had proceeded to squeeze her head and limbs through the letterbox. Carol was in her seventies when she gave this account of the encounter with Mrs Bendy, and as she related the details of an unexplained incident which had occurred neary sixty years before, I noted the goosebumps rising on her arms as she must have relived the terrifying experience. 'Her head was white, and the only way I can explain the way it came through that letterbox is the way a big lump of soft white playdoh or plasticine would if you shoved it hard enough through a rectangular gap which measured about eight-and-a-half inches by three inches. And one of her arms also started to squeeze through as I ran into the kitchen and looked desperately for the keys to the door which led into the garden. I finally found the key and I went into the garden and climbed over a fence where a neighbour's dog almost savaged me. I ran and ran and bumped into a policeman on Cherry Lane, and I could hardly speak. I told him about the woman coming through the letterbox, and the strangest thing happened; he said, "On Queens Drive?" as if he had heard about this thing before. He wanted me to go back with him to the house but I went hysterical and so he took me to a colleague who must have been on another beat, and then he went to the house. He found the kitchen door in the back garden open and he went into the house and found the children crying upstairs. There was no sign of the thing that had started to squeeze through the letterbox. I never babysat for the Griffiths family again.'

Everyone said the girl had imagined the entity because it was impossible for any person to squeeze themselves through a letterbox, but Carol had terrible nightmares about the entity for years. Two more babysitters allegedly witnessed the same weird apparition of the (ectoplasmic?) old lady who could somehow squeeze through the letterbox but not quite get herself entirely through the door, and the Griffiths even had their house blessed by a priest, but "Mrs Bendy" continued to ooze herself through the letterbox on various occasions right up to the time when Ethan lived at the address.

Mrs Bendy is typical of some of the entities mentioned in this book, and while some think she might be a mischievous re-enactment ghost, going through the same behaviour (as some apparitions do) I believe that some mysterious mind manipulator might equally be at work; perhaps an higher intelligence that is conducting an experiment in behavioural psychology on young minds. There is something almost *staged* about these cases, many of which are documented in this book. Just who or what is behind these experiments remains a mystery to me, but perhaps the same hypothetical intelligence behind Mrs Bendy and other apparently paranormal entities is also responsible for the reports of aliens, angels, Bigfoot, demons, fairies, ghosts and other mysterious denizens that are glimpsed on the outlands of our known world.

Tom Slemen

THE SECRET ZOO

In 2007, an elderly woman named Hilary told me a fascinating story about a series of supernatural incidents which took place in the summer of 1969 at a shop run by her late husband Jack. The shop was in the West Derby area of Liverpool and sold everything from shoelaces and cigarettes to soap powder and breakfast cereals, and was very typical of the 'Open All Hours' kind of shops of that era that were once found on every street corner before the widespread proliferation of supermarkets. Jack, aged 56 (but looking much older) and 32-year-old Hilary lived in one of the five rooms above the shop, and, in June 1969, Hilary hit on the idea of letting three of the rooms out to lodgers to bring in an extra bit of money, and so, Jack decorated the rooms and put notices advertising their availability in his shop window. One room went within days to a woman in her seventies named Esther, and a week after this, a quiet bachelor in his early forties named Stan took another room. The third room was eventually taken by Mrs Jackson, a beautiful Geordie woman who looked as if she was in her late twenties or early thirties, and she had her son with her, an unusually quiet boy of five years of age named Andy. Mrs Jackson explained that she had recently split with her husband and only intended to live over the shop until she was offered a house by the council. Jack was not at all keen on having a child living on the premises as he thought he might be a bit too noisy, but the boy – like his mother – was no trouble at all and Mrs Jackson paid her rent as regular as clockwork. Mrs Jackson didn't work and yet she always seemed to have money, and as much as Hilary tried, she could not elicit from her lodger just how she *did* make a living. Jack speculated that she might have been left money by a relative in a will. Old Esther took a liking to Andy and often bought him sweets, and even Stan the bachelor would pat the boy on the head whenever he passed him and his mum on the stairs going to and from his flat.

One scorching summer's day in early July that year, Jack was leaning on the counter, daydreaming as he thought back to the summers he had enjoyed as a child in the early 1920s, when suddenly he saw something greyish walk into the shop out the corner of his eye. Jack thought he was dreaming for a moment, because a huge male lion had just strolled into his shop, and this fearsome animal was of a bizarre grey colour. The beast growled, as it looked about, and the vibrations from that rumbling snarl vibrated through Jack's chest. The out-of-place predatory big cat was facing away from him – it hadn't seen Jack yet. Jack turned slowly and as he headed for the doorway to the stockroom, he felt icy shivers run down his spine, and expected the lion to come leaping over the counter at him. He closed the door behind him and stacked milk and lemonade crates against that door. He listened, and about five minutes afterwards he heard a little girl – it was 8-year-old Lucy from around the corner!

'Jack? Are you there?' she was shouting.

Jack removed some of the crates and opened the door an inch to see Lucy's face peering over the counter at him. 'Jack, can I have a quarter of erm -'

'Is the lion still there?' Jack asked, wiping sweat from his eyelids.

Lucy looked about and smiled, thinking it was some joke or a game. She shrugged.

Jack stepped out of the stockroom, leaned forward and looked over the glass top of the counter, then glanced at the shop doorway. 'Lucy, did you see a big grey cat in here just then love?'

'No Jack,' came the reply.

'It must have left just before you came in!' Jack reasoned and he lifted the hinged door of the wooden counter which was at a right angle to the glass one and he went out of the shop and looked up and down the sunny street.

The monochrome cat had gone.

Hilary listened to Jack's account of the incident and flippantly asked if the lion's name was Parsley (after a Lion puppet character which was on the telly at the time in a children's serial called *The Herbs*), but Jack began to shout and bawl and his wife realised he really had seen something strange. This was the first time he had shouted at her in their married life.

Two days after this, an old man named Albert was buying ice cream blocks at the shop when both he and Jack saw some sort of small tailed monkey jumping from a high shelf onto the neon light fittings of the shop – and this monkey was also of the same grey colour as that lion. Albert laughed and asked Jack how long he'd had the little primate and flabbergasted Jack gasped, 'Where did that come from?'

Next thing that monkey had vanished.

'It – It's gone,' Jack gasped, turning back to face his elderly customer.

'They say we descended from monkeys, don't they?' old Albert rambled, and looked about the shop, saying, 'You better watch he doesn't get out; the cars are going faster in this street. Everyone's in such a damn hurry nowadays.'

Jack was lost words and he looked at the neon light hanging from a chain above and saw it was still swaying.

The monochromatic lion was later seen by many in the area prowling alleyways, and Hilary almost fainted when the colourless cat brushed past her on the stairs to her flat at the shop one evening. Then a curious discovery was made. Hilary visited Mrs Jackson to collect the rent one morning and noticed little Andy's childish sketches of a lion, a monkey and other exotic animals in a drawing book – as well as a number of black and white photographs of a lion in a magazine. Mrs Jackson explained that Andy loved wild animals and hoped to become a zoo keeper one day. When Hilary mentioned the strange grey lion and monkey that had been seen in the house as well as outside, Mrs Jackson seemed lost for words, and she went very pale and looked rather shocked. The mystery then deepened when two well-dressed men visited Jack at his shop and made enquiries about Mrs Jackson and her son.

Jack asked the men to identify themselves and they

claimed to be Special Branch officers, and each produced wallets featuring their mugshots on cards but the print on the cards was too small to make out.

'What's she done?' Jack asked, naturally worried.

'We can't say, it's classified,' one of the officers replied, 'but you'll have to take us to Mrs Jackson's room.'

'Mrs Jackson's out,' Jack remembered, and one of the Special Branch men said he'd still like to see the room.

Jack called for Hilary and after telling her who the visitors were, he told his wife to stay behind the counter while he took the men up to Mrs Jackson's room. As he took the men up the stairs, Jack explained that he did not have a spare key to his tenant's room, but one of the officers told him that they had a 'special key' that would allow them entry. Jack knocked at Mrs Jackson's door, just in case she was in, but received no reply, and then one of the officers produced some sort of key which he fiddled with before inserting it into the keyhole. He turned this key and the lock clicked. The second officer then gave Jack the fright of his life by producing a pistol. The officers barged into the room, and then told Jack he would have to wait outside.

Jack wondered if the duo were really Special Branch men, and so he sneaked downstairs and voiced his suspicion to Hilary, and she left the shop to go and telephone the police from a public call box, just to see if the visitors were bona fide Special Branch men. Hilary received a visit from a police patrol car about fifteen minutes later but by then the men had gone. A policeman told her that enquiries had been made and as far as anyone knew, no officers from Special Branch were investigating any woman in Liverpool. To make matters even more mysterious, Mrs Jackson didn't return to her flat over Jack's shop, and never called to even collect her own clothes or the clothing she had recently bought for her son.

Moreover, the weird grey lion and the mischievous monochrome monkey were seen no more. Hilary wondered if Andy had been some 'special child' who perhaps had the gift of somehow projecting and producing realistic images of the animals he loved through some unearthly power. The child had only access to black and white images of the animals in that magazine, and he and his mother had an old black and white television set that Jack had given them, so perhaps the boy drew on the monochrome images of the lions and monkey he had seen on TV shows such a *Animal Magic* to project his "psychic holograms". The case is a real puzzler.

TARDIS REPORTS

You might think you're sitting still as you read this book, but you and the other 7 billion people of the world are hurtling through space at 2.7 million MPH as the Earth orbits the sun, whilst the sun circles the galaxy at 0.004 per cent of the speed of light. You're not aware of this spatial motion because your mind is too wrapped up in your day to day cares and concerns, and you're probably as equally unaware of the scale of time in your universe too. The present estimate for the age of the universe is 13.7 billion years. Comparing your lifetime to the age of the universe has been calculated as the longest time you can hold your breath compared to your lifetime. In other words, one breath is to one lifetime what one lifetime is to the age of universe. Time, then, is as vast as space, and we are just talking about 'time past'; Einstein revealed that the future is also out there, but we are very small and short-lived in this Cosmos and don't realise this, just as we were once ignorant of the world's curved surface (because we are 10 million times smaller than the planet). Astronomers presently estimate that there are 100 billion habitable Earth-like planets in the Milky Way, and 50 sextillion in the universe, which means it's very likely that intelligent life has visited the earth in the past, and that future visitations are also highly likely. So much for visitors from the vast reaches of space – but how about visitors from the mind-boggling expanses of time? Could the people who eventually achieve time travel in the future somehow 'retrograde' into the past ages and visit us? I believe these hypothetical time-travellers from the future can visit us, and I have some strange cases in my files about mysterious entities who seem to be real-life Timelords who have visited our era and other ages in the past, and I even have reports of someone from elsewhere meddling with history. A former policeman named Bill once told me the following strange story after listening to my discussion about timeslips on the Billy Butler Show on BBC Radio Merseyside a few years back. In the summer of 1955, a hackney cab almost crashed into an old-fashioned wardrobe standing in the middle of a zebra crossing on Liverpool's Scotland Road. No one knew how the wardrobe came to be there, and stranger still, it could not be moved and it couldn't be opened, despite the many attempts of a local locksmith. The keyhole in the wardrobe seemed to be merely of some decorative value, and did not provide access to a lock. Traffic was diverted around the wardrobe, and Bill, the young policeman, sent for assistance. He believed the wardrobe had perhaps fallen from a removal van and somehow righted itself by chance, but then a curious crowd gathered near the tall piece of furniture and a few observers noticed something odd about the wardrobe's mirror: it was partially transparent – it was a one-way mirror – just like the ones you see in movies that are supposedly used in police interrogation rooms.

'Someone's in there!' a teenager declared, and several other people said they could see green and red lights behind the mirror – as well as a very faint silhouette of a man which moved about. Bill moved the people from the road onto the pavement, and a bus passed, and suddenly, that wardrobe was no longer there. No one saw it vanish, and people just seemed bemused and baffled by its sudden departure. This incident reminds me of a 'phantom shed' that was seen in neighbouring gardens of several houses on Queens Drive West Derby in the 1960s. The shed was there one moment, then gone the next, and hoaxers were blamed (and I will detail an incredible story concerning this mysterious itinerant shed later in this chapter), but could the Scotland Road wardrobe and the phantom shed have been some sort of real-life Tardises from a future age? These disguised time machines would blend in naturally with their environment - but some Timelord must have got the coordinates wrong for the wardrobe!

Back in the early 1950s, there was a rather sinister woman in her fifties known as Mary Treen who claimed she could accurately read palms – for a price - and she did not have a fortune-teller's caravan up in Blackpool or even a cheaply-hired room to give 'consultations' to clients. There's an old joke: if psychics are so good, why don't *they* call us? Well, Mrs Treen did this; she went about Liverpool with a type of supernatural protection racket, a menacing paranormal patter in which she obliquely suggested that bad luck would fall upon those who did not cross her palm with silver. Her most famous client was alleged to be a young man named Brian who was working for £5 a week at the Times Furnishings store on Lord Street. Mary managed to get a dining table at this store at a ridiculously low price by telling Brian that his life would change when he met three men in a cellar. He would have riches and fame undreamt of, but he would also have a dark shadow hanging over him, and the journey to world fame would start in the cellar and end on a roof. The man was Brian Epstein, and he met the three Beatles (not including the then drummer Pete Best) in the Cavern's cellar, and of course, the world-shaking band ended their unparalleled career on a roof – recording the *Let It Be* album on the roof of the Apple office, Saville Row, in London. Well, I could write a book about the terrifying predictions of the prophetess Treen, but what follows is quite sinister. One August afternoon in the phenomenally scorching summer of 1959, Mary Treen called at a house not far from Holly Lodge Girls' School, off Liverpool's Queens Drive, West Derby, and a 12-year-old boy named Bobby answered, and immediately sensed the caller was creepy. Mary, who had her white hair scraped up into a bun, was all dressed in black, and her dark eyes looked quite unnerving.

'Is your mother in?' she asked.

Bobby nodded and went to fetch his mum, a 35-year-old housewife named Liz.

'Ah, I wonder if you'd like to buy any lucky peg dolls love, or whether you want me to read your palm?' said Treen, leaning close into Liz's face. Liz knew from an old superstition that bad, even fatal consequences were said to befall anyone who snubbed a Romany person during his or her doorstep call. So Liz immediately went to fetch her purse, and she returned and placed a few half-crowns in Treen's hand. Treen seized her palm and seemed to recoil in horrified shock. 'Oh! No, you keep the money! Oh!' she shrieked. The coins fell and jingled on the floor.

'What is it? What have you seen?' Liz asked, losing her breath at the ominous reaction of the gypsy woman. Little Bobby cowered behind his mum in the hallway, and he looked terrified at the antics of the strange caller.

Mrs Treen backed away and tripped, landing on the path. She quickly got to her feet, shaking her head, saying, 'I'm sorry.' And she turned and hurried away. The sun was blazing in a clear blue sky and yet a terrible shadow was cast over Liz's life from that moment on. She told her husband Terry about the incident and he gave her a lecture about the evils of superstition and how she shouldn't have even listened to the gypsy. He unsympathetically told Liz to put the whole 'stupid business' out her mind, but the housewife couldn't, and had terrible dreams each night about someone closing in on her, ready to kill her. The dream always ended where she knew her killer was behind her, and she would wake in tears and would start to cry out. Liz started to go to church and she would pray to God to protect her from the terrible thing in her future which the gypsy had foreseen. The nightmares stopped after about a week, and Liz's life was returning to normality, when, one sunny Saturday afternoon, Bobby came bounding into the kitchen. He told his mother a shed had appeared in the back garden, out of thin air. Liz had been putting the washing on the line and hadn't seen such a shed a few moments ago, but an excited Bobby dragged his mother out to see it, and she and her son could not believe their eyes. The door of the shed opened, and out came two peculiar-looking little men, about three feet in height, and they had long foreheads and both wore strange orange one-piece suits. Behind them in the shed, were coloured lights 'like those on a Christmas tree' is how Liz described them. Bobby was laughing at the little men, who seemed to be twins, when suddenly, everything froze. Liz could not budge an inch, and she felt as if she was dreaming. In her mind, one of the unearthly men spoke directly to her in an accent she had never heard before. He told Liz he had come to save her. On this day a maniac was about to take her life in a ghastly way, and the murder would be unsolved for decades, and Liz would be known all over the world because she was a victim of this 'strange murderer' who would kill her in a very heinous fashion, but just how the killer would do this, the diminutive stranger did not specify. The killer was already in the garden, the little man told her. Liz then recalled the recurring nightmares she had been having of the menacing presence being behind her. The voice in her mind said he had 'come back to save her.' Suddenly, everything went black. Liz thought she was dead. She could feel nothing at all, no sensations, and she didn't know where she was. But then she found herself back in the kitchen. Bobby ran in and said a shed had appeared in the garden. This looping sequence of events happened again and again, and seemed to go one for about an hour, and Liz felt very ill in this Limbo of recurrence, but then she snapped out of it, and when she went into the garden, there was no shed there, and Bobby sulkily told his mum, 'You slowcoach, you would have seen it if you'd have hurried up!.'

Liz asked Bobby if he remembered the little men, and the boy shook his head with a puzzled expression. For a few weeks after this traumatic and inexplicable incident, Liz kept experiencing déjà vu and she would spook her husband by telling him what he was going to say or do. Liz told me this bizarre but intriguing story, and asked me to withhold it till she died, and she sadly passed away ten years back. She never even told her husband the tale, fearing ridicule, but she felt that somehow, those little men had perhaps come back in time and prevented her murder, and I think that too, and I also think these 'time-meddlers' might have abducted or somehow 'removed' the unknown savage killer from history – hopefully for good. I never mentioned this story on air, and yet, a few years later, I was on a phone-in programme on an independent radio station in Liverpool one night, and a caller named Maxine told me a strange story which immediately made me think of Liz's experience. Maxine, who lived in the Clubmoor area of Liverpool, said that on six occasions in 1964, she had looked out of her kitchen window and seen a shed at the bottom of her back garden. On each occasion when she and her husband or sister went out to look at the shed, they would find it gone. I openly wondered if the shed had been some apparition from the past, but Maxine said it wasn't because she would always find a square of pressed grass at the location where the shed had stood. That same night on the radio phone-in, we received many more calls from listeners who had also seen a strange shed in their gardens which had appeared out of thin air, and all of these incidents took place in West Derby – except for one. A lady in her sixties named Peggy said she and her entire family had seen a shed appear in the back yard of her home on Camborne Grove, Gateshead, Tyne and Wear, in June 1964. Peggy's husband and his brother tried to open the door to this shed for fifteen minutes or so without any luck, and the men also discovered that the tinted window to the shed was unbreakable. There was a typical summer downpour that day and the family went inside, but when the brothers came out a few minutes later with a toolbox, ready to tackle the mysterious shed's recalcitrant lock, they were highly surprised to find that the shed had gone, leaving only a dry square on paving stones to prove it had ever been there. Peggy's cousin Bob had been walking up the alleyway outside the yard at that time and he had not seen anyone loading a shed into a van or any activity whatsoever, which deepened the mystery. Strangely enough, in May of that year there was a spate of UFO sightings across Gateshead and according to local newspaper reports, a 14-year-old lad saw what he initially assumed to be children, standing on and around a haystack. These figures were, he estimated, about two and a half feet in height and all dressed in green. Some of these strange little figures appeared to be digging into the haystack as if they were searching for something, the boy said. Then other people saw these small beings, and one of the 'elves' as they were called, was even seen riding a cow!

Getting back to Liverpool, a caller to the radio phone-in named Richard said he had actually seen the door to the shed in his back garden open, but no one came out, and then, about ten minutes later, the shed vanished before his eyes. This was in January 1965, and Richard was aged fifteen. He told his parents about the shed in the yard and they seemed to think he was joking and never bothered to go and look. Richard lived less than 200 yards from the house were Maxine had seen a phantom shed in her back garden the year before. As in the Gateshead case, there was a UFO flap on in the summer of 1964, and this is really intriguing, as many cities and towns across the country that summer were apparently being visited by the Little People, and this is all documented in newspapers of the day, and some reports even reached the television and radio news bulletins. The *Liverpool Echo* reported on the so-called "Leprechaun Mania" across the city in an article dated 1 July 1964, which was headlined: 'Leprechauns Go Bowling in the Park' – referring to the scores of Little People dressed in odd clothes who had been encountered on a bowling green in the Kensington area of Liverpool by children as well as adults. These 'leprechauns' were subsequently seen in many other areas of Liverpool and beyond, and, of course, the mass sightings were explained away by 'experts' as text book examples of mass hysteria, because the Little People don't exist as far as educated, logically minded people were concerned at that time, and the Leprechaun Mania was seen as just another form of that other mental contagion sweeping the world – Beatlemania. The many people I interviewed over the years who had seen the Little People across Liverpool knew what they had seen, and were incensed at the suggestion that the entities they had seen with their own eyes had been nothing more than the product of mass suggestion. Something inexplicable was behind the reports, many of which were concurrent with reports of UFOs (then termed Flying Saucers by the media). Perhaps the Little People encounters and sightings somehow tie in with the intriguing reports of the sightings of the 'roving shed' in West Derby as well as the one in Gateshead (where there were also reports of Little People). What mysterious agency or person was behind the appearances and disappearances of those sheds? The Liverpool housewife Liz claimed the two little people who came out of the one in her garden had told her they had 'come back' to prevent her murder, so is it possible that the shed or sheds (for we have not determined whether all reports are of the same shed) were some form of time machine, designed to blend in with the suburban environment without being conspicuous? In other words, are these sheds just one outward form of a time machine that is not unlike the fictional Tardis depicted in the long-running science fiction television serial *Doctor Who*? Art and literature often imitate life; long before the laser was invented, HG Wells described the Martian heat ray in his novel *The War of the Worlds* and Jules Verne described many of the inventions we have today in his books - such as the *Nautilus* submarine in his classic novel *Twenty Thousand Leagues Under the Sea*. The shadows of approaching inventions often seem to manifest themselves in such works of science fiction, and the Tardis of *Doctor Who* will probably become a reality – sooner than we think. Research into physical time travel is going on as we speak, in the United States,

Russia, and many European countries, including the UK. A time machine would not only be a historian's dream, it would be a military tactician's worst nightmare, for a time machine would allow an enemy to manipulate history to destroy or subjugate his rival in a very insidious way. A Neo Nazi organization with a time machine at its disposal could go back in time and warn Hitler of all the mistakes he would make to prevent him from winning World War Two, and it would even be possible to give the Third Reich thermonuclear and biological weapons to achieve their aims. An anti-West terrorist organisation could theoretically even send an intercontinental ballistic missile back in time to nuke 17th century America back in the days of the *Mayflower* and the Pilgrim Fathers, thus contaminating North America with radioactive fall-out and setting back the colonisation of the US by a century. The possibilities of a time machine in the wrong hands are too terrible to fully contemplate. I am probably wrong, but sometimes I can't help wondering if someone has managed to send a nuclear weapon back in time. On the last day of June 1908 at around 7.15am, something described as cylindrical flashed across the skies of Russia. It was not seen to descend from a great height (as a meteorite would) but instead it travelled in a horizontal manner, and what's more, unlike a meteorite, this object *changed course* after travelling northwards for about 200 miles. At a place called Kezhma it turned right and started to travel east for about 150 miles, then turned a sharp left – as if it was a guided missile, heading west. It then travelled a further 150 miles – and exploded in mid air. The heat was so intense it incinerated a herd of reindeer and knocked down the trees of a vast forest as if they were matchsticks. And then a mushroom cloud rose – the type of cloud that would be seen decades later over Hiroshima and Nagasaki. Black rain fell, and many animals miles outside of the blast radius developed strange scabs and became ill – as if they were suffering from radiation poisoning. The flight path of the Edwardian nuclear missile seems to indicate that it came from either China – or what is now North Korea. Over a century of hypothesising has led to scientists and science-fiction writers wondering if the Tunguska Explosion (so called after the name of the Tunguska River close to the site of the detonation) was caused by a comet or even a nuclear-powered spaceship which might have developed engine trouble and ended up crash-landing in a remote part of Russia. Even Arthur C Clarke, the famous writer of science fiction and science fact (who was normally terrified to stick his neck out and admit to any Fortean phenomena) opted for the Tunguska explosion being caused by the icy fragment of a comet. Clarke never explained how a piece of interplanetary ice could take on the form of a cylinder which changed course twice in such a dramatic fashion. Also, how would a piece of cometary ice explode with the force of a nuclear weapon in mid air and leave the surrounding area radioactive for decades? No comet was seen in the skies by any of the world's observatories before the mysterious Russian explosion, and not one witness saw the cylindrical missile come down out of the sky as a meteorite would so – or a piece of falling comet. The enigmatic missile which wreaked so much devastation and caused radiation sickness among the wildlife around the blast site was only ever seen travelling along *horizontally* at a low altitude – as if someone had launched a missile not that unlike a modern cruise missile – which almost hugs the ground so it can slip under the enemy's radar. But who on earth would have had such a sophisticated guided missile back in 1908? Is it possible that at some time in the future, some terrorist or some enemy of Russia, might find a way to send a nuclear missile back into the past? Incidentally, had the missile arrived several hours later, it is computed that it would have struck Edwardian London – the heart of the British Empire. The Royal Family and the Houses of Parliament would have been wiped out and history would have taken a drastic new course. Admittedly, this is all just fanciful thinking on my behalf and I cannot back this possibility up with any definitive proof, and unless some future expedition to Tunguska finds the remains of our hypothetical missile (which would be extremely unlikely) we must classify this as a far-fetched idea. Getting back to the idea of time machines disguised as contemporary objects (similar to the Tardis concept), I will now present the following strange story which came my way quite a few years ago.

The Britain that four million demobbed men came home to between the summer of 1945 and the Christmas of 1946 had changed, and the people the servicemen returned to had changed as well. A man we shall call Rick returned from the War, and he had also undergone a drastic change, in looks, in personality and attitude. He had been cocky when he was called up, and was now war-tamed; mentally scarred and aged beyond his 27 years by the unspeakable horrors he had witnessed whilst separated from his wife Maureen and their 6-year-old daughter Jean for so many years. The day Rick returned to his Liverpool home, a man Jean called Uncle Jimmy fled the house via the back door and vanished into the cratered streets of post war Everton. Maureen was seven months' pregnant by this man, but surprisingly, Rick was very forgiving and just wanted a hot dinner on the table each day and a few chickens for the backyard to supply him with fresh eggs. Jean just wanted Uncle Jimmy back and asked her mum when Rick was going home. After the birth of her baby, Maureen nagged Rick into selling his demob suit for a fiver. She wanted to go on a holiday to Blackpool, and the fiver made that possible. Blackpool had emerged almost unscathed by the Nazi air raids because Hitler had given specific instructions to his Luftwaffe to spare the resort because he intended to use it as his personal leisure complex after a successful invasion of mainland Britain. The three piers and the Tower therefore looked just the same as they had when Rick and Maureen had courted here before the war. It was like old times again, and the long-separated couple rediscovered their love. Then Christmas loomed, and Jean wanted toys and Maureen hinted at the gifts she fancied, even though money was hard to come by and rationing of everything was still in force. Rick also developed a bad gambling habit, and his new job as a painter was a poorly-paid one. He turned to an infamous Scotland Road loan shark with connections to a kingpin who virtually ran the underworld of North Liverpool. Rick soon frittered away a thousand quid on the dogs, horses, poker, innumerable expensive gifts for Maureen and countless dolls and toys for Jean, and through also throwing his money around like confetti in the pubs of Everton, always paying for other people's drinks. Unable to repay the loan with its whopping 70% interest, he was visited by two sharp-suited ex military policemen. If Rick didn't pay up within a week it was curtains. Rick sent Maureen and the children to his aunt's house in Kensington and then he went on the run, but the debt-collecting heavies somehow tracked him to Bootle, and on a lonely street one night, one of them drew a pistol as Rick begged for mercy with his back to an air-raid shelter wall. He closed his eyes – and fell backwards through that solid wall as he heard two muffled gunshots. He found himself in an immense brightly-lit hall with white walls and a white shiny tiled floor. Rick also noticed the smell of something akin to disinfectant; it reminded him of a hospital aroma. He walked for what seemed like an hour through this impossibly vast place till he found a doorway that came out on Marsh Lane, a mile from the shelter. When Rick turned around he was in the middle of a bombed site – no doorway or anything. He called on his wife and kids, took them to a relative's home in Southport and never returned to Liverpool until the 1970s. Rick could not explain what had happened to him that evening, but it was probably some form of timeslip – or perhaps he stumbled into a real-life Tardis. One of the unexplained but well-known properties of Doctor Who's fictional Tardis is that its interior is transcendentally bigger than its exterior. The postwar incident I mentioned, in which Rick found himself in what he perceived to be a brightly-lit hall with white walls and a matching tiled floor - inside of an air raid shelter - might have been some dimensional illusion inside a possible time machine with a spatial property similar to Doctor Who's police box. Common sense tells us that there is nothing like the Tardis in the real world – that there is nothing in science or mathematics whereby something infinite or incredibly large can be bounded by something relatively smaller and finite. Common sense would have us believe that an air raid shelter measuring 7 feet in height, 18 feet in length and 12 feet in width can not contain a vast hall which takes an hour to cross at a walking pace. In fact, any "hall" that takes an hour to cross could qualify as a town; the elliptical Albert Hall – 272 feet on its major axis – if traversed at a rate of 2.6 feet (the length of an average stride) per second, would take just under two minutes to cross, but Rick estimated he had walked for about an hour, and the average person can cover about four miles in that period.

In his book, *The Middle Kingdom* (1974) the writer Diarmuid McManus relates how, in 1935, a young Irish girl was sent on an errand in Mayo, and at one point in her journey, she was walking down the slope of a hill (Lis Ard, a so-called Fairy Fort). The girl then bumped into something; her hands felt an invisible wall, and she followed the curvature of this wall with her outstretched palms and discovered it was some sort of massive unseen enclosure. Hours passed, and the girl tried to get out of the circular-walled structure to no avail, and although four search parties passed close by (one within twenty feet) no one heard the girl's frantic cries for help. Sometime later, in the wee small hours of the morning, the girl discovered that the invisible prison had vanished, and she ran home exhausted and in tears. Given the location of this unearthly incident in relation to the "Fairy Fort", the Little People were duly blamed. The girl later said she was disoriented because she seemed to be walking for some time but never left that "magical" circular area. The commonsensical view of something like the fictional Tardis having an impossibly large interior tells us that it simply can't be, because it contravenes the most basic laws of geometry: you can't pull a colony of rabbits out of a top hat and you can't fit a grand piano in a shoebox. It would seem that there is nothing in the worlds of science or mathematics that even hints at something like the larger interior of the Tardis – but surprisingly, there *are* a few caveats we should look to. In mathematics there is a curious fractal known as the Koch Snowflake, and this is a fractal – a type of geometric scale-defying pattern which looks the same no matter how far you zoom in on it and magnify it. The Koch Snowflake, discovered by the Swedish mathematician Niels Fabian Helge von Koch around 1904, is a continuous curve without tangents. The fractal is created according to simple repetitive steps (making it ideal as a computer model). Firstly, you take an equilateral triangle (a triangle with three sides of equal length), and you divide each side of the triangle into three sections and after erasing the middle third of the sections, you put a smaller equilateral triangle there on the erased section, and on the first iteration you will form a "Star of David" pattern, but when you take one of the six projecting triangles and apply the same technique of dividing one side of the new triangle into thirds and creating even smaller triangles, you soon come upon a very strange and intriguing shape which you could keep refining by applying your middle third triangle technique to. You have a fractal with an *infinite* perimeter – a perimeter without end. This would seem to fly in the face of Euclidean geometry and common sense. Let's say we put this Koch Snowflake in a basic two-dimensional rectangular box to represent the famed police box manned by the famous Timelord. The box is, let us say, 9 feet by 5 feet, giving it a total (two dimensional) area of 45 square feet and a perimeter of 38 feet. And yet, within the finite area of our time machine, and contained within its finite (38 feet) perimeter, we have an object with a finite area but an infinite perimeter! This is not just a long perimeter, such as a coil of fine wire placed in the box, the Koch Snowflake perimeter has no end; it can easily span the width of our galaxy and even the universe, and this is a mathematical truth, although, admittedly, this is just a little bit of mathematical recreation – but the principle behind it is sound. A real Tardis would be created using technology we have barely dreamed of yet, possibly an extension of having some sort of holographic walls to create a seemingly impossible virtual space in its interior. This would be a high-tech version of the magician's wardrobe with mirrors placed within it to create the illusion of unaccountable depth. So much for the scientific possibilities of a real-life Tardis, but what about the higher knowledge of the Occult (an ancient word which means "hidden knowledge")? I have investigated and researched many stories of the paranormal which occasionally hint at higher dimensions of the space-time continuum, and some of these reported incidents have touched upon the seemingly impossible transcendental expansion of space within a finite confined area, and some of the following stories illustrate this baffling concept.

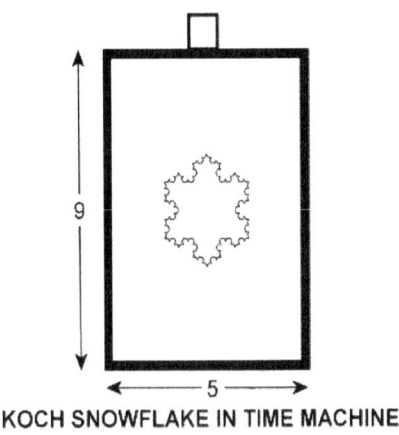

KOCH SNOWFLAKE IN TIME MACHINE

LOST IN A STOCKROOM

So many of the old high street stores and shops have now departed from Liverpool, and a lot of them disappeared long before the advent of the online shopping revolution. We had stores like C&A, Hendersons, Waring & Gillow, Wades, Freeman Hardy & Willis, Richard Shops, the Army & Navy Stores, the House of Holland, Bunneys, Owen Owen, Blacklers, Littlewoods, and of course, good old Woolworths – to name just a few. The following strange story took place in one of these long-vanished shops back in an era when timeslips and the topsy-turvy subatomic goings-on of quantum physics were virtually unknown to the person in the street. It was the afternoon of Saturday 1 August 1959, and Roy Hamilton Martin, the 27-year-old assistant manager of a well-known clothing store in the city centre of Liverpool, was looking forward to the coming Summer Bank Holiday on Monday. Single and free, Roy planned to spend a holiday down in Torquay with a few bachelor friends for some serious drinking, "skirt-chasing" and sunbathing. Already the four regions of British Railways were running 2,000 extra main line trains to every part of the country for the great getaway, and the air exodus had already started with hundreds of British European Airways planes taking to the skies, mostly for the Continental resorts. So, for Roy, there was only "this savvy" to get through, and then the blissful Summer Bank Holiday. However, something very strange took place that afternoon, and it is something that has never been explained. At 2pm young Janet Sperry from the lingerie department upstairs visited Roy in his office and said she thought there were rats in her stockroom. Roy said he doubted this but Janet said she and two of the girls had heard scratching and squealing sounds coming from the room. Roy reluctantly investigated, and he gave a wry smile as he went into the stockroom alone and walked the absolute labyrinth of a meandering path between towering shelves stacked with the intimate apparel of underwear and nightclothes. Roy never knew the room was this big, and he turned a dimly lit corner and found himself in a massive space the size of a hangar. Straight away he knew such a huge space simply couldn't be accommodated by any part of the building – it was a physical impossibility; nor could this vast hall be part of some neighbouring store, because the assistant manager knew the rough layout and cubic capacity of his place of work, and what he was seeing did not add up one little bit; it did not make mathematical sense at all. Roy's footsteps echoed as he walked the cavernous enclosure, and he suddenly saw a figure - a man of about his own age in a smart suit -

walking ahead of him, some fifty yards away. 'Excuse me, there!' he shouted, and a strong echo of Roy's words came reverberating back, but the figure walked on without responding, and so Roy yelled: 'Hey! Excuse me!' and raised his arm – and the figure in front did the same. Then Roy gradually realised the man walking with his back to him looked very much like *himself*. When Roy halted, the stranger halted, and when Roy waved his right hand, the figure did *precisely* the same. This naturally unsettled Roy so he turned and walked back, and looked over his shoulder – and saw that the man was following him now – but he was looking over his own shoulder – as Roy was as he gazed back at the man. It was some sort of weird mirror image, but not a normal reversed image like the one we see when we look at our reflection.

Roy turned away from the doppelganger and hurried away through the maze. He wanted to get out of this accursed place and back to the safety of the store, but he could not find the stockroom. Instead he became lost in a bizarre black void surrounded with strange undulating abstract forms and shapes which seemed to be made from some light blue liquid. Web-like strands of this material stretched across the blackness, criss-crossing bizarre surreal structures of the same stuff which twisted and curled, and large elliptical black holes opened and closed in the blue morphing substance as Roy looked on. Had Roy experienced this phenomenon today he would have thought someone had slipped him LSD, but in 1959 such drugs were largely unheard of. Roy actually wondered if he was losing his mind; he had been under a lot of pressure at work in recent months, filling in for a senior colleague who was off sick. Perhaps this was all the product of a breakdown, Roy wondered, yet he somehow knew this was not the case. At one point he ran off into the blackness, away from all of the filaments and structures, but now he found himself feeling very disoriented, because he could not feel the floor beneath his feet; it was as if he was walking on air. By a faint silvery light from some unknown source, the assistant manager could see the time on his watch was now 2.16pm, but he felt as if he had been stuck in this unearthly place for an hour. After about ten minutes of walking the darkness, Roy began to shout for help. His voice echoed back off something: a wall he could not reach for some strange reason. Then he heard what sounded like a loud deep creaking sound. It sounded ominous, as if something was about to break or fall on him, so Roy tried to run away from it. The creaking became fainter, but then Roy heard faint whispering voices, although he could not make out what they were saying. The voices were talking quickly in a very excited and distressed manner, and Roy formed the impression that the unseen whisperers were only young. Around 2.25pm, Roy heard someone calling his name. It sounded like the voice of Janet Sperry. Roy hurried in the direction of the voice and gradually saw several dim bulbs in the blackness, and these turned out to be the bulbs hanging from the ceiling of the stockroom. Roy Hamilton Martin breathed an immense sigh of relief as he found himself among the stacks of lingerie. He found his way out of the stockroom, and saw that a clock on a wall said it was 2pm. Roy pulled back his white cuff and saw that it was indeed 2pm – again! This was impossible, as he had first entered the stockroom a little after 2pm. He gripped the handrail on the stairs to steady himself as he went down to the next floor, and finding himself perspiring a little, he dabbed his forehead with a handkerchief. Under the curious eye of a cleaner, who thought he looked a little flushed, Roy went back to his office, took a deep breath, and opened the window for some fresh air. He tried to make sense of what had just taken place in the stockroom. Had it all been some strange illusion? He had never suffered from hallucinations before, and could not put the freakish experience down to some fever, as he had felt in good health before he had gone into that stockroom. The only thing he'd had on his mind all day had been the plans to get away to Torquay.

Janet suddenly barged into the office and said there were rats in the stockroom - *exactly as she had earlier.* 'You came in earlier and told me that – didn't you?' Roy asked, all confused. It was like an intense form of déjà vu.

'I haven't been in here today,' Janet told him and thinned her eyes. 'Anyway, there's something in the stockroom. It sounded like rats squealing and scratching. There's definitely something in there.'

Roy felt a nervous spasm in his face. He shook his head. This time he refused to go into the stockroom. 'Don't be silly, Janet, there are no rats in the stockroom.'

'And I'm telling you that there are!' Janet assured him with a stern look.

'Then ask the cleaner, Mr Johnson to go and have a look, I'm very busy,' Roy replied, and Janet left in a huff, slamming the door of the office behind her. The cleaner had a look in the stockroom, and found no evidence of any rodents and he did not report any strange phenomena in there either. Roy never set foot in that stockroom again. He was only too glad to go on holiday that month, and not wanting to lose his job, he told no one about the weird experience he'd had. He told his son about it twenty years later, and his son, Malcolm, later told me about the strange incident. I believe that Roy walked into some rift, or some portal which gave access to another dimension. All of the things he described – the enormous black void and crazy geometrical shapes – and also the odd creaking sound and the whispering voices – are what many people have perceived when walking into these warps in the space-time continuum. I have written about a similar incident which was even mentioned in the staid and sober pages of *The Times* of London. This was the curious case of the 'hole' which opened up in the floor of a room in the Victoria Hotel, Bristol, in the early hours of 9 December 1873. An off-duty soldier from Leeds named Thomas B Cumpston, and his Liverpool-born wife Ann Martha Cumpston, had been sleeping soundly in the hotel room, when, about one in the morning, Mrs Tongue, the hotel manager, heard excited voices coming from the Cumpston's room, and went to investigate. The couple said they had heard strange noises and voices in their room, and believed it to be haunted. Mrs Tongue convinced the couple they had both had a nightmare and somehow pacified them enough so that the couple returned to their bed. At four in the morning, Mrs Tongue was startled from her slumbers by loud screams of murder and gunshots coming from the room where the Cumpstons were lodging. She put on her night-gown, lit an oil lamp and hurried in her bare feet to the room to see what the matter was this time. Outside the door of the hotel room, Mrs Tongue heard Mrs Cumpston exclaim: 'Keep that knife away from me!'

The hotel manager burst into the dark room and found Mr and Mrs Cumpston exiting the window in their nightclothes. They dropped twelve feet and rushed barefooted to the railway station, where they told the night superintendent at the railway, a Thomas Harker, an incredible story as he sat drinking his cocoa in the booking office. Mr Cumpston said he and his wife had just escaped from a den of thieves and had almost been waylaid by them. Now Mr Cumpston feared the blackguards would follow him to the station. Mr Harker took the couple into the parcel office and sat them by the fire, and here he asked them to go through the story again. Mrs Cumpston said her husband had got out the bed after feeling the bed open up. A black hole opened in the mattress. She tried to pull him up as she heard echoing voices crying out. 'My husband has a revolver, and he fired at them!' Mrs Cumpston said, and Mr Harker asked Thomas Cumpston if this was true. 'Yes, I'm a soldier,' he replied, and produced the revolver. He said that he and his wife had jumped out the haunted bed and found another hole opening up in the carpet on the floor. Mr Cumpston fell down the hole and heard screeching voices, and his wife somehow pulled him out of the hole. He grabbed his service revolver and fired first into the ceiling to warn the strangers in the hole, and then he fired several shots at the people in the abyss, before instructing his wife to get out of the room by jumping from the bed to the windowsill. They then opened the window and escaped from the room by dropping onto the pavement below. The voices were heard at the window above, so Mr Cumpston, on the advice from his hysterical wife, fired a shot at the window, and then the couple ran off for help.

Mrs Tongue meanwhile, left her hotel in search of a policeman to report the bizarre behaviour of the Cumpstons and the gunshots, and she encountered Police Constable 310 on his beat at Bath Parade. She informed him of Cumpstons' antics and told him how the couple had headed for the railway station. The policeman went straight to the station and found the Cumpstons seated comfortably before the fire in the parcel office with Harker. After listening to the seemingly far-fetched tale from Mr and Mrs Cumpston, the policeman said that the Victoria Hotel was a respectable establishment, and not likely to be the place where a den of thieves would be found, but he went to the room the Cumpstons had vacated and found no bullet holes; only the blankets of the bed were in disarray. The entire incident was 'explained' away as a collective hallucination, an hallucination that must have been *shared* by Mr and Mrs Cumpston.

The Cumpstons – like Roy Martin Hamilton in the Liverpool store – were lucky to have made it safely back to everyday reality, but others who have stumbled into time-space warps have not been seen since. Thousands of people go missing without a trace every years across the world, and some of the vanishing acts seem like almost paranormal mysteries for a while until new information and findings clears the mystery up – and this may hopefully happen with the case of Flight

MH370 – a Boeing 777-200ER aircraft carrying 239 souls which vanished, seemingly into thin air on 8 March 2014. The plane took off from Kuala Lumpur International Airport, bound for Beijing, and less than an hour after takeoff the plane was reported missing. Despite one of the most intense multinational search efforts ever launched. People of fourteen nations were on the missing plane, and yet the Boeing seems to have fallen off our maps into some limbo, and at the time of writing, not a trace of any wreckage of the missing flight has been found in the sea or on land. Most of the families, friends and relatives of the 239 people onboard the missing plane have given up any hope of finding them alive – for it was once speculated that terrorists might have hijacked the aircraft and landed it somewhere – but this now seems very remote indeed. Closure for many of the people who lost loved ones on Flight MH370 will not come until the wreck of the plane has been found in the depths of the sea or on land in some remote and uninhabited region. Hopefully this aviation mystery will soon be cleared up, but there are other cases of people vanishing in much more mysterious circumstances.

INTO THE TAPESTRY

At a booksigning at Cheshire Oaks in 2002, one of the people who queued to have a chat with me was an Australian named Roger Harrison, the 35-year-old son of a Liverpool man who had immigrated to Australia and settled in Perth in the 1960s. Roger told me a very interesting story with a Liverpool connection that had taken place at Mandurah, Western Australia in 1932. The story had been told to him by his father-in-law, Pete, who had only been a 5-year-old boy when the weird incident happened. One blazing hot January afternoon in 1932, a man with a Liverpudlian accent, who gave his name as Harold Williams, called at a lodging house in Mandurah, run by a widowed man named Foster. Foster smelt whiskey on the breath of Williams and seeing he was rather scruffily dressed, was rather reluctant to give him lodgings, but times were hard, and Mandurah was experiencing something of a recession at the time with the closure of the local cannery and a decline in other businesses too. Today, Mandurah is one of the top tourist destinations in Western Australia, but in the early 1930s the local economy in the town was in dire straits. Mr Foster asked for a deposit and a week's rent in advance, and Williams begrudgingly complied. However, when he was shown his room he said it was too small, and demanded a bigger one, and after much arguing,

Foster put a bed in a bigger room next to his own bedroom, and said he would clear out all of the old furniture (mostly left by previous lodgers) cluttering the place in a few days. Around three in the morning, the lodger Williams was awakened by strange pipe and drum music. He thought it was coming from outside at first, but upon opening his window fully he saw there was no one about on this moonlit night – and then he realised that the rhythmical odd-sounding music was coming from a corner of the cluttered room he was in. Behind an old wardrobe Williams found a rolled-up six-foot length of tapestry of some sort, depicting a group of three weird-looking life-sized naked dancing men with globular heads, large black circular eyes and smiling crescent mouths full of sharp triangular teeth. They were white, and contrasted sharply against the dark green background of the fabric. The music was somehow *coming from* this dusty tapestry, and it faded after a few seconds, leaving an uneasy silence in its wake. Foster suddenly burst into the room in his vest and underpants and he snatched the roll of hand-woven fabric from Williams and told him to stop mooching and to get to sleep. Foster then hid the tapestry in his wardrobe when he got back to his bedroom but when he was asleep, Harold Williams sneaked into his room and stole it, probably thinking the antique-looking arras was worth a good few bob. Plus he was intrigued as to how musical sounds could emanate from the cloth. That morning around 5am, Foster was awakened by terrible screams from Williams next door. The landlord got up and went to see what the matter was, and upon opening the lodger's door, he saw a very frightening and surreal sight: two of the weird white figures from the tapestry had somehow stepped off their cloth and they were dragging a screaming Mr Williams across the room. They dragged him into the tapestry hanging from a picture hook as he reached out to the landlord with a look of sheer horror on his face. The tapestry then fell to the floor – and Williams and the three-dimensional versions of the figures embroidered on the cloth had vanished – but the two dimensional representations of the three figures were still visible on the tapestry as they were before. Foster knew no one would believe his story and never notified the police of his lodger's disappearance. Harold Williams was never seen or heard from again, and Mr Foster was so shaken by the uncanny incident he began to attend church, because he thought the Devil was behind the sinister goings-on. The tapestry had been left at the house by an old lodger after his death around 1927 and just what it depicted, and its present whereabouts – remain a mystery.

After Roger Harrison told me this story, I told him that many strange supernatural things had happened across Australia over the centuries, from the days of the first settlers to the present day, and Mandurah was certainly no stranger to paranormal goings-on over the years. Just a few years before the tapestry incident, a teenager named Beryl and her family saw something very unearthly one evening in 1930 at their Mandurah home. This incident was documented in *Modern Mysteries of the World*, an excellent book by the much-respected writers and researchers on the paranormal, Janet and Colin Bord. In their 1989 book, the Bords mention an intriguing account of what is thought to have been some form of alien visitation. The witness to the unearthly occurrence was teen Beryl Hickey. Beryl recalled that a small being, about half a metre in height, had appeared in her home at Mandurah one night in 1930. Beryl describes the entity as looking like a baby, but not a baby human. It was pink and had large ears, a wide slit for a mouth, and its skin glistened as if it was coated in some oil. The thing had bulging eyes which seemed to be covered in some film, and it made a strange squeaking sound when it was confronted by Beryl's father – who, being a very religious man, thought the being was the work of the Devil. He threw the net he used to catch prawns over the tiny entity and it emitted a scream. It was dragged outside and released back into the night from which it had come. As far as Beryl knows it was never seen again, and her father warned her and the rest of the family to say nothing of the creature. Beryl did tell a friend but later forgot all about the weird incident, and she only recalled it some fifty-two years later when *ET - The Extraterrestrial* was released, because the alien reminded her of the baby-like being which had somehow gained access to her childhood home in Western Australia. Just what the thing was will probably never be known. It could have indeed been the baby or child of aliens who were either visiting that night or had possibly crashed in one of the remote areas around Mandurah. Given the description of the strange beings that somehow came out of the tapestry at the Mandurah lodging house two years after the "ET" incident, it's equally possibly that some of these entities are not from outer space at all, but from some parallel world or some other dimension – and an intriguing question is: how long have these things been paying us visits? It's possible that the visits date back to the first aboriginal settlers – and even before that, when – as some legends hint – an even more ancient (and very mysterious) people inhabited Australia.

A SCOTTISH WEREWOLF

One cold autumnal evening around 11pm in 2010, a 35-year-old Liverpool man named Greg Aldbury left his aunt's house on King John Road, Newcastle upon Tyne. Greg was suffering from an ankle injury (from playing soccer) at the time and he walked a short distance to the stop where he could get the bus to his girlfriend Jenny's home on Holytree Crescent, about a mile away. Greg would have normally walked to his girlfriend's house, but didn't feel up to it because of his sore ankle. He stood at the bus stop, which is located outside the rather modernistic-looking St Teresa's Catholic Church, and as Greg waited for the bus, a man of about thirty approached and sat on the long plastic bench under the bus shelter. He had a good head of black curly hair, and was about six feet in height but of a slim build. He wore a green jacket - of the type that Greg associated with the coats sold in the old Army and Navy stores - and the man also had on a pair of grey cargo pants as well as a pair of Doc Marten boots. The stranger got up off the bench, walked up and down, and in a Scots accent, asked Greg what the time was. 'Ten past eleven,' Greg replied and the man smiled and said, 'A Scouser eh?' And he talked about a Liverpool girl he had courted for a year back in his twenties.

The moon was full on this chilly November night and the Scot kept looking up at it as he talked. He complained about the bus service, when suddenly, an attractive-looking girl who seemed to be in her late teens or early twenties came up Heaton Road in high heels and a very short skirt, and she waved to a Hackney cab - which never stopped.

'Cor, take a look at that, man,' the Scot said, and he went into some very coarse details about the things he'd 'like to do' to the young lady. Greg was certainly no prude but he found the man's talk graphic and sickening. Getting no response from Greg, the Scot asked him if he was gay, and Greg said nothing. The Scot then continued his heinous descriptions of what he'd do to the girl, and said something which made Greg's flesh creep. 'I could eat that b****, no problem, no tenderising needed.'

All of a sudden, he made a strange growling sound from the back of his throat, as if he was bringing up phlegm, and then his hands grasped at his throat, and he made choking sounds. Greg watched in disbelief and terror as the man's face – and body – began to change into something hideous. The Scot vomited a milky fluid, projecting it with quite some force into the road - as his face seemed to bulge forward, and his nose extended and his face darkened to a ruddy brown colour. Simultaneously the man bent over as he became crookbacked, and the young lady who had been attempting to flag down a cab screamed as she witnessed this strange metamorphosis of his head and body. Luckily for her, a Hackney cab halted at that moment further down the road and she ran straight to it and got in. As the cab moved off, the Scot turned his ghastly transformed face to Greg, and the Liverpudlian could see this face was no longer human – it looked like the face of an Alsatian – or a wolf; the long snout, the gaping jaws of sharp teeth, and reddish eyes. The arms of the Scot seemed to have become longer, and Greg could see thick black hair on the back of the man's hands.

Greg ran off in agonising pain from his injured ankle, and he heard the thing give chase as it growled. Greg swore and shouted for help, but there was no one about on this stretch of Heaton Road at this time, and this was odd because the road seemed unusually quiet and devoid of both pedestrians and traffic.

Greg looked back and saw the man was no on all fours, and seemed to be tearing off his green coat. Greg crossed the road and hid behind the hedge of a house. The thing slowly passed by him and halted at one point, and Greg had the feeling that the nightmarish figure knew very well where he was hiding, and was ready to pounce, but he heard what sounded like spitting sounds, and then the hybrid – or whatever it was – was heard to move off back across Heaton Road, headed for a place called Armstrong Park. Greg waited for what seemed like an hour until he heard a couple walking past, and he jumped out from the hedge, startling them, then limped all the way back to his aunt's in a dreadful state. Greg's auntie had never known her nephew to tell lies or to entertain even the remotest interest in the supernatural, but she could obviously see that he had been thoroughly frightened by something. She tried to explain the "werewolf" away by suggesting that some student prankster had somehow donned a mask and had staged the whole thing, perhaps while some hidden confederate filmed the stunt for a YouTube video, but Greg was absolutely certain what he had seen, and he knew that young lady had also seen the lecherous Scot turn into something truly demonic. To this day, Greg has nightmares about that autumnal evening when he believed he encountered something that has been reported since the days of the Romans and the Ancient Greeks: a werewolf. From a physiological viewpoint, the metamorphosis of a human into a wolf – or any other animal for that matter – is surely impossible, yet there is a large corpus of well-documented testimony from people of all walks of life throughout the ages who have allegedly encountered werewolf-like beings. In some cases, many of these reports are undoubtedly cases of clinical lycanthropy - a recognised symptom of a medical disorder whereby the individual *thinks* he or she is a wolf or other wild animal, but other accounts are difficult to explain, such as the legendary Beast of Gevaudan, a massive bullet-proof wolf-like monster that terrorised 18th century France. Getting back to the Heaton Road werewolf encounter, Greg told me how, at one point as he fled from the transfigured man, he noticed that there was a strange quietness all around, and he did not see anyone passing by nor did he notice any traffic on a road that is a well-travelled thoroughfare in Newcastle. Stranger still, about a fortnight before this incident, there was a timeslip incident which was later reported to me. A couple from Durham named Ian and Denise, visiting a relative in the area, where fascinated to see an old-fashioned ice cream parlour on Heaton Road. Ian wanted to go into the quaint old corner shop to try the ice cream but his partner Denise reminded him they were already late and were expected to be at her mother's house soon, so they walked on. When the couple visited the ice cream parlour at 4pm, they saw that it was no longer there, and in its place there was a modern type of mini-market there instead. Denise told her father about the incident and as he had lived in the Heaton Road area as a young boy, he clearly recalled that there was such an ice cream parlour which once existed on that corner of the street where the mini-market currently stood. How does one incorporate a timeslip into the werewolf report? There may be no connection at all, but I feel that there is something akin to the 'Oz Factor' – a term coined by Jenny Randles, a respected researcher into the sphere of the paranormal. Randles had noted that many people who had encountered UFOs or other paranormal phenomena had talked of distinctive feelings of dislocation, alienation, sudden sensory isolation and timelessness during their experiences, as if they had been 'sucked out of reality'. Randles coined the term after thinking of the parallel between people who had found themselves in this altered state of consciousness and the fictional Dorothy who was taken by a whirlwind from her monochrome world of everyday reality to the multicoloured land of Oz in the iconic film *The Wizard of Oz*. I wonder, but I may be very wide of the mark, if Greg and the unknown lady who witnessed the "werewolf" on Heaton Road, had had their minds manipulated by some higher force which was carrying out some psychological test upon them to see how they would react. And perhaps a fortnight before this hypothetical test, the same force tinkered with time to see how a modern couple – Ian and Denise – would react to an ice cream parlour from a bygone age. I quizzed Denise and Ian separately about their apparent timeslip experience, and asked them if anyone else – any passers by – had seen the old-fashioned ice cream parlour, and both witnesses said that they had not seen a single person pass them until they were quite some distance from the shop, and Ian clearly recalled that not a single vehicle passed by on a normally busy road, either. My theory about some superior intellect from elsewhere conducting psychological tests on people is probably mere paranoia on my behalf, but I'm just trying to makes sense of two bizarre incidents which happened on the very same road within two weeks.

HENRI

One drizzly grey afternoon in October 1956 Enid, an eccentric 57-year-old woman of Walton, Liverpool, buried her niece Helen's clown doll Henri because, as far as Enid was concerned, Helen, at the age of ten, was not only too old to mollycoddle a doll, the whole thing was unnatural. Helen was a born ventriloquist, throwing her voice so Henri appeared to talk, laugh and cry, and even the parish priest thought there was something eerie about the child's closeness to the doll, which measured about two and a half feet in height. Helen became so upset, she suffered a fit when her balmy aunt told her that Henri had been buried in a special little grave in nearby Anfield Cemetery. The girl yelled a shocking swear-word at Enid and said she hoped Enid would drop dead, and then she cried so much she threw up, so Enid locked her in her bedroom and told her she was going home to her mother and father first thing Monday morning. Helen kicked up such a fuss at the council-owned house on Swanston Avenue, neighbours alerted the police. A young constable assumed Enid was joking about the burial of the doll, but the spinster aunt said she had 'laid it to rest' in the box it had been bought in three years ago at a shop in Cardiff. 'You're not allowed to do that, miss,' the policeman said, 'it's against the law, like.'

'Oh what a blasted carry-on, its only a little grave!'

said Enid. 'I'll dig it up tomorrow.'

'Yes, miss, you better had,' the copper advised, and finding the whole matter rather creepy, he was only too glad to leave the house.

But Enid never did retrieve the doll from its 'grave', and poor Helen was duly sent packing to her home in Orrell Park, and never saw her beloved Henri again. Then, in 1966, Enid died from a massive brain haemorrhage, ironically within close proximity of the buried doll as she travelled on a bus close to Anfield Cemetery. After the spinster's death, a family moved into the council house on Swanston Avenue, and the youngest of the newcomers was a 10-year-old girl named Julie, a rather introverted girl with a stammer. One October evening just before Duck Apple Night, Julie's older brother Kenny sat down for tea and claimed that some "big lads" had dug up a little man in the graveyard; this was Anfield Cemetery, just a few hundred yards away.

'What have I told you about yapping at the table?' Kenny's father fumed and told him to shut up, but later that evening the woman next door got talking to Kenny's mum and she mentioned the same macabre rumour about the gang digging up a little man. That night, at half-past twelve, Julie was startled from her sleep by raps at her bedroom window, and when she peeped through the curtains she thought it was a little kid on the pavement below. He seemed to be throwing tiny stones up at the window. She rubbed the sleep from her eyes – and saw the boy was actually a weird pale-faced doll in a clown's costume and a cone-shaped hat. She went to her mum and dad in a right state and having a stammer, Julie had a difficult time telling them what she had seen on the pavement outside. Her parents patiently waited though as they were accustomed to, and Julie finally told them about the little clown-like figure. The girl's parents naturally thought Julie had experienced a lucid nightmare, but when they went to the window and pulled back the net curtains, they both saw the creepy little entity too. The girl's father opened the window and saw that the thing was apparently crying, and its sinister face was twisted in sorrow.

'Helen! I've come back!' came the squeaky voice from below.

Julie saw the hairs rise on her father's arm – a sure sign that he was scared of the night visitor, and the girl also saw her mother was frightened, and so she began to cry.

The child's father went and found an old huge hobnail boot from the back of his wardrobe, then went back to the window and threw it down hard at the unearthly entity. The doll screamed when it was hit by the boot, and seemed damaged. It fell on its back, then levered itself up with its right arm. The other arm and one of its legs seemed broken and loose. At this point a dim light went on in the bedroom window of an old woman who lived opposite, and this old woman came to the window and saw the strange events unfolding on the other side of the street.

Julie's father wanted to go downstairs to grab the poker from the grate and then go out and attack the weird doll, but Julie and her hysterical mother begged him not to.

'Helen, I thought you loved me!' the doll screeched, and fell down as it backed away. An alley cat then fled from under a car parked a few doors away, and as it ran past the doll, the clown emitted a scream as if the stray feline had startled it. The doll then somehow managed to limp away into the darkness, looking back now and then.

Julie and her family lived in mortal fear of seeing the little clown doll again, and later moved house because Julie began to suffer from terrible nightmares about the entity and also started to wet her bed. Without a doubt I believe the haunted – or possessed – doll which visited the family that night was Henri, the doll that was buried in Anfield Cemetery, and I am told he is still occasionally seen in the neighbourhood, but whether these reports are just urban legends derived from the strange incidents in the 1950s and 1960s is hard to determine.

THE SCARLET ROOM

On the outskirts of Liverpool there's an old rather remote sandstone house that stands near to Knowsley Lane, about half a mile north of Woolfall Heath, and up to 2009 this ancient dwelling was subdivided into three flats. In 2007 the occupants of the house were a woman in her seventies named Mrs Gurney, a 32-year-old graphic designer named Paul, and two university students in their early twenties named Samantha and Megan. Megan moved into the flat at the house first in 2006, but thought it would make more economic sense if she shared the rent with her friend Samantha – a media student who had left the flat she had shared with her boyfriend in Huyton after catching him in the arms of another girl. On the very first evening at the flat at the former farmhouse, Sam – as Megan called her – had been carrying her belongings from her car in suitcases into the hallway of the house when she had noticed something quite odd. When she looked into the old mirror at the bottom of the stairs, next to a hat stand, she noticed that this mirror did not give a true reflection. Instead, it duly showed a reflection of the carpeted stairs, but at the top of these stairs in the mirror image, there were three doors instead of two. Sam turned away from the looking glass and glanced up the stairs to see that there were only two doors up there: the one leading to Mrs Gurney's apartment and the one to the rooms Sam shared with Megan. The flat where Paul the graphic designer lived was on the ground floor and accessed further down the hallway. With her eyes thinned and her eyebrows crooked with disbelief, Sam looked back into the mirror, and there, as clear as day, were three doors at the top of the stairs. Sam went up the stairs with her cases and looked at the section of the wall where the third door had been in the false reflection. She tapped on that part of the wall – and heard that it sounded hollow. Her curiosity went through the roof. Was there a secret room behind this section of the wall? She wondered, and later when Megan arrived home, Sam told her about the reflection of the three doors in the hall mirror. Megan didn't believe her, so Sam almost dragged her down the stairs to the mirror in the hallway and gazed at the reflected stairs, and she saw, to her great astonishment, that the third door was not visible now.

'It was there before, Meg, honest!' Sam told her friend with a very earnest but baffled expression.

'Come on you,' Meg told her with a dismissive sigh and a shake of the head, 'you better unpack.'

After Sam had unpacked everything, she sat down with Meg and they each had a glass of wine and watched TV. At one point, around 11.40pm, Sam went into the kitchen, which was a very dreary and old fashioned one, and not at all like a modern fitted kitchen. She took a pot of yoghurt from the fridge, and then she suddenly had the eerie impression that someone was standing behind her. She turned quickly and for a brief second, something dark and shadowlike flitted away towards a section of the wall to the right of an old cabinet. This spooked the young lady and she quickly rejoined her flatmate and sat on the sofa, where she kept eyeing the kitchen doorway. In between scoffing Pringles as she watched TV, Megan noticed the way Sam kept looking towards the kitchen, and asked her what she was looking at. Sam told her she thought she had seen a ghost in the kitchen, and Megan smirked and, thinking her friend was just winding her up, she replied, 'Shut up.'

'I swear on my baby brother's life, I saw something, like a shadow – and it went into the wall,' Sam retorted, and then she gazed back at the doorway to the kitchen.

Megan got up off the sofa and walked over to the doorway to the kitchen, and Sam walked gingerly behind her. Megan asked her where the ghost had gone into the wall and Sam pointed to the section of old faded wallpaper next to a cabinet containing plates and upturned wine glasses. 'There,' she pointed at the wall, 'just darted into it dead fast.' That part of the wall sounded hollow, incidentally.

Megan took one of the upturned glasses from the cabinet and suggested contacting the ghost with a makeshift Ouija board. This proposal really scared Sam and she backed away into the living room and swore. Meg thought it was funny seeing her friend so scared and she shouted out: 'Come out, come out, whoever you are - in the name of the Devil!'

'Shut up you stupid idiot!' Sam cried, and she switched on the lights in the living room. Megan laughed, and went to the toilet. Sam went downstairs and checked that the front door was securely locked, because she actually sensed that there was something evil about on this night. She then turned away from the door and happened to glance in the mirror in the hallway again. There was that third door again. Sam quickly ran up the stairs and went to her bed where she felt her heart palpitate. The bedroom door burst open and in came Megan wearing her Adidas jacket with the hood up. Sam screamed and then threw a paperback at her clowning friend. That night, Sam had a vivid dream that she was on the stairs of the house, and she could see the three doors at the top of the stairs. The third door, which could usually only be seen in the mirror, started to slowly open, and although Sam was afraid to see what was behind that door, she found herself walking up the stairs towards it. Upon reaching the landing, she saw a rosy light shining from the open door, and she walked into the room there. What she saw was horrific. A woman around Sam's age – in her early twenties - with long straight black hair, was tied with thick rope to an X-shaped cross, bound by her wrists and ankles, and a man in a pointed hood which covered his face, and a weird long robe which went down to the floor, was torturing the woman. He had cut a "Glasgow smile" – a long incision leading from the edges of the girl's lips to her ears - so it looked as if she had a huge grin, and the woman was screaming to Sam for help. The man in the hood turned, startled by Sam, with a huge knife in his hand, and he said: 'This isn't what you think! She's a witch! An evil witch! I *have* to kill her! Get out of here!'

Sam screamed and ran – then woke up in a cold sweat. This dream was replayed every night for almost a week. She would see the third door open to reveal a scarlet room with the hooded man torturing a woman he alleged to be a witch.

Then the dreams stopped, and a few months later – on the evening of Halloween - Sam was in the flat alone, waiting for Megan to arrive with a few friends for a 'Duck Apple Party' – when something terrifying happened. Sam had her iPod on and was in the kitchen listening to music through her earphones, when a reddish light went on behind her. She turned and saw the red light was coming from a doorway to a room with scarlet walls. A partially materialised figure came out of this room into the kitchen, and Sam could see it was the very witch she had seen in her recurring nightmares. She was naked and she had a loop of rope coiled loosely around her neck, and the entity grabbed hold of this rope trailing from her and tried to loop it round Sam's neck as she shrieked with laughter. As Sam struggled to get the rope off, she felt the icy bony hands of the ghostly woman grip her. Sam screamed – and suddenly, a tall figure came out of the scarlet room. It was the man in the pointed hood who had tortured the witch in the horrific dreams. As Sam screamed at the top of her voice, the hooded man pushed her aside and his gloved hands gripped the witch's neck. Sam slipped the rope off and bolted out of the kitchen and a minute later she found herself running down the road outside the house. She refused to set foot in that house again. That evening, when Megan and her friends went into the kitchen, they saw the name "ELIZABETH SHORT" spelled out on Scrabble tiles on a coffee table. A woman of that name was horrifically tortured and murdered in the 1940s in the United States. Her killer – who cut Miss Short in two, severing her at the waist, after carving a ghastly smile on her face, leading from the edges of her mouth to her ears, was never found. I do not advise you to Google this unfortunate murder victim's name as the search engine will bring up some disturbing images of her appalling injuries. The significance of the murder victim's name – if that's what something – some spirit in the farmhouse was referring to with the Scrabble tiles - is unknown. There are rumours that the former farmhouse in Knowsley was once the scene of a witch execution in the 16th century and that a young woman with the surname Bates was put to death by a local priest for killing many with her dark witchcraft. For some reason, in 2009, the landlord of the cottage gave his tenants notice to quit, then boarded the doors and windows up. The cottage still lies vacant…

THE HOUSE IN THE PARK

That sunny Sunday afternoon, on 17 August 1958, the great parabolic dish of the Jodrell Bank radio telescope in Cheshire was turned to the western skies, attempting to pick up the signals from an American probe that was supposed to fly from Cape Canaveral to the nearest world in space – the moon, but unfortunately the rocket carrying the moon-bound probe exploded shortly after take-off in the skies of Florida. Ironically, a sinister event was unfolding in Liverpool's Sefton Park that very day which suggested that there are other undiscovered worlds nearer to ours than the derelict ones of space. Jane Banks was just aged nine at the time but even now at the age of 65 she remembers the surreal and scary incident as if it had only taken place yesterday afternoon.

Jane left her home on Rosemont Road, Aigburth and walked to the nearby house of her 12-year-old cousin Simon Noakes on North Sudley Road, They then made their way to meet a friend – a 9-year-old girl named Siwan (Susan in Welsh, pronounced Shoo-an) Williams. Siwan attended the same school as Jane and she and her family had only recently moved to Liverpool from North Wales. The three children met in the park, not far from the majestic domed Palm House (which had recently been re-opened after its panes had been shattered by a German bomb in 1941). Simon had brought his beloved leather "casey" football but the girls didn't want to play footy on such a hot day. They collected various flower petals and planned to make their own perfume. Simon soon got bored of the maidenly duo's flower-gathering and suggested calling the park keeper names from the bushes. The girls just tutted condescendingly and Jane, in a haughty imitation of an adult, said, 'Be quiet boy'.

Frustrated as to what to do, Simon "volleyed" the ball with a kick that sent it into the upper branches of a wych elm. He tried to retrieve the casey by climbing the branches but it was too high up – but while the lad was nearly 30 feet up, he noticed something quite odd: there was a little terracotta bricked house about 300 yards away – and he had never noticed that house before. He quickly shinned down the branches and ran to tell the flower-gatherers about his discovery, and was so eager for them to see the peculiar house, he dragged poor Jane by her arm, saying, 'Hurry up! Come on!'

Simon and the girls walked along complaining about his heavy-handed tactics, but when they saw the pointy gabled house standing exactly where Simon said it would be, they smiled and wondered if anyone lived there. There was a red front door and two oval windows above it. 'Shall I knock and see if anyone answers?' Simon asked with a mischievous grin, and he played with his front loose tooth.

But the red door suddenly opened – and out came a man in an outlandish clown costume of some sort, with a pointed hat and a ruffled lace collar. His face was white as snow and he had black x-shaped eyes. 'Hello!' he said to the children, and they all noticed he had a musical instrument resembling a gold cornet in his hands now. As he sat on the doorstep, he played this cornet and as beautiful mellifluous music came out of it, so did large soap bubbles! Simon grinned and went to walk to the clown but little Siwan yelled, 'No, come back Simon!' in her sweet Welsh accent. Jane also sensed there was something not quite right about the clown and that house. Simon walked on, but suddenly a huge stray mongrel the children often saw in the park tuned up, and began to growl and bark at the clown, distracting him, and he stopped playing. The clown chased the dog, which ran off yelping into a wooded area, and while the clown was gone, Simon walked to the doorway of the house – and an awful smell greeted his nose; the disagreeable odour of blood and meat of the kind he had smelled at the butchers. Siwan suddenly let out a terrible scream and she ran off crying. Simon instinctively started to run from the out-of-place house too, and Jane also turned and fled, but they both then looked back – and saw the clown was chasing them, and he was no longer smiling – he looked livid. The children ran into an adult couple and told them about the house and the clown, but when Jane looked into the distance, the house had vanished. Siwan, who was said to be psychic, said she had screamed because she had seen a horrible giant face appear on the front of the house, and the windows became eyes and the door became a huge mouth – as if that dwelling had been alive. And what of that sickly odour of blood Simon had smelt? Had that thing masquerading as a house been some creature from elsewhere which – heaven forbid – consumed the curious?

When I mentioned this account of the weird house in Sefton Park on a radio programme I'd been invited onto to discuss the paranormal, I received calls, letters and emails from many other people who had seen similar strange things in parks across the UK. A woman in her early sixties named June Roundtree got in touch with me to recount a very strange and frightening incident which took place in Derby's seven and-a-half-hectare Arboretum Park, probably the oldest public park in England, which dates back to around 1840. June was 5 years old at the time and lived in Wilfred Street, which is quite near to the park. It was a hot Sunday afternoon in early May 1954, and June was playing with her older sister Marie and a friend named Barbara, when she decided to hide from them. June could hear her sister Marie and Barbara shouting her name as she giggled behind a tree. The child sneaked away and ran behind another tree in the park, then turned – and saw something which immediately caught her full attention. A red "wigwam" stood in a clearing about thirty feet away – an actual coned-shaped tent of the type June had seen on westerns on the television, and as she looked on in awe, she saw a man come out of the wigwam with a massive feathered headdress of the kind worn by the old Sioux chiefs. June cannot remember what else the man was wearing but she did recall that he was white and was definitely not an actual Native American Indian. The man in the colourful headdress beckoned with his hand for June to come to him, and seeing that he had a kind smiling face and did not seem sinister in any way, the 5-year-old first looked back, hoping that Marie and Barbara had seen the man and the wigwam, but there was no sign of the girls. June walked up to the man and he said, 'Come into my tent,' and as he said this he stepped aside and waved his right hand in the direction of the wigwam, which had some angular red and black designs upon it. June sensed she shouldn't go into that tent, and she looked at the entrance to the wigwam, which was of course, just an opening with a flap of canvas or cloth hanging beside it. June thought she saw something with enormous owl-like eyes within the dark interior of that tent, and that creepy thing seemed to be waiting for her. 'Go on, go in!' the "Indian Chief" urged the cautious girl, but June turned and ran as fast as her legs could carry her until she found her sister and friend, and she told them about the strange man in the feathered headdress and his wigwam, but of course, June wasn't believed. Marie and Barbara went to have a look for the tent and saw it was indeed where June said it would be, but there was no sign of the man wearing the costume of the Indian chief to be seen. Then, all of a sudden, that tent was gone. One moment it was there and then Marie glanced back and saw it had vanished. A few days after this, the wigwam and the weird man masquerading as an Indian chief was seen again in the very same spot, and this time he was seen by Marie and her schoolfriend Penny. The stranger asked the girls to come into the wigwam but they refused. The man became annoyed and apparently told Penny that a man she knew would be killed "by forked lightning." Penny asked him who this man was and the eccentric but creepy man gave her the full name of the man who Penny knew because he lived in her street near the park. Penny told the man she was going to tell her parents what he had said and he laughed and went into the wigwam. The girls then walked away, and Penny glanced back – and that tent was nowhere to be seen. She told her mother what the stranger had said about a neighbour being killed by forked lightning, and a few days later on Wednesday May 12, the neighbour that the man in the wigwam had named, a 35-year-old man, was umpiring a cricket match at Raynsway, just two miles from Arboretum Park, when rain stopped play. As the man came back onto the pitch and wondered whether play should resume, he was struck by lightning, and taken to hospital, but was declared dead on arrival. When Penny heard about the tragic incident she suffered a breakdown and had nightmares about the man in the wigwam in Arboretum Park for years. Penny lives in Cheshire now and can still recall the eerie man in the Indian headdress, and feels he was a demonic child-snatcher of some sort. She recalled how, in the presence of the man, there seemed to be a strange quietness hanging in the air, and once she and Marie walked away from the clearing the sounds of other children playing in the park and the hubbub of the traffic in the distance seemed to return.

These are just two of the many cases I have looked into regarding these bizarre and frightening entities which seem to target children in parks. I believe they are undoubtedly paranormal in origin, and I wonder if some of the many cases of inexplicable child disappearances over the years could be the work of these beings.

SPIRIT AUNTS

Many years ago in Liverpool there was a real pedigreed prognosticator – a bona fide fortune teller who – according to her many clients - could really peer into the future and many were convinced she could talk to the dead. This soothsayer, who was only in her twenties, had a tiny consulting room on Mount Pleasant over a watch repair shop, and one Saturday morning in August 1969, a 37-year-old woman named Mary paid her a visit. 'There are two women with you – aunties,' the psychic told Mary straight away as she came into the little office, and she shocked her client by giving their first names as well as some impressive information. 'Hilda passed over in 1950 and you lost Wendy three years ago,' the mystic asserted, and Mary nodded, mouth wide open, astounded. 'Look, Mary, I'm not feeling too good today, and seeing as you have the gift, talk to your aunties yourself.' The psychic then said she had morning sickness – she was expecting. She had not foreseen this symptomatic bout of illness raising its ugly head this morning because the fortune teller tended to block out glimpses of her own future for personal reasons.

'Oh, sorry, I'll come back when you're better,' Mary said, somewhat disappointed, but as she was leaving, the young clairvoyant said: 'Mary – that is your name, isn't it? Talk to them as you used to – and then listen closely, and I swear you'll receive a reply from them; really believe though.'

Mary was very intrigued now, and later in Coopers on Church Street, she sat sipping coffee and she looked around, then, convinced that none of the people at the other tables in the café were within earshot, she whispered: 'Auntie Hilda? Auntie Wendy? Are you there?'

A pair of hands suddenly came round Mary's head and gently clamped her eyes. 'If you gotta go, go now – or else you got to stay all night!' the eye-clamper sang, and Mary blushed and her heart palpitated. It was Paul, 11 years her junior, and that Manfred Mann song he sung played on the radio *that* night nearly three years ago when she was weak, after the Christmas do at work. He hadn't changed a bit, and just seeing him made her feel twenty again. As they caught up on each other's lives, Mary distinctly heard her Aunt Hilda in her right ear saying, 'Don't be a trollop Mary, you're married!' The last time Mary had heard that voice was in 1950 – the year she lost Aunt Hilda - when she was eighteen, but it was instantly recognisable after all that time. Then came the softer timbre of an equally distinctive voice – that of her younger Aunt Wendy in her left ear: 'Oh be quiet, you prude, Hilda, her husband treats her like a slave! These are liberating times!'

'Mary?' Paul seemed concerned at the way she was distracted. 'You okay?'

'Oh, yeah, yeah – I'm okay, sorry,' Mary's eyes swivelled left and right, caught in the clairvoyant cross-conversation. 'So, are you with anyone now?' she asked Paul, and he jokily replied, 'Yeah, I'm with you,' then smiled and shook his head. He reached across the table and clasped Mary's hands. 'I liked what we had, can we do it again?' he asked, and now the smile had evaporated from his face and he seemed so serious.

'Tell that womaniser to get stuffed!' said Hilda out the ether, 'The cheeky bee! He's only after one thing! I've got him taped!'

Wendy loudly disagreed: 'You've had your life, Hilda, now let Mary live hers! Marriage makes or mars a woman, and it has certainly marred our Mary! She's too good for that tyrant!'

'You seem miles away,' Paul was irritated by Mary's sudden brown study, for not being at all psychic, he could not hear a single word being spoken by the ladies who had long passed on. 'You alright Mary? Mary?'

Mary turned her attention back to the living. 'Paul, I'm too old for you; you deserve someone your own age.'

She didn't hear what Paul's reply was because of her bickering aunties, and Paul stormed out of Coopers thinking she was ignoring him. The unwanted advice of the two spirit aunties continually plagued Mary for weeks, then one day she went to see the fortune teller who had first suggested using the 'gift' – and how Mary thought that word was such a misnomer – it was more of a curse in her case.

'Why would you want to block them out?' the young psychic gave a quizzical smile.

'They're advising me about *everything*,' Mary told her, and gritted her teeth as she looked left and right at the places in mid air where the voices of the aunts seemed to originate. 'They advise me on what I eat, what I watch on the telly, how often I should go to the toilet, and they tell me what the neighbours really think of me. They even appear in my dreams and tell me when to wake up. Plus I don't like the idea of them watching me when I'm having a bath!'

'Ah, I see,' the fortune teller said, and she could hear Hilda's faint voice saying: 'Oh don't be silly, Mary, you don't want us to stop talking to you, girl, we're just offering you advice.'

The mystic told Mary to try various meditation techniques to focus on certain mandala-like images in an effort to block the voices out, but Mary just knew these esoteric suggestions wouldn't work – and they didn't when she attempted them. In fact, ironically, a third voice began to come through, albeit occasionally, after these failed exercises – the gruff voice of her late grandfather! And he had a very old-fashioned attitude towards everything in Mary's modern life.

And then one day, many weeks after this, Mary went to the dentist for a check up, and during the examination, the tooth doctor suddenly remarked: 'Ah, who are those two ladies with you?' Mary was stunned. The dentist – a man in his forties named Donald - had seen the dead since he was four. As he became older, he also began to hear the voices of the dearly departed, and over the years he found out how to 'block them out' so he could get on with his day to day living, although now and then he'd relax and the odd voices of the dead – and sometimes their images - what we call ghosts – would become detectable. Mary was naturally fascinated by the dentist's knowledge of the spirit world and of course, she was even more captivated by Donald's claim about being able to shut the pesky spirit voices out, and the dentist promised he'd teach Mary this technique – preferably over dinner, he suggested.

'I'm married, Donald,' she told him.

'We'll just be having dinner – as friends, Mary,' was his reply, 'nothing more. Just friends.'

Within the space of a year Mary divorced her husband and married that dentist.

FRENCH TOAST

Certain strange stories come my way from time to time and sometimes I notice that these tales seem somewhat familiar; they have been reported to me before, and the outcomes of the stories have been the same but different people were involved with each telling. The sociologist would confidently say that such recurring stories are just urban legends – and sometimes they probably are – but in these cases the witnesses were interviewed at length by myself and two of them were people who are not in the business of fabricating yarns: a doctor and a priest. In the late 1950s there was a café called Sissons on Liverpool's Bold Street, and one afternoon a doctor and his pretty 15-year-old daughter Miranda stopped off at this café after a trip around the shops. The doctor's wife was in hospital, recovering from a caesarean, and he and Miranda had been buying her chocolates and various gifts. A spectacled old woman at the table next to the one the doctor and his daughter were seated at was grumbling about the long wait for her French toast, and Miranda, who had a mischievous streak, began to wind the old lady up by telling her she should complain. 'Do you think I should?' the oldster asked, and Miranda beamed a sidelong grin at her father, who shook his head, gesturing for her to stop stirring things up and getting the poor old dear agitated, but the girl turned to the lady and said: 'Oh yes, I'd complain; you've been waiting for ages haven't you? French toast isn't that hard to make. Maybe they're ignoring you!'

'Ignoring me, eh?' the old woman screwed her face up and then began waving her walking stick in the air at a waitress.

'Miranda! Stop it!' the doctor warned his daughter, who looked ready to burst into laughter. The waitress told the old lady she had not ordered French toast, but the pensioner insisted she had. Miranda chortled over her milkshake. When she and her father left Sissons twenty minutes later, the old woman was still arguing with the staff at the café about the 'disgraceful amount of time' she had waited for her French toast.

That night, Miranda was in bed, sound asleep, when something awoke her. She opened her eyes. At first she thought her father was leaning over her, asking her to get up. He often did this because Miranda was a heavy sleeper, but when the girl focused on the face she saw to her horror that it was the face of that old woman from the café that was looming over her, and the elderly lady had such a look of hatred in her eyes behind a pair of wire-framed glasses. 'You're not laughing at me now, are you – Miranda?' she said in a suspiciously-sounding low voice – a *male* voice in fact. Miranda froze in fear; how had the old female impersonator got into her bedroom? Suddenly the face of the eerie intruder changed into something truly horrifying – so terrifying in fact that Miranda managed to emit a single scream before passing out. Her father in his room next door heard the scream, followed by a man's laugh, and heavy running footsteps, and when he barged into Miranda's room there was no one there except his daughter who was having a seizure on her bed. The doctor searched the landing and hallway and the other rooms of the house and found no evidence of an intruder. Miranda recovered from her terrifying ordeal and the doctor made enquiries about the "old lady" at Sissons but he discovered that the staff there had only seen her that one afternoon and didn't know who she was. The exact same thing happened years later in the 1960s when Sissons became the El Cabala Café; a woman made a scene because of an inordinate wait for French toast and 13-year-old Cecelia Jones on a neighbouring table - who found the cantankerous old lady funny - was also visited by her at her Old Swan home that night. In the 1970s an old lady who looked to be in her mid-seventies, complained about the unreasonable wait for French toast in Swinnertons cafe in Chester, then that very night, she appeared in the bedrooms of several of the children who had smirked at her melodramatic behaviour. I mentioned the aforementioned cases on a radio programme I was invited on to talk about the paranormal, and received many more almost identical accounts from listeners who believed they had either encountered the creepy old woman or knew someone who had. Around 1971, a 12-year-old girl named Brenda accompanied her grandparents to a café called the Sorrento on Coventry's Gosford Street one rainy afternoon. Brenda had been shopping with her granddad and grandma, and the latter had suggested that rather than going to all the trouble of cooking the tea when she got home, they could have a meal at the Sorrento. The trio had only been at the café for about five minutes when an old woman, who, Brenda recalled, looked like the actress (Irene Ryan) who played Granny Clampett in *The Beverly Hillbillies* TV comedy series, began to shout at her table in the corner. 'Where is my French toast? Where is it?' the old woman cried at one of the waitresses. Then she began to ask for a glass of water, and said she would be writing to the newspapers to tell people about the long time she had been waiting to get served. Again, the waitress told the old woman she had not received her order for French toast, but the old woman, who wore NHS wire-frame spectacles and had her grey hair scraped up into a little bun, turned to Brenda's grandparents and asked: 'You two remember me ordering French toast don't you?'

Brenda's grandmother seemed somewhat embarrassed at being drawn into the customer's complaint and sheepishly said nothing, but her husband shot a puzzled look at the old woman and said, 'I don't, sorry.'

Brenda giggled when the woman came over, leaned on the table and seemed near to tears over not receiving her toast. 'All I wanted was my French toast, and they won't give me it,' she said in a broken voice. The old lady's sickly sweet perfume assaulted Brenda's nostrils and she disrespectfully pinched her nose and waved her hand in the air. She then burst out laughing and went red, and her grandmother told her off. Eventually the old woman left the Sorrento, saying she'd go to another café from now on where people were served.

All the way home on the bus, Brenda kept imitating the old woman to make her grandmother laugh. 'Where's my French toast? I'll have you arrested for this!' the girl said in a silly soprano voice which bemused her grandparents. The mocking girl also made fun of the crabby old woman's 'cheap perfume'.

Around 11.15om that night, at her terraced home on Coventry's Avon Street, Brenda's mother told her daughter it was time she went to bed, and the girl went to brush her teeth, then changed into her pyjamas. She took a *Bunty* comic to bed with her and tried to read it by the light of her bedside lamp, but dozed off after a few minutes. She awoke at about one in the morning and noticed that the bedside lamp had been switched off. Brenda's mother had turned it off after looking in on her daughter at midnight and seeing her fast asleep. Brenda lay there in the darkness and was about to turn over and go back to sleep, when her little button nose detected a very familiar sweet smell – the scent that old lady had worn in the café. Straight away, Brenda somehow knew that old woman was there in the darkened room, and as she lay stock-still in the bed, she heard a faint rustle of fabric close by – and she felt a cold tingle down her spine. Then came the sensation of the mattress to her left being pressed down gently – as if someone was climbing onto the bed. Brenda then heard someone mutter the F-word close to her ear, and this person sounded male. Brenda's parents never swore and this person did not by any stretch of the imagination sound like her mother or father. Brenda let out a scream and ran from the bed. She ran to the bedroom of her parents and shook her mother awake to tell her of the intruder in her room. When the girl's mother and father entered Brenda's bedroom they immediately smelt the same cheap perfume their daughter had reported, and Brenda saw that someone had torn her copy of the *Bunty* in two and left it on the bed. Brenda became hysterical and told her mother that the old lady from the café had been in her room and she refused to sleep in her own bed for days.

Just who – or what - the creepy old woman character is remains a mystery. I have many reports of her - with only minor variations in her description – seen over a large area of Britain that stretches from Coventry, to Chester and Liverpool, to Hull and Norfolk – but if these widespread incidents concern the same old lady, then she certainly gets around, and she's been at this sinister lark for a long time by the sound of it - and why on earth does she say the same thing about the unreasonably long wait for French toast? The case remains a real puzzler.

BLACKPOOL'S PHANTOM TSUNAMI

One late afternoon in the summer of 1957, holidaymakers on Blackpool beach probably sighed and shook their heads when the blue skies suddenly darkened and thunder rolled in from the Irish Sea. They probably assumed it was one of those typical unpredictable changes in the English weather we are so accustomed to. Patty Whittaker, an 8-year-old girl from Liverpool's Norris Green area, is one of many who were on the beach that August afternoon when something took place which remains unexplained to this day. She was eating candy floss and eyeing the Punch and Judy show with her 12-year-old cousin Michael, and Patty's mum and dad were about fifty feet away with her baby brother John, who was seated on one of the famous donkeys of the beach. There came a tremendous roar in the distance, quite unlike any thunder Patty had ever heard, and she looked out to sea towards the source of the frightening noise, and saw peculiar dark clouds appearing in the blue sky. The effect reminded the child of the way spots of ink 'blossom' and spread when dropped in clear water. Out of this heavenly turmoil, long bolts of forked lightning struck the sea, and as Patty squinted in the sharp cold salty wind that was now stirring, she saw what looked like the misted coastline of an island that had not been there before. Her parents also saw this strange 'mirage' and Patty's father Ray estimated that the island was about five miles off – to the west – which was impossible, as there is no land that far out from the Fylde coast. All of a sudden, that island was seen to tip over, as if something had pulled a gargantuan plug out the bed of the sea, and as the unknown island rose vertically, the lightning repeatedly struck the landmass, which began to crumble as it tipped into oblivion. As the rumbles of this baffling and scary apocalyptic event reached the Blackpool shore, the air was full of gasps of awe and shock from the hundreds of tourists dotted about. Then came screams, because as the island plunged into the waters, the sea bulged and huge foam-topped waves headed inland. Pandemonium broke out. I doubt most in those days had heard of a tsunami, but that was what the people on the beach were witnessing that afternoon. It would have been impossible to outrun that wave of death, but those nearest to the waterline scrambled for the sands. A powerful blast of wind-driven sand almost toppled the Punch and Judy tent, and Patty's candyfloss was torn from its stick. The donkeys giving rides cried out in fear, somehow sensing the unnatural disaster at hand, and Patty's mum and dad snatched little John from the back of the animal and then ran to their daughter and her cousin Michael – who was gazing in horror at the thundering tidal wave as it rolled in against a nightmarish backdrop of the last vestiges of an island slipping into the deep while lightning, acting as if it had a malicious mind of its own, continually struck the sinking upturned terrain. Some on the beach who were present during this strange cataclysm thought they heard a distant cacophony of what sounded like a thousand screaming voices. A 22-year-old Wallasey woman named Liz who was close to the waterline, said an old man told her not to be alarmed, because what was happening was just 'something from the past' which he had seen many times before. The old man was subsequently proved right, because the tidal wave which came hurtling inland never reached the beach as an hammer-blow from the sea – instead, a gale-strength blast of air hit Blackpool, and then as it died, the blue of summer returned to the skies and people looked seawards in disbelief, for now there was not a trace of the sunken island – just glittering golden waves and skimming gulls. Not long after this the weather changed again and an 80 mph squall struck Blackpool and actually blew down a giant Ferris wheel on the Pleasure Beach. What did people see that August afternoon in 1957? No one can say for sure, but I'd hazard a guess and say it was the ghostly re-enactment of the demise of the legendary island of Kilgrimol – a veritable Atlantis on our doorstep which most local historians know nothing of. A long time ago, back in the days before the Roman invasion, they say, Kilgrimol was a beautiful island 7 miles off the Fylde coast, and was about a quarter of the size of the Isle of Man, some maintain. The inhabitants of this island turned to all sorts of perversions and worshipped dark bloodthirsty gods, and a ring of powerful magicians (including a young Merlin) decided to bring down the wrath of Mother Nature upon the wicked Kilgrimolians, and in a very short space of time, lightning bolts seared the island and the bed of the sea floor yawned open and swallowed up Kilgrimol…

GRANDFATHER WEREWOLF

On the outskirts of Liverpool, wedged between Huyton's Victoria Road and Seel Road you will find a Congregational Church (founded in 1890) and a number of unremarkable bungalows, and a little further to the east you will see the sprawl of Huyton Creative Learning Centre. Back in 1932, on the fields adjoining the learning centre, an airstrip was built for the use by Huyton Hill Preparatory School – making the (private) school the first one in Britain to have its own airfield. The landing strip was the brainchild of the school's headmaster Hubert Butler, a Flight Lieutenant of World War One who wanted his pupils to gain practical knowledge of aviation at first hand, and the schoolboys often journeyed from the 25-acre aerodrome to Speke Airport for instructional days out in the school's own plane. Unfortunately, Nazi reconnaissance planes noticed the Huyton Hill airstrip and targeted it for future bombing missions, but the school headmaster fortunately evacuated his pupils to the Lake District upon the outbreak of World War Two. On 19 November 1940, the private school was damaged by a high explosive German bomb, and was subsequently demolished in 1946. So much for this little morsel of Huyton's orthodox local history, but next we come to a sinister little-known incident concerning the Huyton airfield. Around the 1930s when the land earmarked for the airstrip was being surveyed, a tiny cottage adjoining the school field, which was located in the shadows of a wood, was seen as a possible future obstruction, and the single tenant of this cottage, a woman in her sixties known only as Mrs Husha, is believed to have been subjected to an underhand campaign to drive her from her home. Her persecutors did not know that this woman was reputed to be a witch of fearsome talents. It is said that several people who sent Husha anonymous hate mail all died around the same time, including a man who had his arm and shoulder blade torn off in a gruesome accident at Cronton Colliery. People in the area soon realised that Mrs Husha possessed the dark faculty of casting the so-called Evil Eye upon her enemies, and there were rumours that some local bigwig was prepared to resort to murder to get her out of the way. Nothing short of a conspiracy took place with interested parties using influential friends to evict the suspected witch, but no one could even find an ordnance survey map with her cottage marked upon it nor could a record of the dwelling be found in the Land Registry. I mentioned this strange case on BBC radio once and subsequently interviewed a number of people on air who remembered Mrs Husha. They said that the cottage seemed to disappear around 1931, and all that could be found on the spot where it stood was a rectangle of faded grass; not even a trace of any foundations was visible. It transpired that Mrs Husha was part of some type of coven in the area, and all sorts of strange and seemingly far-fetched – but apparently well-documented – stories about her have been uncovered. In 1970, a 9-year-old boy named

George, who lived at his semi-detached home on Huyton's Rupert Road, went mooching in the loft one day, and discovered an old purple hardback of a few hundred pages entitled 'Nursery Rhyme Tales', and finding the illustrations of well-known characters such as Goldilocks, the Three Bears and Jack and Jill quite captivating, he took the book up to his bed that night and read it under the covers with a torch he had got for his birthday. That same night, the boy's grandfather, whom George had been named after, paid a visit. Grandpa George was not a popular man, for he had quite a reputation as an outspoken reprobate who caused trouble wherever he went, and even his own daughter, Jane (little George's mum) became a bag of nerves whenever he visited, as he was usually drunk, and on this night he'd obviously had a bit too much to drink. He called at the house on Rupert Road at ten, and Jane and her husband wouldn't open the door at first, but George threatened he'd kick the door in if they refused to open it – so they did, and after barging into the hallway he said he was going to see his grandson. He went upstairs and George junior pretended to be asleep, because he was scared of his drunken grandfather, but George senior knew he was really awake and pretended there was a spider on the bed. Little George's eyes shot open and his granddad laughed and said he'd sing to him to get him asleep. At some point George senior noticed the old book of nursery rhymes and said he'd read them to the lad, and he did, but as he read on, he saw that these nursery rhymes and their illustrations were horrific and quite disturbing. He also noticed that in the middle of the book there were strange verses, and they read like spells of some sort. Jane and her husband knocked on the bedroom door and told George to go, and he said he would be going after he had read his grandson a bedtime tale. The couple then went downstairs grumbling. The grandson is now in his fifties, and he told me what happened that night in 1970, and he assures me that he did not imagine it because his parents also witnessed the terrifying incident. George senior began to recite a verse in the old book, and that verse mentioned a wolf and also the words 'I will go in my Master's name'.

All of a sudden, the boy's grandfather cried out and made awful choking sounds. George senior had a good head of curly snow-white hair and a thick white beard. This beard seemed to grow up his face before the little boy's eyes, and the child also saw his grandfather's eyebrows sprout, thicken and join in the middle. Then all of a sudden, the granddad's mouth opened wider and wider, and his dentures shot out, pushed out by the emergence of huge pointed teeth and fangs. As these teeth emerged from the old man's gums, blood poured from them and he cried in agony. Then the grandfather's face became like that of a wild animal with greenish eyes. Little George screamed as he clung on to his teddy, and he ran from the bed and out of the room. He was so afraid, he hid in the cupboard under the stairs down in the hallway, and listened to something growling on the stairs as his mother screamed. Some time later the boy's father opened the cupboard and took George to his aunt's house miles away. The boy never saw his grandfather again after that night and he never set eyes on that purple book again. Years later, George's mother told him that she was part of a coven, and that the book he had found had belonged to a Mrs Husha – a former head of the coven. According to Jane, that night in 1970, her father had accidentally quoted a spell the witches of old had used to transfigure themselves into various animals such as hares, dogs – and even wolves. Her father had afterwards died from shock when his body returned to that of a human. What became of Husha's spell book – which was disguised as a volume of nursery rhymes – is a mystery.

THE INDESTRUCTIBLE ARTHUR BROWN

Some readers may recall the cult television series *Captain Scarlet and the Mysterons* which starred the eponymous Captain Scarlet as an indestructible agent of World Security Command, Spectrum, because he possessed a 'retrometabolism' which allowed him to make a rapid miraculous recovery from any injury sustained from guns, explosions, fires, and so on. Whilst Scarlet is fiction, there have been a number of amazing real-life cases where people have cheated death against incredible odds. One night in 1944, 21-year-old Flight Sergeant Nicholas Alkemade, a rear gunner in an RAF Avro Lancaster bomber, was returning from his thirteenth raid on Berlin when a Junkers 88 crippled his plane. Alkemade returned fire and the Nazi plane plummeted in flames. Alkemade's elation was short-lived however, because the Lancaster bomber was on fire with no hope of recovery and ready to fall 18,000 feet to a certain doom for everyone on board – unless they bailed out. 'You'll have to jump for it! Bail out! Bail out!' crackled the pilot's voice over the plane intercom. The other six crew members bailed out – but Alkemade couldn't get to his parachute because of the flames and he watched it burn. Rather than be burnt to a crisp, he tore off his melting oxygen mask and somersaulted through an opening, 'You've had your lot!' he told himself and watched the stars above as he fell. He calculated that his fall from 18,000 feet would mean that he'd hit the ground in one and a half minutes. 'Won't be seeing my sweetheart Pearl, anymore,' he muttered, then passed out from the cold. He didn't feel the impact. He opened one eye and saw the stars shining through the alpine branches. He had survived a 3-mile drop, and deciding he deserved a cigarette, he lit up. 'Nix parachute!' the German rescuers remarked and could not believe Alkemade had fallen 3 miles and merely sustained a twisted knee, but his claims were later confirmed. Nearer to home, there have been other unearthly examples of apparently indestructible people. In the mid-1970s, a car collided with a JCB near Liverpool's Ullet Road one afternoon. The vehicle lay in pieces and a teacher passing in his car went to give first aid to the 74-year-old driver of the smashed vehicle, as his clothes were on fire. The old man, Arthur Brown of Birkenhead, got up and laughed as he patted the flames out with his bare hands. He was taken to hospital but had not suffered a scratch or sustained the smallest burn. I mentioned this incident in one of my newspaper columns in the 1990s and Arthur's daughter, Helen got in touch and told me about her father's other incredible brushes with death – which she puts down to his guardian angel. In 1916 Arthur lied about his age and had signed up to serve for king and country in WWI at the age of 15 and survived the detonation of a German shell which landed thirty feet away and killed three other soldiers. In the 1920s he saved a dog that someone had thrown into the River Mersey, but slipped, climbing out of the river near the landing stage, and fell back into the water. The current pulled

Arthur under the landing stage, where he somehow survived in an air pocket. He then managed to swim back to safety after narrowly missing the propeller blades of a ferry boat. In May 1941, in the darkest days of WWII, Arthur was near the Huskisson Dock, looking for his cousin (an ARP warden) quite unaware he was in close proximity to the *SS Malakand*, a Brocklebank cargo liner packed with over a thousand tons of bombs and shells. Flames from nearby sheds that had sustained damaged from enemy bombing spread to the *Malakand*, and one of the greatest explosions in Liverpool's history took place. The blast destroyed the entire Huskisson Dock and parts of the *Malakand* were found two and a half miles away. Arthur was blown twenty feet into the air and woke up on a major road where fire engines were narrowly missing him. He sustained a sprained wrist. In 1971, Arthur was close to the Hotel Riviera on the Costa del Sol when it caved in as workmen were installing a tennis court on the roof. He was partially blinded by the dust from the debris but was otherwise okay. Then, in the following year, he was standing on the seventh-floor veranda of a hotel complex at Pineda, Spain, when he stumbled and fell over the balcony. Arthur's daughter screamed and closed her eyes. She heard a faint thump. Arthur had landed on a thick hedge and bounced into a swimming pool, dislocating his shoulder. Arthur married in the following year at the age of seventy, and there were was only one further close shave with death when he crashed into the JCB in Liverpool. He passed away peacefully six years later, aged 82. He told his daughter that his mother Mary had taken him to a church as a baby and asked God to look after him because he was a continually sickly infant. Perhaps Mary's prayers were answered and some guardian angel *really did* watch over Arthur Brown.

IT HAPPENED ON HALLOWEEN

No book on the paranormal would be complete without a chapter on strange incidents which have occurred on Halloween, that date in our calendar when, according to a long-held tradition, the worlds of the living and the dead overlap for a while, and all manner of spooky incidents are likely to take place.

In the September of 1976, that fondly-remembered year of the endless summer, standpipes and the drought, Ava and Vincent, a Liverpool couple in their early sixties, put an advertisement in the local newspaper's vacancies column for a young person to help with their busy toy shop near London Road. The couple interviewed seven applicants and chose a 17-year-old girl named Donna, who lived in the city's Wavertree district. Donna's take home pay was £30 per week and she worked from 9am till 5pm, Monday to Saturday. The best-selling toys at the shop that year were the Hot Wheels die-cast model cars, the red track-suited Six Million Dollar Man action figure, Pocketeers (handheld non-electronic games involving mazes, ball bearings and magnets), and Stretch Armstrong – an elastic action figure in blue underpants.

By mid-October of that year, Ava noticed that the shop's account book didn't quite add up; toys were obviously going missing on a regular basis. Vincent said it was all down to shoplifters but Ava suspected young Donna of theft, and told her husband she was going to keep watch on her through a hole in the thin partition wall to see if her suspicions were correct. Vincent had a row with his wife over this plan, and called her paranoid. All the same, Ava drilled a small hole in the partition wall and from the office (which Donna was not allowed to enter) and the shopkeeper kept close watch now and then in the hope of catching the shopgirl red-handed. A few days later in the afternoon, Ava was peeping through the hole when she saw a scruffy-looking lad of about 9 or 10 years of age come into the shop, followed by a girl aged about 7, and she was dressed in a little straw boater of some sort and a dark blue or black dress. The boy went behind the counter as Donna was gazing – apparently in a daydream – through the windows at the street outside. The little girl went to the counter and picked up a tiny doll there while her confederate grabbed a few boxes of Matchbox cars. Ava rushed into the shop but the children were gone when she got there and she chided Donna for not noticing that the kids were thieving. Donna said she had seen no one come into the shop and seemed baffled. On Saturday 30 October, Ava was serving at the shop after letting Donna have the half-day off, when in walked the two pilfering children she'd seen just over a week ago. Once again the lad walked nonchalantly behind the counter but this time Ava stood in his way and said "And where do *you* think you're going?" The boy, who was barefooted, recoiled in shock. 'You can see me!' he said, and turned to the little girl and shouted: 'Run Madge!'

The two children ran out the shop – through the closed glass door. Only then did Ava realise they had been ghosts, and she gazed at that door in shock for a while, then went into the office and told her husband what she had seen. He told Ava she'd been overworking herself an awful lot lately and suggested that she had been seeing things.

'I am not seeing things, Vincent,' Ava told him sternly, 'I saw two ghosts today, and I wonder if they've been stealing our stock?'

'Oh come on Ava, this is silly – ' Vincent shook his head and tried to explain the visitation away but Ava wasn't having any of it. She knew what she had seen with her own two eyes.

'I wonder if they'll come back,' she gasped, and goosebumps rose on her arms.

They did indeed come back. The two ghosts came peeping in at Ava a week later through the shop window but neither Donna or Vincent could see them. Ava wondered why only she could see them; was she psychic?

Several months later the old woman who had owned the shop before Ava was told of the ghosts, and she said: 'Aye, I used to see them. Madge Kirby is the little girl; she told me she was murdered across the road a long time ago, but the lad never said who he was, but I got the feeling he'd died on the road outside the shop a long time back.'

Madge Kirby was abducted in Kensington in 1908, aged seven, and they later found her body in an empty house on Great Newton Street, just across the road from that toyshop. What's more, the child had been wearing the very items of clothing Ava had seen the ghost wearing – the straw boater and the black dress.

Ava endured the ghostly visits for a month and then moved to new premises on the other side of town.

And now for another strange Halloween tale...

In the early hours of Sunday 6 October 1963, several residents living in the vicinity of Liverpool's Newsham Park were awakened by eerie chimes and what sounded like xylophone music. Those who were curious enough to leave their beds glanced through windows and saw an eerie blue light which hovered over the park at treetop level before drifting east towards Lister Drive, and not long afterwards the 33,000-volt oil-filled generator at Lister Drive power station exploded, and the resulting disruption of current in the local grid triggered burglar alarms from Kensington to Knotty Ash. Three days before, a policeman named Ken had been on his beat in Tuebrook, and at 3am he had been walking up Green Lane with nothing but a full moon for company when a well-known local drunk nicknamed "Jegger" startled the PC by jumping out on him from Moscow Drive. 'Hey PC49,' Jegger said, rather disrespectfully, 'you won't believe what I just saw.'

'Pink elephants ,' Ken remarked and told him to get home or he'd be nicked for being drunk and disorderly. Jegger shook his head and told the annoyed constable: 'Close! Pink, but no elephant! I have just seen a fairy, up there – as true as God's in Heaven! All in pink she was.' And he pointed up poorly-lit Moscow

Drive.

'I'm warning you, Jegger – ' Ken was saying, when he noticed a bright light hovering over the front wall of one of the terraced houses of Moscow Drive, about 300 yards distant. 'That's her!' Jegger turned and saw the sparkling light with a blue halo. 'She's all spotty.'

The policeman proceeded cautiously up the street, squinting at the light, which was now floating towards the mouth of an alleyway. With every step, the policeman's logically trained mind tried to make sense of that hovering light. When he reached the corner turning onto the alleyway he could see that the object round the corner was throwing off quite some light, and he could also hear a child's female voice singing a song called *Starry Eyed* – made popular by local crooner Michael Holliday a few years back. Ken peeped around that corner and saw what the drunk had tried to describe: a little blonde girl of about six years of age, wearing a pink ballerina outfit with a ruffled tutu – and she also wore a pair of fairy wings and held a wand with a bright star – and that had been the source of the light. What's more, this child was floating a few feet off the ground. It was an unnatural yet magical sight, and Ken simply couldn't believe his eyes.

The 'fairy' noticed the peeping PC and with anger she screwed up her angelic – and very spotty – face, then pointed her luminous star-tipped wand at him. Something that felt like static electricity crackled across Ken's face and an intense light momentarily blinded him. When his vision returned the little floating girl had gone. Ken mentioned the incident to a colleague at the station who warned: 'Better say nowt lad or they'll have the trick cyclist [psychiatrist] putting you away.'

Other people in the area around Moscow Drive saw that ghostly girl in the ballerina outfit and the fairy wings, always after dark. A brother and sister in their seventies got the shock of their lives on Halloween night at 11pm when they went to their window after seeing a light hovering outside their second floor flat. On this occasion the fairy was wearing a witch's hat as she hovered over their backyard wall, and the apparition waved to the oldsters as they peeped out through the curtains. An Automobile Association mechanic fixing a lady's car on Green Lane that night also saw the eerie girl drifting across the rooftops of houses as she waved her wand.

Not long after these reports, the policeman Ken was off duty, shopping in the popular Blacklers store in town with his wife, when he happened to see that little girl – the fairy – with her mum, and she looked at Ken in such a sheepish way that he knew she recognised him. Ken approached the girl's mum and found himself asking if her daughter had a ballerina outfit. The mother nodded knowingly, and added: 'And a pair of fairy wings.' She explained that Petula had just got over a nasty bout of measles and had been delirious each night, and in that state neighbours had seen her 'double' hovering about. The mother then added: 'She takes after her grandmother – she used to be able to do that – be in two places at once.'

'I don't know what you mean,' Ken admitted, and felt the hairs stand up on the back of his neck when he looked down at Petula, for she was looking at him and her dark eyes seemed to stare right through him. She showed an intelligence that was far in advance of her young age.

'She's a very special girl, Petula,' the mother cryptically remarked, 'that's all I can say, really.'

'Yeah but how did she – ' Ken was asking when mother and daughter moved away quickly into the milling crowds of Blacklers.

Ken's wife, Diane, asked him what that conversation was all about and her husband told her she would never believe him, although he later did tell his wife what had happened, and she didn't doubt him. Diane thought the only explanation lay somewhere in the sphere of the supernatural, and she was probably right. In the world of the occult there is a well-documented phenomenon known as bilocation – the ability of a person to project his or her etheric double to distant location by sheer willpower, so that the person appears to be in two places at once, and the Church of Rome even recognises this unearthly talent, because several priests have experienced it and even practised this projection, sometimes to say Mass in two churches at the same time. The most famous case of a bilocating priest was when St Alphonsus Liguori preached in the pulpit one morning, then, after Mass, sat in his armchair, then somehow projected his double miles away to be with the dying Pope Clement XIV. Maria de Agreda, St Anthony of Padua and even Pope Cyril VI are just some of the Christian personages who have experienced bilocation, and even atheists have displayed the eerie talent too. In October 1923, when the Russian communist revolutionary Valdimir Ilyich Lenin was seriously ill in Gorki, he was seen six miles away in the Kremlin at Moscow sorting through his documents. It has been noticed that bilocation sometimes happens when a person is ill, and this would make some sense of the "spotty fairy" projected by the Liverpool girl Petula in 1963, for during the alleged projections, the child was suffering from a bad bout of measles.

And now we look skyward for the next creepy Halloween story...

On the humid Wednesday night of July 27, 1966, 13-year-old Susan Rayne was walking down Grove Street in the Edge Hill district of Liverpool, on her way home from her boyfriend's house in the Paddington area. The time was 11.30pm and the young teen perceived an unusual stillness in the night air; not a single person had passed her yet and the roads were unusually quiet. Susan was dreading the telling-off she'd receive from her mum at her home on Mulgrave Street because she should have long been home at half-past nine, but had got carried away listening to Beatles' records in her boyfriend Rodney's bedroom after having a lovely day out together at New Brighton. As Susan walked along, she saw that the moon was in a waxing gibbous phase - a little more than half full – and against the lunar body, something was silhouetted, and this something was moving up and down. The movement caught the girl's peripheral vision and she glanced up to see a very eerie and unnatural sight: a silhouetted figure of a man was rising up past the face of the moon with his arms and legs bent in a weird posture. A moment later the shadowy figure fell back down again – but then he went up again, strikingly contrasted against the glow of the moon, which was currently at chimney-pot level. In the stillness of this muggy July night, Susan Rayne felt a cold chill in her very bones as she eyed this surreal sight, and she thought she could hear distant manic laughter – some sort of faint screeching hilarity, and it seemed to be coming from the direction of that gravity-defying freak. Rather than continue on her way and risk being seen by that silhouetted loony, Susan dashed down Cambridge Street and went home via a long meandering route, and upon reaching her home close to midnight, she expected her mum to scold her, but her mum and two older brothers and a neighbour named Mrs Jones were all in the back yard of the house, and they were all watching the very same figure which had spooked Susan earlier. He was still moving up and down against the moon, which had now sunk below rooftop level and had taken on a reddish hue as it glowed dimly through the settled strata of dust and pollution from a hot day's end. 'Mam, I'm sorry I'm home late, but Rodney's Gran's not well…' Susan fibbed to clear herself - but her mum, who was engrossed in the strange goings-on in the night sky - just turned to her and said, 'Have you seen him?' before looking back at the strange spectacle in the skies somewhere over Sefton Park. 'Yeah, how's he staying up?' Susan asked, so relieved at the way the unearthly scene was defusing her distracted mum's wrath.

'He's on one of them trampoline thingies,' Mrs Jones opined, arms crossed, but Susan's mum shook her head and said, 'No, Pat, it'd have to be on a roof for him to get that high. Can you hear him laughing as well?'

They all listened carefully, straining their ears. Screeching, almost theatrical laughter could be heard echoing in the distance. It scared Mrs Rayne. 'Mam, can we go and see where he is?' Mrs Rayne's 15-year-old son begged, and his 17-year-old brother added: 'Yeah, we'll go and see where he is mum!'

But Mrs Rayne shook her head and the lads moaned. Minutes later, the silhouetted madman was gone and the tired-looking moon was soon lost in the thick low-lying clouds of the dusk.

Three months later, the bizarre and unsettling silhouette was seen again, and this time the figure was seen across a large sweep of south Liverpool. On the night of Halloween of that year – 1966 – there was a full moon, and this time the sinister figure was contrasted quite clearly as an ink-black silhouette against the bright lunar disk. Just before the inexplicable leaping figure put in his appearance that night, many people remarked how there seemed to be something hanging in the air that Duck-Apple Night (as British people used to call October 31st). Everyone spoke of an unusual spooky atmosphere being present in the chilly autumn air, and many spoke of the disconcerting feeling of being watched by something or somebody – and then around 10.15pm the first rumours circulated Liverpool that the demonic laughing leaper was active once more. The superstitious and the downright curious opened windows and skylights and looked moonward, and there he was, rising and falling in what seemed to be slow motion, a silhouette of a man with his body in various contortions, as if – as some suggested – he was *possessed*. A parish priest advised a group of women ogling the weird acrobat from Windsor Street to go home, for the holy man believed there was something Satanic about the figure in the sky, but the women, like most of the observers that Halloween night, could not help themselves, and were drawn to the spectacle because it was so scary yet compulsive. Who the hell was this person jumping up and down and how was he able to do it? Was it all some hoax or, as the priest had suggested, was the Devil himself behind all this?

Susan Rayne watched the silhouetted gymnastic shadow-man that night, and she noticed how louder his laughter was than on the last occasion when she had seen him in the summer – as if he was nearer. A gang of teenagers set out to get as close to the unexplained tumbler as possible, but they found that no matter how far they walked, he was always just a small silhouetted figure, although the gang did claim to hear him laugh hysterically and even swear as he did back-flips and somersaults.

Hundreds of people saw that creepy moon-flitting figure until the full moon of Halloween sank into the hazy horizon that night, but just who – or what – he was remains a mystery. Some said he was a male witch, or perhaps a practising occultist, or even the Devil himself. I once mentioned him on a radio programme and scores of listeners phoned in to vindicate the tale.

From moon-silhouetted figures we next move to the case of an invisible man who features in our next Halloween tale…

There are so many strange tales of Liverpool's Adelphi Hotel, and I have collected hundreds of them. Some of the stranger ones have found their way into my

Haunted Liverpool series of books, but I doubt there are as many tales concerning the world-famous hotel that are stranger than the 'invisible man' who visited it on several occasions.

I have interviewed many people who passed on the strange story from relatives who worked at the hotel in the early 1920s, when the following incidents are said to have taken place, and from these accounts and from hard research (which has involved the scouring of the newspaper archives and so on), I have gleaned what you will now read. In the early hours of Friday 18 March 1921, Patrick Hartigan, a well-known horse trainer, was at the Adelphi for the Grand National, but sadly, during the night, he somehow stumbled as he opened his third-floor hotel window and fell to his death. During the police investigation into the accident, a Liverpool detective named Williams discovered several MI5 officers were staying at the fully booked hotel, pretending to be guests, and Detective Williams was told that the intelligence men were watching two armed members of the Sinn Fein movement who were supposedly posing as guests, but Williams smelt a rat. Not long afterwards the manager of the hotel called Williams in to investigate several strange burglaries at the Adelphi, and when Williams interviewed a maid named Jane Johnson, she told him that 'someone invisible' smelling of whiskey had brushed past her on his way from the bedroom of a wealthy guest who'd just had her expensive jewellery stolen. 'You mean a ghost?' Williams asked, with a sceptical smile. The maid, Miss Johnson said the 'presence' had said, 'Excuse me m'dear,' and she had recognised the slurred Scottish accent – it was Mr

Merriwether, a man of about sixty who had only booked into the hotel a week back. Merriwether was supposedly blind and always wore dark spectacles, but had once removed the glasses to reveal no eyes in his head – just black holes – according to the hotel bellboy, Andrew. What's more, the intelligence officers seemed to be keeping Mr Merriwether under close observation. Then one night there was a gunshot in the foyer and the agents and detective Williams supposedly chased Merriwether – who had stripped himself naked. The man's nude body was said to be invisible, except for the 'whole-head' mask and a bowler he wore. Merriwether was rather sprightly for his age, and he ran out of the hotel foyer and onto a foggy Lime Street, where he cast off the hat and mask and vanished into the night vapours. Was Merriwether some supreme magician or some genius who had achieved genuine invisibility? There were quite a few witnesses that night who saw the strange incident, and there were even more who saw the eerie and frightening antics of the alleged invisible man when he returned to Liverpool and the Adelphi Hotel in particular in October of the following year – days before Halloween. On this occasion, the young maid Jane Johnson was crossing the foyer, coming into work at around 8am when she saw a vaguely familiar man booking in at reception. Although he sported a black felt wide-brimmed hat and wore spectacles with smoked glass in them, as well as having a huge bushy beard and moustache, Jane realised it was Mr Merriwether, the 'invisible man' the police and MI5 agents had chased from the hotel the year before, but she said nothing, just in case there was a slim chance that she was mistaken – but the man before her had the same facial profile and had the same heavy fame as Merriwether. The man saw Jane looking at him and he smiled at her and nodded. Jane then realised it was indeed Merriwether, but couldn't bring herself to report him to the authorities, and she changed into her hotel uniform in the staff room and went upstairs to clean some of the 400 rooms of the hotel. On the third storey of the Adelphi, Jane was confronted by Merriwether in his latest disguise. He asked her if she remembered him and Jane said she did, and asked him how he had performed the invisibility 'trick'. The old man said it was no trick, and that he had somehow acquired his invisibility after being struck by lightning when he was forty while on board a sailing ship in the North Sea. He had gone into a week-long coma after being struck, and after his recovery, he began to feel strange, and one day suffered a seizure. Not long after this he felt 'very peculiar and not at all real' and realised he had no shadow as he was about to get into a bathtub. When he looked in the mirror he saw that he wasn't there – he had no reflection. He lifted his hand to look at it but saw nothing, and soon realised he was invisible. These bouts of invisibility sometimes lasted for days, but gradually, over the months, the strange condition ceased, but then Mr Merriwether discovered he could voluntarily become invisible by willpower, and after becoming transparent in this way the invisibility lasted for about an hour.

Jane didn't believe the old man's claims, so he took off his expensive-looking brown leather glove – to reveal he had no hand. This invisible hand clasped the maid's hand and she felt faint and recoiled in horror.

Merriwether told Jane not to be afraid; he would never hurt her or anyone, and was only wanted by the intelligence service because they either wanted to know how he had achieved invisibility with a view to recreating it for their own agents – or they perhaps wanted him to become one of their agents. Merriwether ranted on about how evil the world would become with invisible soldiers and undetectable killers, and why he would rather kill himself than assist any military organisation or espionage service. He then admitted he had to steal to support himself, but assured Jane he only stole from those who could afford their losses – the rich. He replaced his glove and begged Jane not to report him, and the maid said she wouldn't tell on him but asked him to keep away from her, and the old man did this. The maid then read of a number of baffling thefts in Liverpool which had the police baffled, and all of the thefts occurred in the homes of moguls and rich aristocrats or in warehouses owned by the most wealthy magnates in the West. Then, on the evening of Halloween, something bizarre took place, there were screams and shrieks in the foyer of the Adelphi Hotel when a naked old man appeared in the midst of a number of gentleman and ladies, and Jane realised the nude man was Mr Merriwether. She caught a fleeting glimpse of him hurrying out of the foyer and onto busy Lime Street, where people stared either in shock or amusement at the old streaker as he ran towards Copperas Hill. He was supposedly chased by a policeman but managed to evade capture and possibly willed himself invisible again. Detectives searched the hotel room of Merriwether, who had booked in as Mr Davis, and found nothing but suitcases crammed with strange masks and expensive suits – but no proceeds from his crimes. I admit this all sounds rather far-fetched but years later, when Merriwether would be at least in his seventies, he was said to be active again in Liverpool, and this time many newspapers detailed a series of peculiar crimes that were put down as nothing short of supernatural. Across the world, from the *Liverpool Echo* in northern England, to all of the newspapers in America and Australia, there came sinister accounts of the baffling thefts, and this report, from the *The Recorder* in Port Pirie, South Australia, for 3 July 1929, is typical:

"A PHANTOM THIEF"

'A phantom thief has thrown a big Liverpool (England) business house into a panic. For weeks, goods have been stolen on a colossal scale. Every device to catch the raiders was tried in vain. Concealed watchers spent nights waiting to make a capture. They saw and heard nothing – and in the morning it would be found that yet more goods would be missing. The men who have to stop the thieving say openly it must be the work of a ghost. In three months it is estimated that goods worth £2,300 just vanished – and no one knows where or how. An extraordinary feature of the raids is that goods taken are so bulky, elaborate transport arrangements must have been made to carry them off. Now the climax has been reached. Everyone employed by the firm received a summons to attend a secret meeting. At this meeting a prominent member of the firm announced that "unusual methods" were to be adopted to trap the thief – or thieves. And he added: "The identity of the culprit will make no difference – whether he is a director of the firm or the lowliest employee." But in spite of this the ghost raids have gone on.'

The "business house" was not identified in the report, but further strange thefts in which goods were seemingly spirited away, perhaps by the same 'ghost' *were* identified in the press reports, and these stores were Lewis's and Bunney's. One lady shopper in Lewis's even claimed she had almost been knocked down by the unseen thief, and swore she would never shop in the 'haunted' store again. Most 'educated' people dismissed the stories about the invisible thief as a modern fairy-tale, but it is said that one journalist investigated all of the reports and he also received an anonymous letter from someone in Scotland who named the invisible robber. This man had come from Dundee, and intriguingly, he became invisible after being struck by lightning on a ship that had been sailing from the Orkneys to Aberdeen in 1898. Not long after, the man had become invisible, and the newspapers were afterwards full of reports of the so-called "Dundee Ghost" – and this claim is true; there are numerous reports on the so-called "Dundee Ghost" in newspapers across the land, especially in the *Dundee & Courier Argo* for 15 November 1898. The invisible man had then turned to petty larceny before progressing to bank robberies and bigger crimes. The police suspected the man, who lived on Littlejohn Street, but he boarded a ship at Leith which was bound for the London Docks, and resumed his twisted life of crime in the capital. The journalist contacted the police at Dundee about the far-fetched claims and he was told that the man concerned had been insane and had taken his life many years back. The tantalizing trail then went stone cold for the pertinacious journalist, and we must also give up the ghost (no pun intended) at this point, as there is little more to tell about this fascinating case. Research into high-tech invisibility is being seriously undertaken by scientists all over the world, primarily to provide the military powers with an ability that would tip the balance of power in the Cold War (which resumed in the aftermath of the Crimean crisis of 2014). How would a lightning strike make a man invisible though? It is known that electric and magnetic fields can bend space to a minute extent, and perhaps in the case of our invisible man, when he was struck by what would have been a massive amount of energy, the space surrounding and pervading his body, might have momentarily been bent – albeit fractionally – at right angles to itself, creating a man who was occupying a higher dimension – a fourth dimension, and one that is not subject to the same laws of optics as the usual three-dimensional bodies. This is just a wild guess of course, but the way research into invisibility is progressing, we may know more about this intriguing subject sooner than you might imagine – and heaven knows how such a revolutionary technology will be abused.

Let us now move a little further back in time to indulge in another strange but true tale which touches on Halloween...

In the September of 1932, a beautiful 22-year-old Dublin lady named Florence Chase paid a visit to her 25-year-old Liverpool-born cousin Hazel, who lived in a sleepy, shadowy cul-de-sac near Belmont Road, in the Anfield district of Liverpool with her husband William. When Florence arrived at her cousin's home she complained of irritation to her eyes, and the condition steadily worsened until the doctor was called for. The severe bacterial infection was treated at St Paul's Eye Hospital and Florence was put to bed in the spare room of her cousin's house with a bandage – which was wrapped around her head - covering her eyes. To keep her company, Hazel and her little 4-year-old daughter Clarissa spent a few hours each day talking to Florence as she rested in the bed, and Hazel's husband even rigged up an old crystal radio set and put headphones on Florence so she could listen to various light entertainment programmes being broadcast from morning till evening time. Florence was only expected to stay in bed for a week, and was pleasant enough about her condition. The parish priest also popped in a few times to see Florence, as well as the elderly neighbour Mrs Jones, who brought the Irish girl some of her lovely scones and cakes in the afternoons. Then one evening, Florence was lying in bed when she heard a silky male voice say, 'Florence Chase, forgive me for flattering you, but you have a beautiful name. How do you feel?'

'Who is that?' Florence asked, and smiled. She thought the voice had an almost spiritual quality to it, and asked if it was a priest speaking. 'Oh no, not at all,' the stranger laughed. 'Just a friend of your cousin. My name's Sebastian. The bandages will be coming off in a few days, won't they?'

'Yes,' Florence nodded and smiled. 'I do hope I'll be able to see.' And then Sebastian asked her what colour eyes she had, and Florence blushed and told him they were of a light green. Sebastian then said: 'You are so beautiful, Florence; you remind me of a girl I knew a long time ago. Her name was Verity.'

Florence felt uneasy by Sebastian's smooth talk; she could just tell somehow – call it female intuition – that he was too nice to be true, and so she asked him to call Hazel, but there was no reply. 'Are you there?' she asked, and her bottom lip trembled, for she felt as if her strange admirer was still there but heard nothing – no door being opened or faint footsteps on the floor of the bedroom. Florence shouted for her cousin and Hazel and Clarissa came into the room, but Hazel was baffled at the mention of Sebastian because she knew no one of that name and no one had been seen coming up the stairs to the room.

'There *was* someone here, Hazel, I'd swear on a stack of Bibles!' Florence said nervously and she clenched little Clarissa's hand. 'He must be still in the room, he must!' Florence insisted.

'Alright Florrie, don't get all worked up, calm down please,' Hazel told her and looked about.

'Was it a ghost?' little Clarissa asked, and her big blue eyes rolled about.

'No, it wasn't a ghost Clarissa,' the worried girl's mother reassured her, 'Florrie must have been dreaming.'

'I was not dreaming, Hazel, I was wide awake,' Florence told her sternly, and tried to get out the bed as she added, 'and he must still be in here, hiding somewhere!'

Hazel gently pushed her cousin back into the bed, saying: 'Florrie, because of those bandages over your eyes you haven't realised whether your eyes were open or shut, and that you were dreaming – and you've mistaken a bad dream for being awake, that's all.'

Clarissa knelt down and looked under the bed. 'No one here mummy!' the girl said in a serious tone, and then she got up off the floor and announced that she was going to look in the wardrobe.

'Don't dear,' Hazel told the child, 'this is all so silly.'

'No, let her look,' Florence said, turning her head to the direction of the four-year-old, 'please look Clarissa, and be careful!'

Clarissa opened the wardrobe door and browsed through the jackets and dresses. 'No, Florrie, no one here!' she said, and looked about the bedroom to see if there was anywhere else 'Sebastian' could be hiding. She pulled the long drapes hanging at each side of the window aside and saw no one there, either.

Hazel brought Florence downstairs for a few hours and then took her back to her room and sat with her for a while, reassuring her that the mysterious visitor was nothing more than the figment of a troubled dream, but all the same, Florence instructed her cousin to leave the bedroom door ajar – so she could be heard if she shouted, should the man return. The door was duly left open a few inches. Florence hardly slept that night, and when she did, she had the same dream of a shadowy man walking around her bed.

Three days later the bandages came off and Florence cried when she found her vision had returned, although she used eye drops for a while afterwards. A week later she was returning from a Halloween ball held at her aunt's house in Everton, and as Florence walked down the dead-end street of The Willows in the moonlight, she heard soft footsteps behind her.

She halted and turned – and felt a hand on her shoulder. A tall man in a long black cape stood there with a black trilby, and he had pointed ears and the most sinister grin on his unearthly pale face. Florence initially assumed - or hoped – that he was wearing make-up for Halloween, but then she saw his pointed fangs as his smiling mouth widened. 'Ah, Florence, your eyes *are* so green, my dear,' he said, and leaned forward, trying to kiss her. Florence immediately recognised the silky voice – Sebastian! She screamed and ran, and when she looked back she saw the tall wiry silhouette of Sebastian running off in the opposite direction, faster than a racehorse with his cape bellowing behind him. When Hazel's elderly neighbour Mrs Jones was told about the encounter, she seemed faint, and she had to sit down. She made the sign of the cross, and then she told Hazel and Florence that a man named Sebastian Armitage had lived – and died – in the Willows 40 years ago. He'd had a young mistress named Verity, who had died aged around eighteen from consumption, and her death turned his mind. He became a recluse, never going out of a day, but after dark he would walk the streets and was often seen hanging around churchyards. Then he died after a short illness and his relatives quickly sold his house and all of his possessions – and then there came rumours of his ghost being seen walking down The Willows, always during the hours of dusk, and policemen and milkmen and other people out at night and on dark mornings reported seeing him. Still, people thought these reports were just stories, but then the parish priest bumped into the revenant one evening and upon recognising him, the holy man tried to persuade the ghost to return to the grave, but the caped spectre laughed and hurried off into the shadows. Other witnesses had reported the fangs that Florence had seen, and the general consensus was that Sebastian Armitage had somehow become a vampire because he had turned away from God. Florence Chase was so afraid when she heard of this she boarded a ferry back to Dublin that week and never returned to Liverpool.

We usually associate witches with Halloween, and so, here's a story concerning a certain witch named Violet who is still active today in her sixties...

We may be in the second decade of the 21st century but Liverpool's Gateacre Village still retains a lot of its Old World charm, and when I look at the magpie Tudor gables, the white painted cottages, bucolic mews and sleepy leafy lanes, I have a knack of visualising Gateacre of yesteryear, when it was a very isolated village among sprawling farmlands. Those days of yore and their forgotten peoples sometimes tiptoe back into the present as ghosts with the changing of the season, as the dying embers of the weary sun cast long shadows across the greens. With the arrival of autumn, there is something hanging in the very air over Gateacre; that faint aroma of leaf-mold, mingled perhaps with the incense from someone burning the dead dried leaves of summer past. But there is something else pervading the atmosphere of Gateacre at this time of year, and even the most thick-skinned down-to-earth cold fish of a person senses this supernatural ambience. Long before this land was called England, way before machines divorced us from nature, the folk of those times accepted an unknown force which emanated from the earth, and they used it to heal – and a few used it to harm. These people were witches, wizards and Druids, and they believed that at this time of year, the partition which separates this world from the next one was at its thinnest, and the spirits of the dead were prone to visit. This period was called Samhain – known to us today as Halloween. In the October of 1827, a 12-year-old Gateacre boy named John Callaghan became a highwayman. By day he went on occasional errands for an old reclusive lady named Mary Onions, but by night he donned a sinister black mask and, armed with a sword and flintlock, he prowled the lonely roads leading from the village. It soon became apparent to locals that the boy was a hold-up "man" and that he possessed the Devil's luck, for whenever the authorities tried to capture him, he'd always escape into the night. Elaborate traps were laid to detain the lad, and many seasoned mercenaries were even hired to capture him dead or alive, but the little blackguard always seemed to go to ground awfully fast when the chase was on, and a local priest soon suspected Mary Onions of protecting Callaghan by the use of witchcraft. Other people agreed but nothing could be proved. Then, in March 1828, John Callaghan, now 13, was at last captured after robbing Charles Smith of Gateacre of his pocket book, three sovereigns, a gold watch, seal and ring. At the Lancaster Lent Assizes, John was indicted for highway robbery and the case against him was a cast-iron one, and the boy faced transportation to Australia or a long prison sentence with hard labour – but Mary Onions appeared in the court and suddenly all of the witnesses and Mr Williams, the seasoned prosecutor – suffered from strange spells of amnesia. Williams stated the case in court to the best of his ability, but the Judge said the evidence as presented was clearly defective and that the witnesses were all 'woolly minded' – and so he directed a verdict of Not Guilty to be entered. John Callaghan was released. Now let us jaunt forth over a century, and we will find a certain family living in Gateacre who are descendants of a Lancashire coven. I will not give you their names for various reasons but the family may even be living next door to you. We shall call them the Joneses. Now, in the autumn of 1961, Gateacre Comprehensive (the first school of its kind in the country) opened its doors to 1,530 girls and boys, and one of them was an awkward 13-year-old named Violet Jones, a girl who always seemed to be in a world of her own. She seemed to live in the Victorian era, always dressing in old-fashioned clothes, and was not aware of the modern music and fashion scene. On Monday 23 October that year, the pupils of Gateacre Comp were given a day off because of a nationwide teacher's strike over a Government pay-offer to the National Union of Teachers. Most of the kids at the school were chuffed at this holiday, but Violet turned up at the school gates that Monday morning (as she'd forgotten it was a day off). A few of the lads and girls skitted her because of this, and then two schoolgirls who met Violet as she made her way home informed her that she was invited to the Halloween Party being held at a house in Aigburth at 8pm, but that she would have to come in fancy dress, perhaps as a witch. Violet was quite poor, and certainly had no fancy dress clothes, and felt so down. A boy she liked named Harry was going to that party, she subsequently learned. Hearing Violet crying softly in her room that morning, Glynis Jones, the girl's grandmother, went in and asked what the matter was. Violet told her about the party and how she had no money to get the bus to Aigburth and no fancy dress clothes either. Glynis left the room and returned with a beautiful modern black sleeveless dress, black Chelsea boots, sparkling diamond earrings and even lustrous black silk stockings. She styled Violet's hair and applied some sort of watery make-up she called "glamour" – and Violet ended up looking like a stunning movie star. Something then took place; it seems Glynis revealed that the Jones family were of a long line of special people – witches, and that it was time Violet became one, if she so desired. Almost every one of the girls at the Aigburth Halloween party dressed in witch hats and black robes, and everything was going swimmingly – until a beautiful teenager appeared in their midst. Who on earth was she? All of the boys in the room were literally spellbound by her, and eventually one of the girls – Judy – realised it was Violet Jones, the dowdy drippy drab, as they called her. Where had she got her outfit from? Who had styled her hair? The girls all wanted to ask her but couldn't get near her because of the fawning lads. She danced like the Devil and seemed to leave the ground when she did the twist and the "mashed potato" – and boy could she sing! She knew all the words to Del Shannon's *Runaway*. Then she became what we would now term as "hyper" as the night wore on and the moon rose higher. She was seen to run up walls and back-flip, and when the party ended at 11.30pm, every guy planned to escort her home, but Violet was nowhere to be seen. Then something peculiar happened. Six of the girls left the party and headed home dressed as witches, and the mum of one of these girls was there too as they walked home (having missed the late bus). As the girls chatted incessantly about Violet's antics, they heard laughter overhead. It happened that fast it was hard to take in all the details, but those six 'witches' and a fully grown woman of 35 saw a fleeting glimpse of a young female, sitting astride on what looked like the shaft of a brush as she flew above their heads in the moonlight. They looked at one another in jaw-dropping disbelief; it surely wasn't *that* girl – was it? They all walked on in silence for quite some time. Violet and her family of witches were a little feared by those who discovered (through gossip) what they were, but a many local people consulted Violet in the capacity of a fortune teller in the shed of her garden! On one occasion, just before Halloween in 1970, a 32-year-old woman named Kathleen went to see Violet for advice over her husband, Ernie. She had left him a few months back but had now started seeing him again, and Ernie had even talked to Kathleen about renewing their wedding vows in a big church ceremony. Violet read Kathleen's tealeaves and warned her not to get back with her husband because he had a violent streak, and in the leaves, Violet could clearly see Kathleen lying in a hospital bed, and she felt that this was something to do with the aftermath of a 'domestic' - an old-fashioned term for domestic abuse - usually violence towards the wife from the husband. Kathleen shook her head and said her husband did have a flaming temper but would never go as far as hitting her. Violet then said that there was a woman in the afterlife looking over Kathleen, and she looked very concerned. Violet could see a capital letter D by this mysterious figure in the leaves and Kathleen said that her mother – who had died about 10 years ago, had always guided her while she was alive, and even though Kathleen had called her an interferer on many occasions, her mum had always been right about people and situations that would have proved detrimental to her daughter. Violet studied the leaves for a while then said: 'Kathleen, you will receive a personal message from your mother, and this will happen in the near future.'

About a week later, Kathleen went out with her friends one night on the town, and told her husband Ernie she'd be home no later than midnight. Kathleen, however, lost track of time, and realised it was almost 2am when she was walking to her friend Barbara's flat at a maisonette in Everton. Barbara told her to go home in the morning and said she'd go with her and explain to Ernie that it had been her fault for keeping Kathleen out. Kathleen was given a bed in the spare room of her friend's flat, but she couldn't get a wink of sleep because she kept worrying what her husband would say when she went home in the morning. All of a sudden, Kathleen went ice cold, and had the overwhelming feeling that her life would end soon if she went home. It was a ghastly, stomach-churning feeling that got hold of her, and Kathleen left the bed and opened the window to get a breath of fresh night air. The moon was full and the sky was clear of any cloud. There was a strange stillness hanging in the air. As Kathleen looked out across the skyline of Everton, her sad eyes swept across the moonlit rooftops, and suddenly she got the shock of her life, because a thin horizontal ribbon of cloud was drifting across the sky, high above the moon, and as Kathleen looked on, this cloud broke up – and formed five letters which spelt out the message – LEAVE.

These letters were not vaguely formed but quite distinct, and Kathleen knew at once what the word spelled out in the sky meant – that she should *leave* her husband. She went to wake Barbara up and told her to go to the window.

'Why? What's out there?' Barbara asked, all bleary-eyed, but when Kathleen opened the curtains and pointed at the sky, her friend also saw the eerie word written with wispy clouds, and as the two women looked on, the message slowly dissolved into nothingness.

Kathleen left her husband after that night, and three months later, Ernie began to see a woman named Carla, and a few weeks after she moved in with Ernie, he accused Carla of having an affair, and slapped her face so hard the young lady fell to the ground and knocked her head on the edge of a coffee table. Carla was taken to hospital where she had a nasty head wound stitched up, and she was kept in after she began to have seizures that had been brought on by damage to her skull when she hit her head on the coffee table during the cowardly attack by Ernie. Kathleen knew she would have received the same violent treatment from Ernie had she stayed with him, and she realised that Violet's tea-leaf prediction would have come true if she had stayed with her ex-husband.

OPERATION FIRESTONE

A few years ago in Liverpool I gave a talk about the paranormal at the Adelphi Hotel's Sefton Suite, which, incidentally, is an exact replica of the smoking lounge which once existed on the *Titanic*. The interior decorators who built the Sefton Suite were the very same people who had worked on the ill-fated (and Liverpool-registered) liner. After the talk, I signed books and listened to readers' own experiences concerning the supernatural and the unexplained, and that day I met a man in his early seventies named Mick who told me a fascinating story about an intriguing incident from his days when he was a soldier. In July 1955, Mick was stationed in Wiltshire, at Battlesbury barracks, Warminster, and one afternoon he and six other Army men were despatched to Salisbury Plain to take part in a bizarre experiment which involved Mick and other soldiers looping cables around the ancient ring of standing stones which form the enigmatic Stonehenge. The cables from the stones ran to a row of special high-power generators and various consoles. A klaxon sounded, and Stonehenge was cleared of military personnel, and then suddenly, the boffin seated at the console began flicking switches and turning knobs, and sparks flew from the cables, which started to buzz and hiss with high-tension electricity. All of a sudden, a pencil-thin beam of luminous vapour appeared which came from between two of the huge upright stones of the prehistoric monument, just beneath the lintel which bridged them. More power was applied to the stones, and suddenly the whole of the area and all of Salisbury Plain was criss-crossed with bright beams of laser-like light which could even be clearly seen in the bright July sunlight, and all of the beams seemed to pass through gaps in the ancient standing stones with incredible accuracy, and extended for miles. There were cries from within the circle of stones because a young soldier had somehow strayed into the enclosed area of Stonehenge after the klaxon had sounded, and the lethal-looking beams were missing him by inches. The scientist at the console was given some signal by a captain and he reluctantly shut the experiment down, but the ghostly rays remained visible for about a minute after this, and when they did fade, the clear blue summer skies over Salisbury Plain darkened, and a thunderstorm erupted, the likes of which had never been seen in that area for many years – even though there wasn't a single cloud present. The menhirs of Stonehenge seemed luminous to Mick, and he felt the hairs on the back of his neck prickle with the electrical charge hanging in the air, and there was a distinctive smell of ozone in the atmosphere. Later that day, news came in that a strange thunderstorm had crossed the country - from the direction of Salisbury Plain – immediately after the experiment at Stonehenge, and it had started with 44 men women and children being struck by lightning at the Royal Ascot meeting. Witnesses screamed as the victims all fell down simultaneously with flames issuing from their limbs, and one pregnant woman from Reading died from the strike. Six people met swift deaths elsewhere after being 'blasted' by strange-looking bolts of lightning from cloudless skies, even though it was the hottest day of the year with temperatures almost in the nineties.

In Cheshire and Lancashire, strange balls of light and beams of shimmering light were seen in the skies, and an eerie aurora was seen on Camp Hill, the site of an ancient Iron Age fort in Woolton which is thought to be part of a ley line that connects All Saints Church in Childwall, St Chad's in Kirkby, Walton Church, and Bidston Hill. All of the aforementioned churches were built on sites which were revered by the ancient peoples of this area. The experiment which Mick witnessed at Salisbury Plain is said to have been Operation Firestone, an attempt by the Ministry of Defence to "power-up" Stonehenge – which some believe to have been a prehistoric generator of some sort which fed a network of standing stones which criss-cross the British Isles and parts of France.

Mick later heard from other soldiers that there had been another experiment conducted at Stonehenge two months earlier, and on that occasions, the same mysterious interlacing beams were seen to criss-cross the ancient stones and spread out across Salisbury Plain, and like the July experiment, the weather was affected again, only this time, snow fell! This claim is corroborated by the fact that snowstorms raged across Britain on 17 May 1955, and besides London and many other parts of the United Kingdom, the county of Wiltshire – where Stonehenge is sited - found itself under heavy summer snow. Four inches of snow fell in South Wales, while the four major roads of the Peak District were blocked by snowdrifts. Nine vehicles became hopelessly stranded on the Snake Pass at Glossop, Derbyshire, and even the snowploughs sent to clear a path became stuck themselves. Up on Kinder Scout in the Edale Valley, meanwhile, a blizzard raged that May for sixteen hours and eighteen inches of snow blanketed the area by the following morning. The bizarre out-of-season snowstorms even affected the shipping, with the *Queen Mary* homeward bound from New York with eleven-hundred passengers anchoring off the Isle of Wight in an unsuccessful effort to escape the wrath of the wintry gale force winds. Then, just as quickly as the snow had arrived, a thaw ensued, and after widespread flooding the summer resumed again. The British summer is infamous for sudden changes, and it saved our neck in 1588 when it suddenly turned and blew the Spanish Armada into oblivion, but even today, there are those who remember the day winter returned in the middle of summer, and most recollect the weird way the weather changed that year, as well as the vicious thunderstorms. Perhaps the experiments held at Stonehenge were merely incidental to the drastic changes in the weather, but some believe that the military boffins behind Operation Firestone inadvertently stumbled upon a form of weather control.

A SPOOKY SELECTION BOX

No book about the supernatural would be complete without a collection of Christmas ghost stories, as it was once traditional to tell seasonal tales of the uncanny before a blazing fire with goosefeather-sized flakes of snow whirling down beyond the window panes. Like Halloween, Christmas Eve was said to be one of the few nights of the year when ghosts of the dearly departed and the not-missed-at-all had a habit of intruding upon the world of the living, and in all my long delvings into the sphere of spirits, I would have to agree with this handed-down assertion, for I have certainly noticed an increase in supernatural goings-on around Yuletide. Here then, is my little gift to you, a spooky selection box of seasonal scary stories.

I saw many strange, inexplicable supernatural things when I was a child, and without fail, the adults would say I'd either 'been seeing things', been dreaming or had witnessed a 'trick of the light' – (whatever that is)– and when I look back now, I know I really *did* see things that were not of this world, and I know there are many more of you out there who also saw things in your childhood which were similarly 'explained away' by the adults. Take "Nelly Longarms" – a frightening woman seen by many children in one of the spookiest cul-de-sacs of bygone Liverpool – The Willows – sadly now gone. Hennawood Close now stands near to the spot where The Willows existed, close to the junction of Belmont and Breck Road. The Willows had seven haunted residences, and I have already told you about one of the strange beings which haunted that cul-de-sac in the chapter about Halloween incidents, and let us now return to that long-vanished dead end street to take a look at some of the eerie reports of an elderly resident there nicknamed Nelly Longarms. Like the leaping Victorian and Edwardian bogeyman Spring-Heeled Jack, Nelly was dismissed as a folkore legend, but quite a few people – young and old – reported this lady, and I even have a report from a retired policeman named Jim who said he and a colleague once chased Nelly across the tracks of (the now disused) Breck Road railway station in the summer of 1946. The woman looked about sixty-odd but ran like the wind from Jim and a colleague, screaming with laughter after scaring a gang of children near Townsend Lane. This lady's arms were so long her palms padded against the floor like a primate, and she was dressed in black old-fashioned clothes with her hair tied up in a bun. Despite her age the odd-looking woman bolted across the tracks at the station and narrowly missed an incoming train – then vanished like a puff of smoke. Jim thought the woman had been some young male prankster in drag, but was later told by an elderly neighbour that he had seen the bogeywoman Nelly Longarms. Then, in the snowy December of 1954, about three days after Christmas, 11-year-old Billy Perkins and his 7-year-old sister Hattie, were playing in an alleyway behind The Willows when Hattie threw Billy's prized cricket ball over a backyard wall. The ball had been a Christmas present from Billy's Uncle Stan and so he tried the door to the backyard and found it was unlocked. He and Hattie sneaked into the snow-covered yard and noticed weird long shoe prints about two feet in length in the snow. As Billy studied them, Hattie tried to bowl the cricket ball at a wall and it went through a window instead. The children hid behind a wall in the yard and heard the window-frame grate open. An elderly voice cussed them, and Billy peeped round the corner – and saw an old woman with impossibly long arms which seemed to stretch. The woman went away from the window for a moment, then came back – brandishing what looked like a coal hatchet. Because of her superhuman reach with her impossibly long arm, the hatchet just missed Billy's head and struck the wall, producing sparks. He and Hattie ran screaming out the yard and cried all the way to their home on Boaler Street. No one believed the children's tale, for how could a woman have such long arms? Well, in the world of the occult there is a remarkable phenomenon known as bodily elongation, a weird stretching of the limbs, neck, fingers and even a displacement of the ribs which has been well-documented in ecstatic saints, possessed mediums – and witches carrying out certain obscure rituals, and I believe 'Nelly' was probably a witch. When I first mentioned Nelly Longarms in a newspaper article some years ago I was inundated with letters and emails from readers who had either seen her (or someone remarkably similar to her) with their own eyes, or had heard about her from their parents. A Liverpool-born woman named Janet who now lives in Norfolk, told me how, on the Christmas Eve of 1960, when she was seven years old, she voluntarily went to bed earlier than usual, thinking Christmas Day would arrive sooner along with all of the presents she optimistically expected. However, Janet was too excited to sleep, and lay there in the dark bedroom, wide awake. The only illumination reaching the room was from a distant lamp somewhere at the back of the house, beyond the backyard walls of the alleyways. The rays of that faint lamp cast a small rectangle of light upon the bedroom wall facing the bottom of the bed, and as Janet looked at this rectangular area of light (which had filtered through a net curtain), she was startled at the appearance of a very strange shadow within it. It was the shadow of a head rising vertically on a long pole of a neck, and as the girl looked on in horror, that neck stretched even further, then began to contract again. Janet shot up from the bed, hurried to the window and peeped through the net curtain. Outside in the entry there was a head looking over the wall, and that head – the head of an old woman – was on the end of a neck that looked at least two feet in length. Janet had seen pictures in school books of the Padaung women of the Kayan people of Burma with their stretched necks adorned with columns of rings but this was something else – this woman's neck seemed almost rubbery the way it moved and stretched. Janet ran out of the room and went downstairs to her parents – catching her father in the act as he wrapped the presents of Janet and her brothers. He was furious at the way his daughter had barged in on him and he ushered her into the kitchen where her mother was preparing the turkey for tomorrow's Christmas dinner. Janet blabbed out about the woman with the long neck but her mum said she had just been dreaming and Janet was soon taken back up into her bedroom by her father. Janet urged him to look out the window, to see the weirdly proportioned old lady for himself, but when he did, he saw nothing outside but a tom cat on the backyard wall. He looked at his watch and said: 'You've had a nightmare Janet, now go asleep.'

And he left the room, and Janet lay there, eyeing that rectangle of lamplight on the bedroom wallpaper, dreading to see the return of the old woman's shadow. The child closed her eyes and thought of nice things – of a recent trip to the Christmas grotto in Lewis's and then she opened her eyes – and was struck numb with shock, for there, outside the bedroom window, was a long, long neck – about five feet or more in length, and at the end of that neck there was the head of that old woman with her hair tied up in a bun, and that head was pressed against the window! She appeared to be trying to look into the bedroom. A long arm – much longer than any usual human arm, came into view, and the hand at the end of the arm pressed against the window for a moment, and then the hand started feeling for the base of the window. The window frame rattled, as if the unearthly stretched woman was trying to open it, and Janet suddenly found herself at the door of the bedroom, yanking at the door handle. She ran along the landing and straight downstairs, and with each step on the stairs she yelped and whimpered. She could hear a television show coming from the back parlour, and she headed for that room and burst in, and there was her mother, sitting on her father's knee, kissing him. The startled parents watched a hysterical Janet rocket towards them, and this time the girl's father was furious, and he shouted at Janet and told her she wouldn't be getting any presents from Father Christmas if she carried on like this, but the girl's mother said something must have upset her, and Janet eventually managed to get out an account of what had happened – of the woman with the long neck and long arms trying to get into her room. 'Maybe someone did try to get into her room,' the child's worried mother said, holding Janet in her arms and rocking her and patting her on the back.

'She's been dreaming again love, that's all,' the father said, but then he heard a noise in the backyard. He went to the kitchen to look out the window into that yard, and saw that snow was now falling. There was no one about. When he decided to unlock the kitchen door to see what had made the noise, Janet screamed for him not to, but he went outside, and there on the flags of the yard in the fresh thin layer of snowflakes, her dad saw a long weird shoe print. There was another one about twelve feet away. He never told his wife or daughter about the creepy imprints until well after Christmas. That house where Janet lived was less than a hundred yards from The Willows, where many children had seen "Nelly Longarms" and to this day, Janet believes she was visited by the sinister old lady that Christmas Eve.

It's a sad fact of modern life that a person can vanish

and not be missed. The files of police forces across the world are overloaded with missing person reports and the police forces in the UK certainly have its fair share of them. Merseyside Police, for example, has about a dozen bodies and body-parts which have resisted all attempts at identification – despite DNA tests and extensive investigations spanning many counties and countries, as well as public appeals. The force also has about 530 missing person reports (some dating back to 1972) to clear up, and all of these missing people were someone's husband, wife, son, cousin, uncle, sister, brother, nephew - best friend – and yet they remain nameless and forgotten and seemingly unmissed. What is even more baffling is when not one – but four anonymous bodies – are simultaneously found an hour after they were seen alive and well. This is said to have happened on the Christmas Eve of 1962 when several officers of Lancashire police chased a gang of four burglars – believed to be from the Huyton district of Liverpool – into the snow-covered expanses of Knowsley Park. The men had been responsible for a string of burglaries in the Mossley Hill, Calderstones and Wavertree areas in recent months, and upon this snowy night, the gang had ransacked the house of an old eccentric woman in Calderstones and made off with her jewellery and several items "of sentimental value". The gang were thought to have fled from the scene of their latest crime in a four-door Austin Cambridge, and the tyre tracks of this vehicle were even followed in the snow for a few miles – but then the tracks came to an abrupt dead end off a dirt track in Knowsley Park. At this time, the whole country was experiencing the so-called Big Freeze, a record period of low temperatures and incessant snow that went on till March of the following year. Two policemen branched away from five others (who believed the crooks had hid near a reservoir to the east), and these two officers saw a faint glimmering light about four hundred yards in the distance. As the constables got close to the light they could see it was a little fire in a small clearing in the wood, and it looked as if someone – possibly vagrants, were seated around it. The policemen then made a very surreal and sinister discovery: four motionless men sat around the dwindling flames of the small fire, and they were covered with snow and frost and each had his head bowed and his hands clasped – as if in prayer. 'Alright lad, the game's up!' shouted one of the coppers, but there was no reaction from the seated figures. The police moved in for a closer look with their truncheons at the ready, but there was still no movement from the men. The four faces of the strangers wore peculiar, creepy grins and the eyes were all turned upwards into the forehead, showing almost just the white of the eyeball. No breath vapour issued from the mouths of the strange stock-still sitters, for they were all dead from what seemed to be acute exposure. What's more, the four bodies were so frozen they felt as hard as statues. The inquest into the deaths established that hypothermia had killed the strangers – and yet the hypothermia must have taken effect with remarkable swiftness, as the men had only been in that clearing in the woods for about an hour or less, and three of them wore parkas and woollen garments. It was as if they had all been freeze-dried in an instant. The bodies carried no identification and despite fingerprints being taken, the deathly quartet were never identified and subsequently buried in a communal grave. The getaway car they had supposedly driven – the Austin Cambridge – was never found either, nor was the loot the burglars had obtained that glacial night. Then some strange facts about this bizarre case slowly emerged; the two policemen who had first come upon the eerie scene had noticed abnormally long footprints in the snow, twice the length of the average foot – made by someone who had worn pointed shoes with thin heels. Near to the fire the men had huddled around when they had inexplicably frozen to death, someone had laid out a number of twigs to form a peculiar symbol said by some to have been a "witch mark" – the identifying symbol of a particular coven in the North West. Then it was established that the Calderstones woman who had been burgled by the men was alleged to be an elderly practising witch; so, had she or others of her coven exacted some supernatural revenge upon the four burglars, perhaps for stealing something to do with her Wiccan lifestyle?

In early April 1890 a 10-year-old Liverpool lad named Johnny Wilson went with his parents to spend a week with his Auntie Julia (the sister of Johnny's mum) down in Crewe. Julia lived on Heron Street in Crewe, and it was on this street where Johnny met his first love, a pretty 9-year-old girl named Jessie Jervis. Johnny first set eyes on her when she and a long line of girls were all skipping together as a long rope of about twenty feet was being swung faster and faster by two lads. When Jessie noticed Johnny, a boy she had never set eyes on before, looking at her, she was distracted by him and tripped over the rope, and when she fell, she knocked over a few girls on either side of her. Johnny helped Jessie up and the two got talking. 'Ooh! Jessie's found a boyfriend!' a girl named Janet said in a mocking tone, intending to embarrass Jessie, but the trick never worked, because one of the lads crouched down behind the Janet while another gently pushed her back and Janet toppled over the crouching boy. Johnny and Jessie, meanwhile, moved away from the street gang and went walking together. Johnny offered Jessie some of his boiled sweets but she seemed too shy to eat in front of him. The couple walked and talked all day and then Jessie's mum, Sarah, began to call her daughter's name as dusk gathered. 'I'll meet you tomorrow by the sweetshop over there,' Jessie promised Johnny, and then the girl's older sister, Lillian, who was fourteen, came along the street and told Jessie to get home immediately. Johnny stood there on Heron Street, watching as Jessie went to her home at number eight. Just before the girl stepped inside of her hallway, she looked back at Johnny and he waved, then ran off to his Aunt Julia's house just a short distance away on the same street. Johnny talked incessantly about Jessie for the remainder of that evening, and his mother warned him about making friends in Crewe, because he would be going back to Liverpool in a week. A week is a long time when you're ten, and Johnny didn't think that far ahead. All he knew was that he loved Jessie and wanted to be with her all the time. The young couple met at their rendezvous by the sweetshop and then went walking again, and this time Johnny poured out his heart and told Jessie that, although he had only known her a short while, he felt as if had met a "real-life princess" – and this really touched the girl. They kissed in an alleyway shortly afterwards and made all sorts of promises, typical of young sweethearts. Johnny said he would take Jessie to Liverpool and marry her there, and they'd live in a big house and have horses and later on they'd raise a big family. Jessie said she'd be a ballet dancer and Johnny said he'd buy land and become a farmer. Three days later, Jessie, Johnny and a gang of other children of a similar age, were playing in Bridle Road, when someone suggested they should have a game of hide and seek. Johnny ended up being the seeker, and he closed his eyes and faced a back entry wall as he counted to twenty. The girls and boy darted away from him in every direction and many of them did a good job at concealing themselves. 'Coming ready or not!' Johnny announced, turning from the brick wall, and he caught a 6-year-old girl named Mary, who was peeping from behind a post office pillar box. Johnny then left the street, and caught a boy who was trying to shin up a drainpipe. He then went in search of Jessie, but couldn't find her anywhere. A little boy of about five said he had seen a girl three streets away, hiding in a shop. The little lad was lying but Johnny believed him and went to look, and upon reaching the shop he saw Jessie Jervis at the mouth of an alleyway with a very serious look on her face. 'Caught you!' Johnny said, but Jessie ran off down the alleyway. Johnny sensed there was something wrong, and he ran after her. He saw his first-ever sweetheart run down the entry, then slow down, halt, and run back towards him.

'Jessie, I caught you! What – ' the lad was saying.

Jessie ran screaming – right *through* him.

The boy felt a coldness pass through his body and his bones, and as Jessie went through him, he turned, and saw her run on – then vanish.

When Johnny returned to Bridle Road, he saw a crowd of people, and some of the women there were crying. Johnny tried to push through the crowd to see what they were looking at and crying over, and before he even saw the body, he just knew he was going to see something really bad.

The body of Jessie Jervis lay crushed beneath a pile of timber in the form of thick logs that had been stockpiled outside a timber merchant's shop. Jessie's eyes – those beautiful eyes he had stared in only today and lost himself in – were looking at him, but there was no sparkle in them now, no life at all, they were as dead as the button eyes of a doll. Two men pulled the logs off the little body and dragged her free, but right away the head lolled about – because the neck had been broken. Blood trickled from Jessie's mouth, and all of a sudden, the noise of the crowd faded and the world tilted to the left as the sky dimmed.

Johnny had fainted.

When he awoke he was in a bed at his auntie's home, and for a moment he was alright, but then he remembered what had happened, and recalled that Jessie Jervis was no longer in the world, and he began to cry and yell hysterically. 'I want Jessie! I want Jessie, Mam!'

The coroner, Mr H. C. Yates, was appointed to perform the autopsy, and on the day of the post mortem, the ghost of Jessie Jervis visited Johnny as he lay in bed, and when he saw her she was in tears.

'They're cutting me up, Johnny! Oh it's horrible!' the child screamed, and ran towards Johnny, but he hid under the blankets, and when he looked up, the ghost of his girlfriend had gone. At the inquest, the coroner heard from several witnesses that, upon the day of the tragedy, Jessie had been hiding behind a pile of timber. The owner of the timber business had noticed that the pile of wood looked unsafe because it had not been stacked properly, and so he went to get a prop to support it, but before he returned, he heard a loud trundling noise and a crashing sound, followed by screams, and when he returned to the street outside, he saw the girl lying under the logs with her chest and abdomen flattened and blood squirting out of her mouth. He didn't know that her neck had been broken by one of the logs. The jury returned a verdict of "Accidental Death".

Poor Johnny returned to Liverpool heartbroken. Meanwhile, on the streets around Crewe's Bridle Road, the ghost of Jessie Jervis began to appear, and one Boxing Day, a group of children were playing on the road where the girl had been killed, when someone suggested playing hide and seek. The children noticed that one particular girl was very good at hiding, and only later that day did one of them realise that this girl was partially see-through, and the boy who discovered that his playmate was a ghost ran home screaming. In the 1920s, a boy from Liverpool mistook Jessie Jervis for a real flesh and blood girl and got talking to her, and she told the Liverpudlian that he talked just like a boy she was going to marry. And then all of a sudden the girl began to cry – and vanished. All of those old streets where this strange tale took place are gone now, but the ghost of Jessie Jervis is said to appear from time to time on the housing estate that was built on the site of her tragic death, and for some reason the ghost is quite active around Christmas.

And now let us take a supernatural sleigh-ride through time and space to a certain Liverpool pub, where so many inexplicable things have taken place, and one of them unfolded around Christmas...

The Glebe Hotel public house on Walton's County Road in Liverpool has been the scene of many strange goings-on over the years. In June 1897, 29-year-old Sarah Elizabeth Bastian, a lady with a drink problem, stormed into the pub and demanded a drink, but was refused by the barman. The unfortunate lady had been refused by all of the other pubs in the area, and so she produced a bottle of carbolic acid she'd purchased from a County Road pharmacy, and she calmly poured it into a customer's glass and – before the barman could stop her – she drank the poison in one swift movement. Police were called and a PC Anderson tried to save Sarah by administering olive oil, but the woman later expired in Bootle Hospital. At the ensuing inquest the verdict returned was: "Suicide while temporarily insane".

But that was not the end of the matter, for the solid-looking ghost of the late Sarah Bastian started to make regular dramatic entrances to the Glebe, always asking for a glass of gin, and only the bravest drinkers and staff would stand their ground – most fled when the wild-eyed ghostly lady stormed into the place in her white burial shroud and ghastly pallid face. Eventually after almost six months of the disruptive ghostly visits, a Catholic priest from St Mary's church laid in wait at the pub and when the restless ghost burst into the pub, he offered her a glass of holy water – and the apparition smiled, vanished on the spot, and was never seen again.

On Saturday 23 December, 1967, Mick and Joan, a couple in their thirties, were drinking at the Glebe pub when an old eccentric man – nicknamed Loggerhead – came into the pub. He had a heated debate with an Irishman named Cyril, and when Mick listened in on the argument, it seemed that Loggerhead claimed he had been time-travelling, and Cyril asked him to prove it. 'Here!' the eccentric slapped a coin and a ticket down on the counter – a half a crown, and an old tram ticket. 'Explain them!' Loggerhead cried, 'A brand spanking new half a crown from nearly thirty years ago and a tram ticket! Explain them you bloody doubting Thomas!'

The Irishman drank up, shook his head and headed for the door. Loggerhead made eye-contact with Mick and then nodding to departing Cyril he said, 'He always leaves when I get one over on him. Small-minded he is!'

'Don't get involved, love, let's go,' Joan tugged at the sleeve of Mick's camel-hair coat. But Mick was fascinated by the eccentric's claims. He bought Loggerhead a drink and asked about the time-travel.

'I studied *The Sphinx of Time*, an old book on the occult,' he said, 'bought it at a Cairo bookstall when I was serving over there.'

Mick picked up the half a crown and saw it had King George VI on the obverse, and was dated 1938. Loggerhead pointed his fat forefinger at the coin.

'That's a bridge to the past – if you want to visit 1938, that is,' he explained. 'But if you could get hold of say, a Victorian shilling, that would take you back further – if you know where to stand, like – time has spots like that, see.'

'Spots?' Mick, asked, as Joan rolled her eyes. Loggerhead nodded and gulped his Double Diamond. 'Yes, there's a big spot round here. If you go to the end of Church Road West – the County Road end - at precisely midnight and utter a certain word, and if you will squeeze that coin in your fist and believe 1938 will return – it will, but you must not talk or the year will vanish.'

'And what's this word I have to utter?' Mick was hooked now, but Loggerhead grinned and looked at his empty glass. A few pints later the eccentric whispered the word in Mick's ear. He then went the toilet and never returned. 'Let's go home, Mick,' Joan asked wearily, 'there's a Norman Wisdom film on the telly.'

Mick noticed that Loggerhead had left the 1938 half a crown on the counter and he slyly swiped it into his palm and left. The next day was Christmas Eve, and at midnight, Mick and Joan stood at the end of Church Road West, gazing at County Road as sleet fell. 'This is stupid, Mick,' Joan complained, nuzzling into his coat. 'Don't say a thing, love, I believe this will work,' he said, and he whispered the word Loggerhead had divulged to him, over and over as he squeezed the half a crown in his fist. All of a sudden, Joan's stomach turned over and Mick saw the whole scene before him change. It was no longer midnight, but what seemed to be a snowy grey afternoon, and there were shops on

County Road he had not seen since he was a kid – and trams! The women passing by in ankle-deep snow wore cloches and long fur-collared coats and the men wore trilbies and bowlers. 'Oh Lord – ' Joan murmured, but Mick clamped his hand over her mouth and whispered: 'Don't say anything, or it will all vanish.'

A little golden-haired boy of about seven years of age came trudging through the snow –and Joan saw it was her older brother Stanley! But he was long dead – knocked down and killed in…1938. 'It's my brother, Stanley,' Joan whispered, and tears flowed.

'What?' Mick asked softly.

The lad stopped about twenty feet away and eyed the couple with suspicion. 'Stanley!' Joan tried to call to him in a choked voice – and the whole scene shimmered. 'Sshh!' Mick whispered in her ear and saw her tears. He recalled her sad stories about Stanley's death, and somehow sensing that 1938 would soon fade away, he tossed the half a crown at the wary boy. Stanley picked it up, smiled and said, 'Thanks!'

And then the world of 1938 vanished and the bitterly cold night of 1967 returned. Gone was the snow and the trams, and the only sound was of Joan sobbing. She and Mick walked home in a daze, and decided to tell no one what had happened – and who would believe them anyway? On Boxing Day Joan's mother visited, and she brought up the subject of Stanley's death. She said a strange thing that gave Mick and Joan quite a jolt. 'Stanley was knocked down running to the sweet shop that day, and where he got the money from to buy sweets is a mystery, but whoever gave him the money killed him with kindness in a way because he wouldn't have been crossing that busy road.'

We remain in this era of the 1960s for our next strange seasonal supernatural story, which concerns the resident ghost of one of Liverpool's most famous theatres, and I have it on good authority that this spirit is *still* haunting the place...

Across the globe in recent years there has been a drastic increase in the reports of ghostly black-eyed children. I've had reports from my neck of the woods - the North West of England - about these eerie entities from Formby to Frodsham and Heswall to Hyde, but what are these sinister beings? Some believe they are extraterrestrial, while others have speculated on their origins being in a neighbouring dimension, but there are many black-eyed ghosts which haunt this world. There's a lady in white flowing robes who is regularly seen near Greenbank Park not far from Penny Lane in Liverpool, and all who see her are supposed to suffer extreme misfortune. In the 1960s, a boy who looked about 7 years of age came into the Blackburne Arms on Liverpool's Catharine Street one rainy October afternoon, and the drinkers saw that he not only wore an old-fashioned child's sailor suit of the type worn by children in Victorian and Edwardian times, his eyes had no white or colour to them because the eyeballs were jet black. Most backed away from the creepy boy but an old drunken lady named Mary said to the underage visitor: 'What's your name, eh?'

'Grief,' the boy said, in a weird low voice. He then turned and walked out the pub and vanished. Three of the drinkers – none of them old or in bad health - subsequently died from sudden illnesses that week and many of the other drinkers suffered from long runs of bad luck. Another black-eyed child haunts the Liverpool Empire Theatre, and although local unsubstantiated folklore says she is the ghost of a child who fell from a balcony and broke her neck at the theatre in Victorian times, I have used several fairly accurate psychics on many late-night tours of the theatre and all of them have told me that the girl haunting the place was in fact murdered by a certain actor in a dressing room at the Empire in the 1900s. One medium even sensed that the girl had been buried under the theatre. I am still researching these controversial claims. From December 1966 to early January 1967, Dusty Springfield was in panto at the Empire in Merry King Cole, and on the first night, her co-star, the internationally famous clown Charlie Cairoli did not seem his usual cheerful self. He told Dusty he had seen something 'very strange' in the wings of the theatre during rehearsals, and a few other people backstage talked in hushed tones about 'the girl'. Dusty had a lifelong interest in spiritual and psychic matters but thought Cairoli had probably just seen some young fan who had come backstage, but then, a few nights later, Springfield was just about to make her stage entrance when a voice yelled: 'Dusty!' and it sounded like Charlie Cairoli. Dusty turned to the direction the shout came from – and saw a girl of about 10 years of age dressed in old-fashioned black clothes. She wore a black silken blouse with a high collar and a black dress that went down to her shins, where a pair of polished black boots protruded, and she also had her hair in pigtails. When she turned to face the famous singer, Dusty recoiled in shock because the face of the girl was very pale – almost as white as snow - and contrasted sharply with her completely black eyeballs. Cairoli and the rest of the cast waited – Dusty had missed her cue, and the audience could not only see that Springfield was distracted by something – many of them in the front row also saw the little girl in the wings standing there. That girl vanished into thin air, and there were gasps from those in the audience who witnessed this startling disappearance. The show lumbered on, and afterwards the pantomime was put on twice daily, at 2.15 pm and 7 pm, and the ghost put in more appearances throughout the rest of the show's run, constantly fraying the nerves of Dusty and Charlie Cairoli. One peculiar aspect of the haunting was the way in which only some people could see the girl's ghost. Cairoli could see her plain as day in the wings while a musician in the pantomime could see nothing. The ghostly child was a very talented mimic, and would knock on the dressing room doors and shout 'Curtains are up in five minutes!' which was of course, a lie, but the voice sounded like that of the producer, and caused quite a panic among the performers. Telephones would also ring in the theatre box office and a child would be heard giggling. On January 7 the pantomime ended, and completely fatigued by the supernatural heckler, Dusty Springfield vowed that she would never appear at the Empire theatre – or star in any more Christmas pantos – ever again.

There was another ghost that caused a stir at a major theatre during the festive period in the previous decade, and this apparition also interfered with a pantomime.

There were constant gales of laughter from the

audience during that first performance of the *Robinson Crusoe* Christmas Panto at the London Palladium that December in 1957. Arthur Askey – born in in the Dingle area of Liverpool in 1900 – was stealing the show as a daintily flirtatious Dame named Big Hearted Martha, and Tommy Cooper, in full magician's robes and his trademark fez, played a fumbling magician named Abu who had to do little to get laughs. The critics had foretold the demise of the pantomime – that it was a dying art form – and yet the papers soon reported that attendances for the Palladium show were phenomenal and it was mostly down to the comedic skill of one Arthur Bowden Askey, whose catchphrases "Hello playmates", "I thank you", and "Before your very eyes" were woven into the script. And then in the middle of this hyper-popular panto run, the ghost walked, and Tommy Cooper went to pieces. Unknown to the public, Cooper was deeply superstitious, and those close to him knew for example, that he would not put his fez down on its brim 'in case it trapped a spirit', he would say, on uncharacteristically serious occasions. Tommy would never wear green because he believed in the superstition 'green for grief' and so he had to have a pink Robin Hood costume made for him when he played the folklore hero in a TV sketch. So when the news broke of the Palladium's infamous spectral lady, Cooper was sure it was an omen – either of bad health or a sign that something would go catastrophically wrong during the panto – and Arthur Askey, who was fascinated by the stories of the ghost, attempted to calm the comic-magician down. Arthur was just under 5ft 2 and Tommy was just over 6ft 4. 'It's just a ghostie, lad,' Arthur told him, 'and she means us no harm; she probably enjoys the show.' A reporter got wind of the haunting and asked Cooper if he was superstitious and the towering comic covered up his fear by quipping, 'Oh, definitely superstitious, I won't work a week with a Friday in it.'

Cooper's reply to Askey's assurances about the benign nature of the Palladium ghost is not printable, and Cooper seriously asked a stagehand if they could get priests to hang around in the wings during the panto. David Whitfield, a popular singer of that era, was playing the part of Robinson Crusoe, and three days into the panto he casually asked Arthur: 'Who's that lady in the big bell-shaped dress, always hanging round outside the dressing room door?'

Cooper went cold when he heard this, and accused Askey and the singer of winding him up, and when he finally realised it was not some cruel prank, he was ready to hit the bottle to get some Dutch courage, but Arthur announced he would confront the ghost and see what she wanted. A stagehand said he had seen the 'glowing lady' on and off for years and a medium had told him she was the ghost of an aristocrat – the Duke of Argyll, whose house once stood on the spot now occupied by the theatre (and this is a fact; the street the Palladium stands in is named Argyll Street, after the Duke).

The next evening, minutes before curtain-up, the ghost appeared right in front of Tommy and Arthur carrying a huge bouquet of flowers – which Arthur bravely took off her. Cooper was rigid with fear. After attempting to communicate with the bemused spirit, Arthur asked: 'Can you kindly stay out of sight till the show ends its run, love? Only you're scaring my mate here.'

The radiant lady smiled, nodded and vanished – along with the ethereal flowers. She made no further appearances until the following March.

REAPER REPORTS

I have a folder bulging with reports of Grim Reaper encounters, and I don't know who these ominous harbingers are, or who sends them, but too many people have seen too many of these entities to dismiss the reports as hallucinations. The following story was told to me by the wife of a certain administrator for Liverpool City Council who died some years ago, and I have changed the names and a few details as promised. Trevor, in his late thirties, worked in administration at the Municipal Buildings on Liverpool's Dale Street, and one morning in 1960 his secretary, Mrs Clark noticed him staring intently out the window of his office. 'Mrs Clark, have you seen this?' Trevor asked, without turning from the window. The secretary went to see what he was looking at. A very tall figure in a black robe and hood was standing on the pavement below. Not one person standing at a nearby bus stop or passing by seemed to notice him, despite his outlandish and sinister attire.

'Ooh, *who* is that?' Mrs Clark asked, and shuddered at the sight.

'There are some real idiots knocking about

nowadays,' Trevor said, and he then returned to his desk and worked for a while, but was unable to get the image of the oddball in black out of his mind.

A quarter of an hour on, Mrs Clark went back to the window and looked out onto the grey street.

'Is he still there?' Trevor queried with a smile, expecting the secretary to answer in the negative, but she nodded and replied: 'Yeah, and he's looking up at the window. Oh, his face looks ghastly.'

Trevor got up quickly from his chair and went to see the weird robed man himself. His face, upturned towards the window as the secretary had said, bore a grim basilisk stare. That face was very pale and his dark eyes were like two pieces of coal in the face of a snowman. Trevor felt a weird shudder from his abdomen to his neck. 'Someone just walked over my grave,' he found himself saying.

'Ooh, don't say things like that,' Mrs Clark advised, and she 'touched wood' in a superstitious effort to counteract the offhand comment by pressing her fingers on a bookshelf.

Trevor went towards the door of the office.

'You're not going out there are you?' Mrs Clark asked with a look of utter concern.

'Nah, just going to the toilet,' Trevor told her, but then he slipped outside, his corrosive curiosity getting the better of him – and there was no sign of the man in the black cowl anywhere on Dale Street.

It was early April, and so Mrs Clark suggested the "man in black" was probably a student playing an April Fool prank, but the Reaper-like figure was seen again - by a few other people too - walking along a road in the Childwall district – close to Trevor's house.

This was taking a joke a bit too far, Trevor thought, and he just knew there was something unearthly about this lanky eccentric dressed in a black cowl and hood.

On Monday 2 May that year, Trevor came out of his uncle's house off Picton Road, Wavertree – and there was the eerie figure at the end of the street, waiting for him. Trevor halted in his steps for a moment, then decided to face his fear of the unknown, and so he almost marched towards the entity, determined to see if he was just some warped joker. His car was being fixed so he'd have to bus it home to Childwall today and his bus was due any minute. Moments later, Trevor's bus appeared at the top of the street – and it hit a car head on, and the double-decker toppled over on Picton Road, landing with a mighty crash as it destroyed a shop. Around 44 passengers on the overturned bus were injured and Trevor helped some of them out the wreckage. He turned to see the wreck of the car that had hit the bus. The driver had died – and that Reaper was standing beside the car. Amidst all of the screams and pandemonium surrounding the crash, Trevor looked over at the Reaperlike figure by the car containing the dead man, and he saw him fade away into nothingness. This dematerialisation really frightened Trevor, but he resumed his rescue work among the wreckage of the bus.

Trevor had the feeling he was supposed to have died in that bus crash, and that the figure in the black robes had been some personification of Death waiting for him. Stranger still, Mrs Clark came down with pneumonia days later and almost died at one point, and Trevor wondered if this brush with death explained why she had also been able to see that figure in black when she had looked out of his Dale Street office window. Trevor never saw the creepy figure after that but had nightmares about it for many years.

In September 1958 a Liverpool-born woman living in Birmingham named Mrs Craddock kept having terrifying dreams of an archetypal Grim reaper with his black hood and cowl and a long-bladed scythe. In the recurring dreams, the Reaper would stand at the end of her bed in the semi-darkness, and then he would somehow "zoom in" on her so she could see his ghastly bulging eyes with jet-black irises – and in one of those irises she would see the same weird scene each night – four silhouetted men dancing in a frenzy before dropping down, apparently dead. Then the huge eyelid of the reaper would slide shut and Mrs Craddock would wake up in a cold sweat. Then came some horrific news. During the construction of a factory on a building site at Studley Road, Redditch, a crane was lowering a 60-foot steel girder with six workmen guiding it into place. That girder happened to touch an overhead electric power line carrying eleven thousand volts. Two of the workmen were saved because they happened to be wearing rubber boots, but the other four men suddenly danced about as the lethal voltages coursed through their bodies and made them violently convulse. There was then a massive bang and a shower of sparks, and the two men who wore rubber boots were knocked clean off their feet. The four fatally electrocuted men lay there with smoke rising from their bodies. One of the dead, a 53-year-old man, happened to live just around the corner from Mrs Craddock on Upper Gough Street. When the news of the fatal accident and the description of the 'dance of death' reached the ears of Mrs Craddock she felt ill. Why had she been shown a ghastly preview of the fate of four men? Such recurring premonitions of death are commoner than you think, and those who experience them are often left shocked and bewildered, and sometimes feel guilty for not attempting to stop the foreseen tragedy. In August 2001 a Wirral woman named Helen kept having graphic nightmares of a man smashing down onto a pavement at such a phenomenal speed, his internal organs and bones would strike the dreamer with considerable force and Helen would feel the sting from the man's teeth and bones hitting her like bullets. When the dreams became more and more graphic, Helen went to her doctor, and he eventually referred her to a psychiatrist who noted down all of the events of the gory nightmares. Helen began to recall the terrifying figure of a man in a black hood and a long robe which went down to the ground, and he always appeared in her more sedate dreams which led up to the terrifying ones of the man smashing into the ground. And then the September 11 terror attacks took place, and afterwards, Helen was told that a man she had dated many years before had either fallen or jumped from the North Tower of the World Trade Centre. Like most of the people who fell or jumped from the burning towers that morning, the body of the man Helen knew would have been practically unrecognisable after death and only identifiable through DNA sampling and fingerprinting because of the velocity he would have been travelling (around 155 mph) when he impacted into the sidewalk.

In Victorian times there were several sightings of

another sinister figure which bore a resemblance to the archetypal Grim Reaper in Sniggery Wood, a secluded wooded area between Little Crosby and Hightown in Lancashire. On each occasion when this hooded apparition was seen, a death would occur in the vicinity. On the fine hot summer morning of Thursday July 8, 1880, a farmer saw the weird hooded figure entering Sniggery Wood, and not long afterwards the body of one Robert Rigby, a rabbit farmer, was found lying close to the track of a railway line running past the wood from Southport to Liverpool. The inquest determined that Rigby had been knocked down and killed by a passing goods train but that he had been acting strangely after strolling through Sniggery Wood upon the previous evening. According to the locals, many people entering Sniggery Wood over the years have had their minds turned by some supernatural force that makes them suicidal or murderous, and in the case of Robert Rigby, he spoke of 'a horror' in the wood and of seeing the 'face of the Devil'. Whether this mysterious horror has any bearing on the numerous reports of the monk-like figure in black is not known. A mysterious sniper who fired crudely-made darts dipped in some irritant substance was also active in Sniggery Wood between 1920 to around 1950, and it was assumed that this sniper either used a blow-pipe to launch the darts or some sort of airgun fitted with a silencer, as all of the shots were deadly quiet.

Another local sinister personage responsible (according to the superstitious) for a great number of deaths is the so-called M57 Reaper of Knowsley. This is an abnormally tall hooded figure dressed like a monk, who has been seen both on the M57 and on the hard shoulder as well in fields adjacent to the motorway just before a road accident which ends in a fatality or a number of deaths. I first received reports of something resembling this figure back in 1999. Several motorists saw the eerie hooded figure apparently gliding up Spencers Lane around 8.50pm on the Friday evening of 3 September, 1999, and not long afterwards there was a serious accident on the nearby stretch of the M57, involving two cars. A 61-year-old pedestrian died in this accident. On the Ribblers Lane side of the M57 on the Thursday morning of July 10, 2003 at around 1am, the roadside Reaper was seen again, this time standing on the hard shoulder with his hooded head bowed. Fifteen minutes later, the figure vanished, and there was a crash at that spot which resulted in the death of a 43-year-old man. Just before Halloween of that year, the hooded figure returned to that same spot, and once again there was an incident, this time in the afternoon around 4.45pm, and on this occasion, the driver of the car died. The weather at the time was fine. The figure seems to mostly haunt the part of the M57 that runs near to Spencers Lane, but he has also been seen as far afield as Dunnings Bridge Road, Knowsley Lane, and at the Ormskirk Road turn-off. On the morning of Thursday 2 March 2006, at around 7.15am, the Reaper was seen by dozens of witnesses – most of them motorists on their way to work along the M57 – near to Brewery Lane. One driver told me how he could not see a face in the hood, just a dark shape, and that he felt his flesh crawl when he saw the figure, which he estimated to be about six feet and five inches in height. He had his arms hanging at his sides and his hands looked pale grey in colour. Other people who saw that figure that morning spoke of the feeling of dread they experienced when they set eyes upon him, and about five minutes after the many sightings of the creepy entity, there was a major incident involving seven cars on that stretch of the motorway with one fatality (a 53-year-old driver) and three drivers suffering serious injuries. The last report I have of the M57 Reaper is from Valentine's Day, 2010, which fell on a Sunday that year. A man in his late fifties named Rob told me how he was travelling down the M57 that Sunday afternoon around one o'clock with his grandsons in the back of his car. The children told their grandfather that there was a "man in a brown hood" in a field, and that he had his hands in the sleeves of his garment. About fifteen minutes after this, on that fine Sunday afternoon, there was an incident involving two cars. The driver of the first car was seriously injured, as was his female passenger, and the passenger in the second car, a lady in her seventies – was tragically killed. If you are travelling along the M57 soon – please take extra care – especially if you see that hooded figure.

Reports of Grim Reapers haunting traffic accident black spots abound throughout the UK (and in many other countries too) and I wonder what dark world or plane of existence these hooded harbingers originate from. Not all of these Reapers are inert brooding characters either, according to the many reports I have collected over the years – take the case of the Dancing Monks in Black who have been seen on numerous occasions over the years In Caterham, Surrey. On Sunday 28 July 1963, motorists travelling down the

A22 were bewildered and amused by the surreal sight of eight men dressed in black hoods and cowls running and leaping into the air in the field adjacent to a dual carriageway. What was even more eerie about this spectacle was the fact that the eight oddly-attired figures were moving "strangely and silently" and one witness, a Mr Roberts from Chester, said the figures seemed to move in slow motion, almost reminiscent of the way the astronauts moved about in the low gravity of the moon. Apparently, these sprightly hooded figures are often associated with accidents on the roads of Caterham, and were seen in the area before the Caterham Bypass even opened (in 1939). Three of these creepy animated "monks" were seen on the Caterham Bypass in July 1972 on the day a car carrying the professional golfer Harry Weetman and his wife careered off the Bypass and smashed into a hedge. Weetman never recovered from the fractured skull he sustained in the crash and later died in hospital. Ten years before on the same stretch of road, the running figures in the black cows had been seen, and on that day, a prominent journalist named Arthur George Jenkins was killed on the motorway when his car was involved in a collision with a motorized caravan. In 1979 there was a report of an eccentric farmer shooting at one of these hooded figures near the Caterham Bypass with a 16-bore shotgun – but the entity seemed impervious to the blast and ran off, leaping into the dusk. Who are the ominous leaping monks of the Caterham Bypass then? They could be ghostly revenants of the Augustinian friars of nearby Reigate Priory, which was founded in the early 13th century (but was later dissolved by Henry VIII and later adapted to become a fabulous Tudor house). The Augustinian friars, like all Catholic religious orders, wear a habit made up from a tunic, cincture (or sash) around the waist, as well as shoulder cape and hood, and the habit and hood are usually black. The Austin friars also wore black, and occasionally grey habits and centuries ago these friars would have been a common sight in and around Surrey's Tandridge Priory, which was another religious residence in close proximity to the sightings of the phantom black monks. Just why the animated monks appear when a tragedy is in the offing remains a longstanding mystery.

I NEVER BELIEVED IN

GHOSTS UNTIL…

It's quite amusing how sceptics undergo a type of conversion – a sort of Road to Damascus phase – when they have an encounter with a ghost or a profound supernatural experience. I have seen people who had previously been ardent non-believers in the paranormal turned into disoriented and even gibbering idiots when they have finally come into contact with a supernatural entity, be it a poltergeist or doppelganger or even some innocuous apparition. They feel as if their world – a world of solid trustworthy logic and rationality – has been turned upside down. Everything they believed in has been shown to be flawed, and most of the people who see evidence of ghosts accept the sphere of the supernatural from that point on. These individuals are like the 19th century scientists who believed in the old classical model of physics – that atoms could be thought of as indivisible units like sub-microscopic billiard balls – and that time ticked away simultaneously everywhere in the universe. And then of course, Einstein's Relativity shattered Newtonian dogma and Quantum Physics upset the scientific applecart even more. This chapter is about non-believers who have come into contact with the unknown and realised that there is more to this universe 'than we have dreamt of in our philosophy' to paraphrase a line from Shakespeare…

In the fierce summer of 2007 Sean, a 27-year-old security guard from the south-end of Liverpool, lost his job after the factory he had patrolled for five years went bust in one of those mini-recessions we constantly hear about. He decided he'd try bouncer work, but before he could enquire about any openings in the club scene his 65-year-old Uncle Stan contacted him and practically begged him to mind his rather secluded house near Lady Green Lane, up in the village of Ince Blundell, which is historically in Lancashire but officially in the borough of Sefton. Sean sheepishly told Uncle Stan he had debts to pay and really needed to be working instead of house-minding but Stan said he had bought two airline tickets for himself and a lady friend to go to Florida for a fortnight and how the person who had promised to mind his house had let him down at the last minute. Stan said he'd give Sean a few hundred quid for the favour and let him use his wine cellar – which was huge. Sean agreed, and began the house-sitting period in early August. He soon got bored of the cable TV and the wine and in the afternoon he walked six hundred yards to the nearest pub – the Weld Blundell on Scaffold Lane, where he had ham, eggs and chips and a pint of sub-zero lager on such an infernally hot day. Someone tapped him on the shoulder. It was Roy "Beef" Beefeater, an old friend from his college days in Liverpool. Roy was now working at a garden centre in the area, and the two men caught up on each other's lives. Roy was separated from his wife and Sean had not settled down with anyone and was currently single. Sean was so glad to see a familiar face in Ince Blundell, for he knew no one in the area except his uncle of course. He told Roy where he was staying and said he should come over to the house on Lady Green Lane whenever he could because there was a big well-stocked wine cellar at his disposal. Roy promised he would, and left around 1.30pm to return to work, but Sean, not being too keen on returning to the old secluded house, decided to have a few more drinks. He ended up staggering home some time after 10pm, and dusk was gathering as he watched his swaying shadow on the very narrow sidewalk of Lady Green Lane. He had to halt at one point because he kept veering towards the road. A young female voice startled him and a soft hand felt his forearm. He turned to see a very pretty girl who looked to be in her late teens or early twenties. She had long black hair to her waist and the face of an angel. She wore a greyish tee shirt and dark trousers and tennis shoes. 'You alright, mate?' she asked in a local Lancashire accent.

'Yeah, yeah,' Sean replied, slurred and insensible. 'You're not going to mug me are you?' he joked.

The girl smiled and asked him where he was going and Sean told her his address. She said she'd see him to the door. 'What's your name, and how old are you?' Sean queried as she walked along holding him by the arm. Her name was Prim – short for Primrose, and she was nineteen. Sean told her his name and age. 'What you doing out this time at night?' Sean asked and stepped off the sidewalk by accident, almost falling. The girl just smiled and next thing he knew he was at his doorstep, trying to put his key in the lock. He turned but Prim was gone. The next day at noon, Roy Beefeater called and the two men drank wine and Sean put a pizza in the oven.

'Roy, do you think I'm too old to see a 19 year old?' Sean wondered out loud. Roy said it all depended on the chemistry of the personalities, then asked: 'Why?'

When Roy told him about Prim and how she had

escorted him home and how beautiful she looked, Roy said, 'Sounds fishy to me, mate. Not being funny but what would a young good-looking bird see in you?'

'True,' Sean nodded, 'why indeed? She was lovely though, in ways *and* looks.'

That evening, Sean was at the Weld Blundell pub again, and he got talking to a man of about seventy named Jim who told interesting stories about the many jobs he'd had in his life, but somehow, the course of the conversation turned to the eternal subject of the supernatural, and Jim said: 'You'd better watch out when your going home down that dark lane, Sean; you might bump into the White Lady.'

Sean did not believe in ghosts and flippantly said, 'She a ghost is she?'

Jim nodded and smirked. 'I've seen her – no word of a lie. She comes out onto the roads and causes all sorts of traffic accidents. She was seen when I was a kid and before that. I'm being serious mate.'

'She can stay with me tonight,' Sean joked, 'I need the company, and I'll put some colour in her cheeks if you know what I mean, lad. Hey my uncle's place isn't haunted is it?' Sean gave the address but Jim shook his head and said, 'Nah, not heard of any funny goings on there.'

'I don't believe in all that *Most Haunted* crap anyway,' Sean said, screwing up his face, 'it's all in the mind. When you're dead you're dead – that's what I think anyway and no one will ever convince me otherwise.'

Anyway, the night wore on, and around 11pm, Sean was once again wending his way home down Lady Green Lane, when Prim put in an appearance again. 'Sean, I was just wondering –' she said, shyly. Sean found her coyness endearing; he had not known many girls to blush at anything nowadays.

'Wondering what?' Sean asked, intrigued. Prim fidgeted with her hands and said, 'Do you know the Beatles, being from Liverpool. I mean, have you met any of them?'

'No, I haven't. You into their music?' the former security guard asked, and hiccupped.

'I like John Lennon, he's my favourite.' Prim said and giggled and as she averted her gaze and looked down at the floor, her huge eyelashes fluttered.

A horn sounded and there was a deafening screech. A car had almost run the couple down. When Sean looked about he saw no one else on the moonlit road. He shouted for Prim and looked behind the hedges but the girl was nowhere to be seen.

Sean got home, baffled, and went to bed. He didn't sleep too well, and felt too hot, so he got up, showered and then decided to shave his face – and what little fuzz of hair he had on his head. As he began to shave, he heard movement in the hallway; faint voices and giggles. Prim walked into the bathroom and Sean started at her reflection in the mirror in shock. 'How did you get in?' he asked.

'Sean, I want to introduce you to a friend,' Prim said, and something didn't look right about her; her face looked awfully off colour in the harsh light of the bathroom. She turned to the doorway leading to the hall and said, 'Come in Mary.'

A woman with a face as white as chalk and red-tinged eyes popped her hooded head around the doorframe. Sean could see she wore some type of robe – or a *shroud* of sheets wound about her.

'The White Lady,' Prim explained to a horrified Sean, as if he would be pleased to make her acquaintance. Sean let out a string of swear words and screamed: 'Get away from me you bastards!' And ran between the ghosts, into the hall, but was in such shock he never disabled the alarm and so, as he ran barefooted in his boxers (and face and head covered in shaving foam) down Lady Green Lane, he could hear the wail of his uncle's burglar alarm behind him. He never returned to that house. I began to get almost daily emails from Sean, asking me why Primrose had 'homed in' on him, and if it was some omen. I told him that certain ghosts, especially ones in rural areas, are often simply attracted to new faces in the area because many ghosts are curious creatures; they are also attracted to lights in the darkness, and my old grandmother would often tell me when I was a child to draw the curtains in the evening because, she'd explain in a cryptic way, 'there's all kinds knocking about at night'. She later told me that restless spirits were attracted to the lights of dwellings because of their loneliness and curiosity, and over the years, I have found this to be true. Poor Sean – formerly an fervent disbeliever in ghosts, lived in mortal fear of meeting another one after that night. I have no idea who Primrose was, but imagine she might have been a girl who died during the 1960s, because she said she liked John Lennon, as if she had not been aware of the former Beatle's murder in 1980. The White Lady has been seen by hundreds of people at Ince Blundell for decades, and she seems intent on causing traffic accidents with her sinister antics. She is still active.

One of the strangest forms of apparition is not that

of the dead, but phantoms of those who are alive and kicking, and these phantom doubles are known as doppelgängers – sinister look-alikes that have often been interpreted by occultists as harbingers of imminent death to the person they are mimicking. "Doppelganger" is derived from the German words for doppel – meaning double, and gänger, which means a walker or goer, and the word was first used in a German romantic novel by Jean Paul (Johann Paul Friedrich Richter) in 1796, and later entered the English language in 1851. The Ancient Egyptians referred to a tangible spiritual double of a person which they called the *ka* the vital essence of life which left the body after death, and many other cultures throughout history have propounded similar beliefs. The Cornish and the Norman French peoples believed in the Ankou, a figure that is death in the form of a person, and Norse mythology lists the vardøger – a ghostly yet tangible replica of a person which arrives at the intended destination of that person hours or minutes before he or she gets there. This latter type of doppelgänger, which acts as a type of 'forerunner' who precedes the original person, was first reported in Norway for some obscure reason, and has traditionally been at large there for centuries. Some believe the vardøger phenomenon is common in Norway because for centuries, Norwegians lived in relatively remote parts of their country, and in the absence of electronic communications in those times, nature endowed the Norwegian with a supernatural way to bypass such isolation by allowing them to somehow project their bodily image. However, the vardøger has been reported in other parts of the world, including the UK.

There was a story reported in the papers a few years ago about a "house husband" in Manchester who knew exactly when to start cooking his wife's dinner because her vardøger would arrive home – along with a ghostly version of her car – in the drive outside, and then his real flesh and blood wife would always turn up in her car just over an hour later. The vardøger version would be heard opening the door and walking into the hallway before closing the door behind it – followed by an eerie silence. The husband would start cooking as soon as he heard the clatter of the vardøger's heels coming to a halt on the tiles of the hallway. This phenomenon went on for many years and was witnessed by the husband's friends and relatives.

Throughout the autumn of 1980, John Lennon was seen in various places across New York City – Upper Westside, Broadway, Harlem, as well as West 72nd Street and Central Park Avenue – the thoroughfares near to his home in the gargoyle-crested Dakota building. At the times of these reported sightings and encounters with Lennon, the world's most famous musician was either at home or in the recording studio. A fan impersonating Lennon was ruled out, because the Beatle was seen on several occasions by people who knew him well, and some had asked him why he was walking round New York without Yoko or any bodyguards for that matter, but 'John' never so much as uttered a reply and snubbed them. And then, shortly after the bespectacled impostor went to ground for good, John Lennon was murdered by Mark Chapman. The superstitious therefore wondered if the Lennon twin had been a doppelgänger omen – a warning of approaching death. I have investigated many doppelgängers over the years, but one case that really stands out began one icy February night in Liverpool in 1995 outside the Arkles Pub in Anfield, as a 27-year-old Walton man named Stuart got off a bus. Stuart met a strange wall of silence in the Arkles pub; none of his friends would speak to him, and at first he thought it was a joke, but soon realised something strange had happened. A former old neighbour named Mike told Stuart he had a cheek coming back in the pub after the verbal abuse he had given. 'Whoa! When was all this supposed to have happened?' a baffled Stuart queried. 'Go on, beat it!' Stu's friend from his schooldays, Sean screamed at him, and made a fist. Stuart said he had not been in the Arkles since the previous week, but gave up protesting his innocence and left the pub confused and angry. He walked through sleet to Venmore Street, where his girlfriend Kirsty lived, but as he passed the entry at the top of the street, he heard a voice swear at him and felt something pressed against his back. 'I'll do you in if you try and turn around,' the voice said. 'Giz your wallet and your ring.'

No way was anyone having a ring that had belonged to Stu's late father, and he swung around – and found himself facing his exact double. The mugger even had on the same black Adidas tracksuit, same Nike trainers too. 'What the –' Stuart's anger gave way to astonishment, and at this point, Kirsty, his girlfriend, came round the corner from Walton Breck Road, and she saw the mugger from behind – and the knife – and screamed. Stuart's living replica ran off much faster than Stuart ever could and headed towards Robson Street, where he went to ground awfully fast. 'Did you see him? It was me!' Stuart said repeatedly to his girlfriend. She thought Stu was just in shock. It seems the mirror image then went on a crime spree, and you can imagine how the police reacted to Stuart's alibi when he blamed his doppelgänger, but a week later when he got on a bus on Scotland Road one night, he saw his double sitting in front of him. Stu tapped the eerie figure on the shoulder, and the impostor turned. Their eyes met for a chilling moment, and the doppelganger got up, ran to the door and pressed the Emergency Door Open button. He laughed and ran off into the night near Leeds Street. 'Your twin's an idiot!' the bus-driver told Stuart, and after that night, the creepy carbon-copy criminal was seen no more. Stuart had never given an iota of credence to tales of ghosts and the supernatural, but after the strange episode of the creepy impostor he became an avid student of the paranormal.

The following unearthly sequence of events unfolded near Halloween in 1997. A woman in her late forties in the Gateacre area of Liverpool named Cathy, was deserted by her partner of almost ten years - a pharmacist named Eric. He started to ignore Cathy, and would turn away when she asked him what the matter was. 'Please tell me what I've done,' she had said to him when the bizarre behaviour first started. Eric would say nothing in reply, though. 'Have you found someone else?' Cathy asked, and tears began to fall. She had lost her husband Mike fifteen years before all this and couldn't go through losing love again. 'It's not you, it's me,' he told Cathy, and made out that he wanted a trial separation. He felt trapped, he said, and perceived his life as being in a rut of clockwork routines. A few days later Cathy woke up and found a letter on the pillow where Eric's head would always rest. Cathy cried when she read that Eric had felt he had not found his soulmate after all. Cathy wanted to die, and only her elderly neighbour, Denise, made her pull herself together. Denise reminded Cathy that she had a certain little Sussex Spaniel named Deano who loved her, and that did the trick, but every now and then, Cathy would go into a relapse and start to cry. It was to be a long healing process. Cathy just wanted to be someone else; she felt a failure, and when she saw couples holding hands, she envied their love with a vengeance. Then something bizarre took place. Cathy worked in a travel agency shop, and one day she returned from work and found Deano missing. He should have been in the garden, but he wasn't, and Cathy went to tell Denise that her dog had escaped, but Denise shot a puzzled look and told Cathy she had taken the dog for a walk earlier. 'I've only just come home from work - how could I?' Cathy gasped, but Denise came back with: 'You told me you'd got off work early.'

Cathy thought she was going mad, and this was just the first of a series of strange incidents which almost caused Cathy to have a breakdown. Her friends said they had seen her in various places in the city centre when Cathy plainly knew she had not been anywhere near town. Some of her friends said she had snubbed her and one friend claimed she had received a nasty phone call from Cathy, telling her to stop having affairs with married men. Cathy swore it had not been her, but wasn't believed, because the nasty caller had sounded exactly like Cathy. A friend of Denise, a 37-

year-old man named John Denning, heard about these strange goings-on, and John believed some warped prankster was trying to drive Cathy mad. Cathy was so glad that someone believed that she was innocent, and then something very unearthly took place. One evening, Cathy took Deano on his walkies along Acrefield Road, up Rose Brow and back home again, a distance of just over a mile – and some woman who looked just like Cathy – same hairstyle, same long black coat and same red scarf – followed her every step of the way at a distance of about fifty yards. This had to be the demented "joker", but why was she going to all this trouble to ruin Cathy's friendships? John Denning told Cathy he would follow her the next time she walked the spaniel, and he advised Cathy to take a detour down a certain cul-de-sac known as Runnymede Close, in the hope of trapping and confronting the unhinged stalker. The loopy lookalike did not take the bait, and walked on towards Rose Brow when Cathy and the dog went down Runnymede Close. John Denning chased after the creepy carbon copy of Cathy but the impersonator managed to lose John somehow. John racked his brains, trying to think why the strange woman was doing this – dressing like Cathy and pretending to be her when she made nuisance calls. The lady had to be mentally unstable. On the night before Halloween, at around 1am, Cathy, suffering from acute insomnia, foolishly took Deano for a long walk. She got the shock of her life when that accursed mimic turned up and started to follow her again. Cathy went down the cul-de-sac of Runnymede Close – but on this occasion – so did the stalker, and she began to run after Cathy. Now, at closer quarters,

Cathy saw that the woman looked *exactly* like her – even the hairstyle was identical, but the skin colour seemed pallid, and the strange copycat had dark eyeliner around a pair of piercing eyes that looked insane.

'Get away from me!' Cathy screamed, and the spaniel Deano whimpered at the eerie emulator. Cathy picked up the dog and ran off towards Acrefield Road, where a police patrol car was slowly cruising along. Cathy waved frantically at the car and it accelerated towards her then slowed to a halt. The driver wound down the window and asked: 'What's up?' and Cathy told him she was being stalked and turned to point at the imitator – but there wasn't a soul about.

'You'd better get home miss; walking around at this hour's asking for trouble,' the policeman advised. The next day, John Denning gave very careful thought to Cathy's odd account of the way the 'impersonator' had ran after her, and how pallid she had appeared. John told Cathy there were things called doppelgängers – paranormal beings which imitated people with a view to either destroying them or taking over their lives. People suffering from severe depression, low self esteem – or people unhappy with their lives who wanted to be someone else - had allegedly reported being stalked by these sinister doubles. John's theory really unnerved Cathy, for she had always mocked people who believed in the paranormal, and yet she had seen that weird look-alike with her own eyes, and so, feeling thoroughly confused and worried she asked John if he could stay over with her till these strange goings-on ended. John stayed with her and became very close as a result, and eventually started seeing

Cathy, and the creepy "twin" was only seen on one more occasion – and that was on the day, in 1998, when John and Cathy were married. When Cathy walked from the altar with her husband, she thought she caught a brief glimpse of her sinister counterpart, all dressed in black as it stood among well-wishers and friends at the back of the church.

STRANGE HALLUCINATIONS

Many stories come my way which I cannot explain; they seem to defy logic and the laws of rationality, and the following account belongs to this class of conundrum.

The time was 7pm on Saturday 27 September, 1969 and the place was the leafy suburbs of Poll Hill, Heswall, one of the highest points on the Wirral peninsula. A 13-year-old boy from West Kirby named Ralph arrived at his old uncle's house, and getting no answer, Ralph went into the back garden and climbed through the lounge window, which was ajar. He found his Uncle Eric dead, sitting up in his favourite armchair, his lifeless eyes gazing at the television which was showing an episode of *Dixon of Dock Green*. In shock, Ralph calmly went to the telephone in the hallway and informed his mother, Astrid, that Eric was dead. This uncle, a favourite of Ralph's, was his mother's oldest brother, and Astrid was a cold, scheming lady. She ranted on about her older sister Cecelia getting everything because she was legally Eric's next of kin (as Eric had never married and had never made a will). As Ralph stood in the cold hallway eyeing his deceased uncle through the doorway which led to the lounge, his mum Astrid ranted: 'She'll get Eric's Rolls-Royce Silver Shadow and that Chesterfield, and the Howard Miller grandfather clock…'

Ralph put the phone down on his mother and, still

in shock, he did a silly thing. He located the keys to his late uncle's Rolls-Royce, manoeuvred it out of the garage, and drove homewards on the five-mile journey to West Kirby. His mother would be so pleased at him bringing the Rolls-Royce to her before Cecelia could lay her hands on it! Uncle Eric had often given Ralph driving lessons but it seemed so different now that he was alone in the car with an empty seat beside him. Even in this state of distress the boy was mindful of lighting-up time (7.18pm) and he switched on the headlights of the Rolls-Royce as he joined Telegraph Road. A sky-blue and white Triumph Herald police car cruised alongside the roller Ralph was sat in, and the boy felt beads of sweat pop out of his forehead. Ralph pretended to scratch his right ear and hid his face behind his hand. The police car accelerated away up Telegraph Road, leaving Ralph on a secluded stretch of road with the newly-risen full moon for company. Anyone familiar with Telegraph Road will know there is a one-and-a-half-mile stretch of the highway with nothing but desolate farmland on either side of it once you get past Mere Lane and Oldfield Drive – and this is where Ralph was when he saw the thing in the rear-view mirror. He could not believe his eyes. There was a giant ball – a dark brownish-green globe, about fifteen feet in height, and it was rolling after him along Telegraph Road. He felt as if he was in the bowling alley of a giant, and that huge ball looked very heavy – and deadly, because as it moved in close it seemed to have a metallic finish to its rolling surface. Ralph stepped on the accelerator and watched the speedometer needle swing to 55 mph. The Silver Shadow had a top speed of 120 mph but Ralph was getting nervous handling the vehicle as it approached half that speed. What on earth was that thing? Had it fallen off a lorry and would it slow down soon? Ralph's mind raced and his heart pounded as he tried to outdistance the spherical nightmare. It was almost touching the rear fender now! The village of Thurstaston was just a few hundred feet away now, and perhaps someone there would be able to help Ralph to fend off this surreal but terrifying object. The gigantic ball nudged the car sideways, aiming it at a concrete lamp post! Ralph screamed as the Rolls-Royce shuddered, and suddenly he lost control of the vehicle. He slammed on the brakes and the car swerved, then went through a hedge and shook his bones as it careered across a furrowed field. The boy got out of the Rolls-Royce and tried to run off through the cloud of brown soil dust that the vehicle had kicked up. It was impossible to run more than a few feet without tripping over or stepping into the furrows, and not once did he look back to see if that globular giant was coming after him. He made it to a road and hid behind a tree in the moonlight and listened. He heard a distant thunderous sound like a fleet of steamrollers moving away from him. Eventually he came out from the shadows of the tree and made his way home, arriving back at his house at almost 8.15pm.

Ralph stammered out the unlikely story of the giant ball and its eerie intentions to crush him in that car, but his father and mother exchanged glances and had knowing looks in their eyes.

Ralph's mother then said the Silver Shadow had been run off the road by Cecelia's 'witchcraft'. Ralph didn't understand, and when he asked his mother to explain what she meant she just shook her head and closed her eyes.

Later that evening a grinning Cecelia turned up at Ralph's house – in that Rolls Royce he had abandoned, and when she sat at the family table, the boy noticed something very curious which sent a shiver down his spine: Cecelia was fidgeting with a little dark brownish green ball on her key fob; it looked just like the giant metal ball which had tried to crush him on that stretch of lonely road, only it was the size of a gobstopper.

When Ralph mentioned that ball again to his parents they never made any more references to witchcraft, but said instead that their son had hallucinated the whole episode because of the trauma of finding Uncle Eric's body. Ralph then noticed that Cecelia had somehow won them over, and Ralph had the sneaking suspicion her witchcraft – or whatever power she possessed – had control of his mother and father's minds. Ralph thought it wise to never mention the giant ball incident again until Cecelia passed away in 2010.

Was the giant ball some hallucination in the mind of a 13-year-old who had just found his favourite uncle dead in his chair, or was the weird construct some product of his Aunt Cecelia's witchcraft? We'll probably never know. Some things that are initially explained away as hallucinations are seen by more than one person, and that was the case in the next strange story.

In early December 1965, a 12-year-old girl from Bootle named Maureen Kelly went to stay with her Aunt Rhona and Uncle Alastair at their Victorian three-storey house on Langlands Road, in the Govan area of Glasgow, facing Elder Park. For years, Rhona and Alastair had been promising Maureen she'd be able to spend a Christmas holiday at their home, and now Maureen's parents thought their child was old enough for a fortnight's stay at her aunt and uncle's house. The child was due back in Bootle on Christmas Eve. Maureen was spoilt rotten by her aunt and uncle and the couple's five children all got along well with their English cousin, however, on the third night at the house on Langlands Road something quite bizarre and terrifying took place. Maureen went up to bed in a spare room in which there was an old upright piano. The girl lay in bed as the room was warmed up by a two-bar electric fire, and after about ten minutes, her Uncle Alastair came into the room to tuck his niece in and turn off the electric fire. The time was about 11pm when Alastair bent over Maureen and kissed her on the forehead before saying goodnight. Maureen dozed off and at around 1am she was awakened by what sounded like echoing musical notes somewhere. The girl's head protruded from the warm blankets as far as her button nose, and she looked around the room nervously. Half of the bedroom was in shadow and the other half was faintly lit by the moonlight streaming through the gap in the heavy curtains.

That reverberating music was heard again. Maureen's ears homed in on it this time – it was coming from the old upright piano. The girl hoped it was just a mouse in that piano, but then she saw the long rectangular lid on the top of the old dust-covered piano lift about an inch. At first, Maureen thought she was seeing things – that the semi-darkness was playing tricks on her sleepy eyes, but then the lid opened even further and this was not some optical illusion – the lid was slowly lifting.

Fingers emerged from the gap under that lid and bent as they gripped the piano.

Maureen wanted to scream but was simply too afraid to.

She heard that music again and realised it was the sound of something moving against the strings of the piano as it emerged from the old instrument. The lid lifted as far as it could go and it rested against the wall. At this point, Maureen distinctly heard what sounded like the noise of a great group of people talking, perhaps at a party, because the girl definitely heard the sound of drinking glasses clinking as if someone was toasting something.

Then two long, weirdly jointed arms emerged from the piano via the opening at the top of the instrument. Maureen was so afraid at the appearance of these creepy elongated limbs, she actually felt her teeth chatter, and she closed here eyes tightly for a moment and willed the thing to go away, but when she opened her eyes she saw something terrifying. The entity climbing out of the piano was a man of some sort with either pale blue skin or tight-fitting clothes of the same colour, and the length of his arms and legs were about three times the length of normal limbs. These arms and legs were jointed like the legs of a spider so the man appeared to have three elbows on each arm and three knees on each leg. The uncanny-looking creature's head was egg-shaped and black, and it was not at the top of the torso, but at the bottom, at the crotch, between the gangly multi-jointed legs. The face on this head was a white oval with two ghastly eyes –

red hemispheres of something jelly-like. The creature had no nose, but it did have a grinning upturned black crescent of a mouth with no teeth evident at that point. The unearthly long-limbed entity placed its white long-fingered hands against the wall, and moved up that wall like a spider. The legs did the same, and they had no boots or any footwear at the end of them, just hook-like feet of the same blue colour as the rest of the body. The spidery creature crawled up the wall and onto the ceiling, so its torso and ghastly grinning visage faced Maureen, and there it hung as the terrified girl heard that peculiar hubbub of background noise, apparently coming from the piano. As if the appearance of the spider-like man wasn't scary enough, another sinister entity emerged from the piano too. This figure was not elongated or multi-jointed, but dressed in what looked like medieval clothes. This was a man of about six feet or more who looked a lot taller in a pointed maroon hat which terminated in a little jingly spherical brass-coloured bell. He wore a black balaclava of some sort which went down to the shoulders, and his clothes were pied in two colours, maroon and yellow – rather like the traditional particoloured dress of the jesters of old. He wore black tights and a pair of pointed long-toed shoes which curled inward toward him. The backdated-looking figure tip-toed over to Maureen's bed with his index finger against his lips, gesturing for her not to shout or scream, but the girl emitted an ear-piercing scream, and the bizarre late-night visitors darted back towards the piano and seemed to fight one another as they both crawled into the opening at the top of the instrument. Maureen lay there in tears, waiting for

Uncle Alastair to come, but all she could hear was the sound of the surreal entities moving about against the strings of the piano. Maureen sat up slightly and looked at the door of the room, wishing her uncle would arrive, but instead she saw movement to her left. It was the furious face of the man in the pointed hat, gritting what looked like decayed and blackened teeth. He waved his fist in a threatening manner and issued threats to the girl in a Scottish accent, and some of the words he spoke were later repeated by Maureen to her uncle and she discovered they had been very coarse swear words. The door barged open and in came Uncle Alastair in his pyjamas, and his thinning hair, which was usually carefully combed over his bald head from above his ear, was sticking up.

As he entered the room, the lid on the top of the old upright piano slammed shut, and Alastair heard this and looked reflexively towards the piano. He also heard the faint tumult of voices and other sounds suddenly cease, and Maureen's uncle also heard the sounds of something brushing against the strings and wires of the piano's innards. Alastair hurried over to Maureen, pulled back the blankets and lifted her with his strong arms. He then hurried out of the room and took her to the bedroom of his youngest child, 9-year-old Mary, who was sleeping soundly in her bed. Maureen spent the rest of that night sleeping top-tail in Mary's bed, and in the morning Alastair moved Maureen's bed out the spare room and put it in Mary's room. When Maureen told him what she had seen that night, Alastair said she had just had a nightmare, but Maureen knew what she had seen, and years later when she was seventeen, Alastair visited her and her family at Bootle and after he had enjoyed a few glasses of whiskey, he told Maureen that she had not been seeing things that December night in 1965. She had seen two of three entities that had haunted that house on Langlands Road for about eighty years or more. The bizarre-looking entities were said to be evil spirits conjured up during a séance that had been held in the very room Maureen had slept in, back in Victorian times, and this claim had been told to Alastair by an old man who had lived on Langland Road as a boy. On the afternoon of Saturday 30 October, 1886, a week after the uncanny beings had first appeared during a séance at the house of 71-year-old Lizzie McCulloch, they appeared again, this time in broad daylight, and terrible screams were heard in the house. Mrs McCulloch's body was later found crumpled on the pavement outside of her home. Her head had been split open from the three-storey fall and her brains were all over the pavement. A witness to the woman's death said he had been in the nearby park when he had looked up to see the old woman had been watering plants in her flower box when someone had pushed her to her death. The man who had pushed Mrs McCulloch out of the third-storey window of her home had worn a strange reddish-coloured hat with a point to it, the witness recalled, and this man had also torn the window box full of flowers from the sill and thrown it down onto the pavement as he screeched with laughter. The witness who described this was never called to the inquest on Mrs McCulloch because it transpired that he had been drinking in the park and had a history of alcoholism. The man in the pointed red hat and other bizarre-looking entities were seen in the upper rooms of Mrs McCulloch's house in the weeks following her death, but after a few months of intense ghostly activity at the house, there was a hiatus which lasted for about a year, and the family who had only just moved into the house were forced to flee. Alastair had taken possession of the house in 1955 and had been unaware of its haunted history at the time, but sometimes saw shadows out the corners of his eye whenever he was walking up or down the upper flights of stairs at the house.

Moreover, Alastair said that on the Saturday night of 1 January 1966, weeks after Maureen had been visited by the unearthly trinity of apparitions from the piano – strange shadowy figures had been seen on Langlands Road and also in nearby Elder Park, and hours later, a 19-year-old local lad named Alex Cleghorn, who had been in the vicinity "first-footing" (a Gaelic Hogmanay ritual) with two older brothers, had inexplicably vanished into thin air. One minute Alex was walking along with his brothers, then suddenly he was nowhere to be seen. The three brothers were walking along Govan Road when Alex disappeared without a trace, and that road is on the other side of Elder Park – the very park Alastair's house faces – and just 400 yards from the site of the haunted house. Alex Cleghorn is still missing almost fifty years on, and his disappearance has never been explained. Could there be some connection with the teenager's sudden disappearance and the weird goings on around Elder Park and Langlands Road that night?

When Maureen heard about the strange history of her uncle and auntie's house, she knew beyond all shadow of a doubt that she had not hallucinated the bizarre characters she had seen that December night back in 1966. She still has no idea who they were or why they visited her (and in such a bizarre fashion, emerging from a piano), but she never visited the house on Langlands Road again after the revelation about its creepy history.

The entities and objects featured in this section so far – a giant rolling sphere chasing a car, a spidery-limbed humanoid and an apparent character who seemed to date from the Middle Ages who emerged from the insides of a piano with the latter – have a distinct hallucinatory air about them, and its often very difficult in the world of the paranormal to establish whether some apparitions are products of the witness's mind or whether they have an existence all of their own. The only indications an apparition is real come from physical evidence left behind by the entity or object or from unequivocal vindication of the entity or object's existence by another witness. Many percipients that see ghosts of the hallucinatory kind choose to keep their experiences a secret because hallucinations are widely associated with mental illness, and so, if a reputable person such as an airline pilot or a doctor or Member of Parliament sees something paranormal, he or she will keep quiet about it for obvious reasons. One of the first serious surveys concerning ghosts was carried out in 1889 by the Society of Psychical Research (SPR). The name of this pioneering survey was called the *Census of Hallucinations* and around 17,000 people were contacted. The questionnaire began by asking (in a rather wordy roundabout way): 'Have you ever, when believing yourself to be completely awake, had a vivid impression of seeing or being touched by a living being or animate object, or of hearing a voice; which impression, so far as you could discover, was not due to any external physical cause?'

Some 15,316 replied that they had not, but 1,684 stated that they had. Many of the things reported by people in the census and in later investigations by the SPR made it clear that some very bizarre hallucinatory-types of ghost had been seen by people (and sometimes groups of percipients) who were in full possession of their mental faculties and manifestly sane. Further and more widespread studies since the 1889 *Census of Hallucinations* have reached the same conclusions – that some very bizarre and surreal things are being seen by people who are mentally healthy and these weird things are being seen more than people suppose. A case in point is the strange being seen in an alleyway off Preston's Church Street one foggy evening in November 1894. A well-known drunken trouble-causer of a woman named Annie Ainsworth had just been forcibly expelled from a pub near Church Street in the town around 10pm, and was making her way to a relative's house when she heard someone shout her name. Annie looked around and saw no one except an old woman who was hobbling her way home with a walking stick. 'Annie!' said the voice again, and this time Mrs Ainsworth judged that the person calling her was in a poorly-lit alleyway off the thoroughfare, and so she cautiously went to see who it was. She could see that the person standing in the shadows and fog had on a reddish uniform of some sort with brass buttons, but as she got nearer, Annie Ainsworth let out a scream which was heard over a mile away that night. The person in the uniform was not human – it was something with the head of a cat, and where hands should have been hanging from the sleeves of the uniform, large paw-like hands hung there, and they had very sharp long claws.

The face of the creature was just like that of a feline, and yet it had a wide rather sinister grin, and so it reminded Annie of the Cheshire Cat illustrations by John Tenniel that she had seen as a child in her mother's copy of *Alice's Adventures in Wonderland*.

'Oh be quiet, woman!' the entity said in response to Annie's screams in well-spoken and accent-less voice. The head of this bizarre creature was the size of a human's but had the face of a cat with pointed ears in place of human ones. Annie could not take in any further detail because she turned on her heels and ran. About two minutes later, Annie bumped into a PC Woodacre on his beat and told him what she had just seen, but of course, her claims were hard to take seriously as far as the policeman was concerned because of her reputation for being a drunk. But then there were other sightings of the cat-headed man in the red uniform in and around the Church Street area of Preston over the next few night, and one of the witnesses was impeccable in the eyes of PC Woodacre: Chief Inspector Walmsley – a well-respected hardboiled street-wise police official; the sort of man who was not in the habit of making up silly stories. Walmsley and a policeman named Johnson had heard reports of the strange figure with the head of a cat from an elderly night watchman and had gone to investigate. Walmsley saw the "bogeyman" (as people were calling the strange feline humanoid figure) on

Fishergate and Cannon Street, and like the encounter Annie Ainsworth had, these sightings took place in thick fog. On both occasions when the Chief Inspector closed in on the weird creature it seemed to melt into the darkness. There were a few more sightings of the cat-headed figure in the military-type uniform (which was never identified) and then the entity - whatever it was – was not seen until some 37 years later, and this was at New Cock Yard, a narrow passageway off Fishergate around Christmas 1930. On this occasion the bizarre-looking creature had acquired a long cape, and when it was cornered by several members of the public, the feline-faced man jumped clean over them in a manner reminiscent of that other hoary old bounding bugbear Spring-Heeled Jack. Again, this encounter took place during a December fog, and also after dark (around 10.30pm), and the few brave people who gave chase said the cloaked figure made no sound as it ran off into the night, quickly vanishing into the jade mist.

Hallucinations that take the forms of animals (such as in the previous case where the apparition had the head of a cat) are known as zoopsia, a psychology textbook classification of a psychiatric condition which is mostly experienced by sufferers of delirium tremens – commonly known as the DTs, a condition in which an alcoholic or drug addict hallucinates all sorts of ghastly-looking insects and animals (usually perceived to be crawling all over him or her) during a withdrawal from alcohol or drugs. The term "pink elephants" is a reference to the hallucinatory beings a recovering alcoholic or drug-dependent person can perceive while they suffer from "the shakes" or "cold turkey". People with the DTs and cold turkey often report hallucinatory insects infesting their clothes and body, and some report seeing (and feeling) black rats and sinister-looking snakes. But sane, mentally and physically healthy people have also reported bizarre out-of-place animals which seem to belong to the world of hallucinations. The only difference between these animals is that although they *do* seem to have no apparent reality in the world outside of the head of the person who is seeing them, they are often seen by a second percipient or even whole groups of witnesses. Hallucinations are classed as perceptual illusions, and they are often vivid, even though they have no tangible existence, and they are mostly associated with a psychosis, and so in 2010, when a 7-year-old Liverpool child named Emma told her mother Fliss that the food going missing out of the fridge was being eaten by a huge hairy elephant, Fliss believed Corinne was seeing things and naturally became worried. Children are very imaginative and prone to make up far-fetched stories to get themselves out of all sorts of sticky situations, but Emma was not the sort of child who told even white lies, and if she had been responsible for taking choc ices and half a sandwich cake out of the fridge, she would have owned up. The girl claimed that a huge elephant had started visiting the house, mostly during the early hours of the morning and sometimes late at night. Emma had even named this 'imaginary' animal Ethel, because she somehow sensed that it was a female. Fliss and her husband Alec had left Liverpool two years before and had come to live in north-west Kent at a beautiful detached house in Ebbsfleet Valley. Emma's stories were treated as out-of-character tall tales by her father Alec at first but when a box of iced buns and a birthday cake Fliss had made for a neighbour went missing one night, Emma's ridiculous claims about Ethel eating the missing items proved to be the last straw for the patient parents. Fliss told her husband that she was worried about the state of her daughter's mind and suggested taking her to the family doctor. Alec said he believed that Emma had given the birthday cake away to a boy she had talked about named Rob who went to her school. Emma started to cry and said she was telling the truth about the elephant and so her parents sat her down and listened to what must have seemed like a very incredible tale. Emma said that the deep thuds she and the family had heard a few months back in the middle of the night had been the first signs that something spooky was going on; this was Ethel walking about in the back garden. Emma's mum and dad recalled the mysterious thuds Emma mentioned but believed it was the result of digging work going on in the area, as Ebbsfleet Valley is a new town and is still being developed, as most of the land the town is built on is classed as "brownfield" – land that was previously used for industrial or commercial use, and some of this land was being excavated and cleaned up when the nocturnal bumps were heard by the family. Emma clasped her hands together rather dramatically and said to her mum and dad, 'You've got to believe me, just hear me out!'

'We're all ears Emma,' Alec sighed, and added: 'the floor's yours.'

'Okay, so one morning about three maybe, I got up to get a drink of water, and came downstairs, and

Jimbo [the family's Alsatian dog] was hiding under the table as if something was scaring him, and I could not get him to come out. He was whimpering like this,' Emma emulated the sound of Jimbo's yelps.

'Get on with it, Emma,' the girl's impatient mother urged.

Emma continued her long-winded account. 'And then I turned around, and there – that whole wall on the side of the kitchen, went all funny.'

'How do you mean, all funny?' Alec asked, eyeing the wall his daughter had indicated with a nod.

Emma explained. 'Well it went sort of see-through, as if it was like glass in some parts, and I could see a blue sky and like trees, and I know it was like of a night, but that's what I could see, and then these long pointy things came through it – through the wall, and then what I thought was a big snake, but it was the trunk of the elephant I could see and those long pointy things were its tusks.'

Fliss glanced at Alec, who was gazing at the wall with a puzzled expression.

Emma held out both of her hands at the kitchen wall and pointed with both forefingers and said: 'And then the head of the elephant came right in and Jimbo ran out the kitchen and hid under the stairs, and I just stood there. I was scared but I stayed there because I was so amazed at what I was seeing. And then the end of the trunk, like the tip or whatever it's called, just stroked my face and I froze at first, but it sort of felt wet as if the tip was kissing me. Then I saw her eyes, and she looked as astonished as me, and I swear on my Nan's life that this happened.'

'Don't say things like that, Emma, take it back,' her

mother warned her.

Emma shook her head and seemed tearful. 'I won't take it back because it really happened and you and dad are being mean by not believing me.'

'Emma, can you blame us for not believing you?' Alec chipped in, his hand stroking the kitchen wall. 'You're telling us that a massive elephant came through this solid wall and that your mother and I slept through it.'

'Dad, I know it sounds bogus but I give you my word, it happened!' Emma wiped a welling tear away from her left eye and sniffed.

'And you gave this elephant all the cakes and those buns?' Fliss asked and shook her head.

'She was hungry mum,' Emma replied. 'Don't ask me how but I just sensed that she was, and she was also thirsty because she sucked all the water out Jimbo's bowl and then I showed her the water tap and turned it on and she drank from that as well.'

'And does she still come around or as she found another kitchen?' Alec asked in a sarcastic tone.

There was a pause, and Emma shrugged, then said, 'I haven't seen her for a while. Maybe she's gone back to wherever she came from.'

About a fortnight after this, Emma was playing with her wi-fi game in a downstairs room at the house which had just been decorated. No furniture had been installed in this room yet and the only items in there were a television mounted on the wall and a play station. It was a Sunday and the time was around 8pm and Fliss went into the room to tell her daughter it was time to get a bath for school on Monday morning. As Fliss walked into the room, she got the shock of her life. Her daughter was standing in the middle of the room, and the dog Jimbo was barking furiously – and behind Emma, partially sticking out of the newly wallpapered wall – was the huge head of either an elephant or a mammoth. The huge curved ivory tusks were protruding about five feet or more, and so was the animal's long grey trunk, which was dangling behind Emma, who seemed oblivious to the terrifying spectacle. Fliss let out a scream, and as she did, the enormous head and tusks and trunk retreated back into the wall in one swift moment.

Fliss ran towards her daughter, grabbed her by the upper arm and dragged her from that room as a whining Jimbo followed the mother and startled daughter. Fliss could not get her words out at first, and when her husband Alec came bounding into the house from the back garden, where he had been mending a greenhouse door, he thought Fliss had been attacked by an intruder. He asked Emma what had happened and the girl said, 'I don't know, Dad!'

Eventually Fliss managed to babble out an incoherent description of what she had seen in the newly-decorated room, and Alec went in there immediately and looked around. He checked the windows and saw they were locked, and then Fliss appeared in the doorway of the room and said, 'Oh Alec, I saw it! Emma's telling the truth.'

Alec took his wife into the kitchen and sat her down with Emma and made her a cup of sweet tea, an old remedy for shock, he had been told. He listened to his wife's account of the ghostly elephant, but like most people, was at a loss to explain it. He knew his wife was not at all superstitious, nor had she the slightest interest in the topic of the supernatural – so Alec knew she had seen something real which had genuinely spooked her. Emma assured her mother it had only been Ethel and that she was harmless. Unfortunately – as far as Emma was concerned – the elephant was not seen again, and to date it has not reappeared in the house in Ebbsfleet Valley. Alec mentioned the strange goings-on at his house to a local man named Geoff one evening at his local pub, and Geoff told the Liverpudlian something which really shocked him. Geoff said that in 2003, during the construction of the High Speed 1 rail link from the Channel Tunnel to London, workmen unearthed flint tools – and the bones of a some sort of elephant. Archaeologists descended on the building site – on Southfleet Road, not far from the house Alec, Fliss and Emma now lived in. Alec thought Geoff was winding him up at first and so he Googled "Southfleet Road Elephant" as directed by his friend and saw that everything he had claimed was true. The remains of an elephant, twice the size of today's African variety, were 420,000 years old and this animal had been hunted and butchered by humans with flint tools, some of which were found in the animal's ribcage, along with a wooden spear. This elephant had been four times the weight of an average family car and yet it had been captured and slaughtered by four individuals who had been fighting for survival in the great ice age known as the Anglian Glaciation some four-hundred-odd centuries ago.

Alec told Fliss about the incredible find on their doorstep, but they both agreed not to tell Emma about the way the "stone age" people had butchered the elephant, in case it upset her.

So, this was another case where something which was initially classed as some sort of hallucination was shown to have some basis in reality, and was in all probability, all down to some portal in time itself. Was that how the elephant from over four hundred centuries ago, back when Ebbsfleet was a verdant wooded tributary of the River Thames, able to poke its mighty head into our modern era? We may know more someday.

THE SOUL MATES PHENOMENON

I am a great believer in the soul mate phenomenon – that every person upon this earth has someone who was made solely for them; a person who is metaphysically assigned to one man or woman, and is pushed towards that individual by forces we mere nescient mortals label 'coincidence' and the tragedy is that not everyone ends up with their soul mate, because sometimes ocean-spanning distance gets in the way, and even time, so that the soul mates have to bridge a generation gap. When death intervenes, the devotee who lives on may resort to suicide – or even attempt to turn back the very wheels of time, and that is the subject of this first strange tale. The beautiful American medicine pioneer Susan Dimock, surgeon and physician, was 28 when she lost her life on the Victorian equivalent of the *Titanic* – the *SS Schiller*, a 380-foot long German ocean-liner which sailed from New York, bound for Plymouth (and then Hamburg) in April 1875. On 7 May that year, Susan and 335 other people perished when the *Schiller* went down after striking the notorious Retarrier Ledges off the Scilly Isles in a thick night-time fog. Susan had many admirers, but none who loved her the way Liverpudlian Jonathan Burgess did, and as Susan drowned in the English Channel that night, he somehow sensed the great loss – and it was a loss that turned his mind. He turned to religion, but abandoned it when it failed to bring Susan back, and so he resumed an old interest from his youth – the Occult.

He begged, stole and borrowed the dangerous books of Eliphas Levi, Henri Gamanche, de Gébelin and a dozen other occultists – and then he acquired a large unfurnished attic at a house in the Toxteth Park district of Liverpool and dabbled in the forbidden science of Lucifer. He painted the walls and floorboards of the attic with lamp black pigment and inscribed a circle upon the floor in silver. Around this circle he wrote various glyphs, magical symbols and letters in the Theban Alphabet. Ritual lamps dotted around the great circle were lit, and just before the 'evocation ceremony' was due to start, the door burst open and the irate old landlady threatened to report Burgess to the police for spoiling the décor of her attic with the lamp black, but he pushed her out onto the landing, locked the door, and then, in an almost operatic-sounding baritone voice, Burgess solemnly called upon the 'keepers of a higher knowledge' as he termed the beings he was invoking. The landlady peeped through the keyhole – and saw that the black walls now showed roaring waves and a distant horizon and a dark green and grey brooding sky above. Frightening sounds of crying voices and crashing waves could now be heard coming from the attic, and the seven other lodgers in the house later reported hearing those strange noises. James Kinnish, a close American friend of Burgess, suddenly arrived at the lodging house, and the landlady told him about the strange goings-on up in the attic. Kinnish returned a knowing and worried look, then went upstairs and tried to break down the attic door. He told the landlady Burgess was foolishly attempting to rescue his lost love by going back in time to meet her on the ill-fated ship she'd been sailing on. Burgess hoped to be able to warn the captain about the rocks of the Scilly Isles and save his beloved Susan as well as the lives of the 335 people due to perish – or he would gladly die in the deep with her! After three attempts, Kinnish managed to kick open the attic door – and as he barged into the attic he was swept aside by a powerful wave of seawater. A blast of freezing salty air from the transformed attic struck the landlady, and she could not even conjure up enough breath to scream as she beheld a terrifying dreamlike sight. The attic was no longer a room, for it now somehow contained a heaving expanse of foaming sea, stretching as far as the eye could see, and there was a forlorn-looking Mr Burgess, about thirty feet away, gripping the safety rail of some ship that was sinking rapidly. He went down below the waves still gripping the rails and moments later only his top hat remained, bobbing about. Then came the sound of a ghastly assortment of screams of men, women and children which all ended simultaneously as a mass drowning ensued. The room went black and the landlady fainted. When she awakened in hospital she was told that an unusually heavy rain from a terrific thunderstorm had damaged the roof tiles of the lodging house and flooded the empty attic - and yet Jonathan Burgess and his friend were never heard from again. The landlady told a doctor about the strange mirage inside the attic but he believed she had been seeing things because of the trauma of the destructive flooding. The diary of Jonathan Burgess was later found and many entries in it made it clear that he believed that he had known Susan Dimock as a lover in several previous lives.

Perhaps the Soul Mate Phenomenon can be extended to friends. It's been noted over the years how close friends often die in groups, even when one friend is not aware of the other's death. On Monday 22 September 2014, three New York firefighters who were on duty at Ground Zero during the attacks on the Twin Towers, all died on the same day from cancer. Howard Bischoff, 58, Daniel Heglund, 58, and Robert leaver, 56, all passed away within hours of one another Leaver and Bischoff had been childhood friends in Brooklyn, and the rational explanation for the triple death was that the firefighters had developed their life-threatening illnesses because they had come into contact with the vast clouds of toxic dust released when the Twin Towers crumbled. John Adams and Thomas Jefferson, two of America's greatest founding fathers, both died on the same day in 1826, and it was a very apt date too – 4 July.

The Soul Mate Phenomenon, as I stated at the beginning of this chapter, mostly applies to lovers, and some of these couples have lives that are so interconnected, they are often born on the same day – and even die on the same day, and a perfect example was that of Diana and Kent Kraft, a couple who were both born on 2 September 1941 in South Dakota. The Krafts married in Sioux Falls in 1964, and after a 43-year marriage in which people spoke of them as being inseparable and made for one another, the couple both died on the same day – day – February 9 2008. Diana Kraft, who had been suffering from a neurodegenerative disorder (Lou Gehrig's disease), passed away first, and later that day, her devoted husband Kent, who had been suffering from a heart condition, also died. Such 'entanglement' of the lives of soul mates – sharing birthdays and other significant dates, as well as dying on the same day, are more common than you suppose, but equally fascinating is the mysterious force which has seemingly drawn people to one another. In 2002 there was a self-made multi-millionaire named Connor who, at the age of 36, was still a bachelor – the type of lifestyle he preferred. He lived in a mansion set in hundreds of acres in Somerset and had recently acquired his own private jet. The pilot of this jet was a Liverpool man named George, and he acted as a glorified chauffeur to Connor, taking him to all sorts of exotic destinations across the world, as well as the many cities across the globe where his boss had business to conduct and megabucks deals to be made. Then one morning, Connor called George to his study and told the pilot something which sounded decidedly odd. Connor had had a dream in which he had seen a woman – a beautiful woman – and he somehow felt as if he knew her. This woman looked as if she was around 25 to 30 years of age, with long dark-brown hair. She had been wearing a flowing dress down to her knees which had a blue and white daisy pattern on it, and she had been walking barefoot through tall grass in a field which struck Connor as being somewhere in the American mid-west. The young lady had been carrying what looked like a large spiral-bound book – perhaps some sketchbook – and she had a little dark-furred terrier running behind her. George was puzzled as to why his wealthy employer had summoned him to discuss a dream; he had seemed a rather level-headed man to the pilot. 'I have got to find her, George,' Connor said, and George noticed that his boss had a map of the United States spread out on the ink-blotter of his desk.

'Find a girl that you saw in your dream, sir?' George asked, with a slight sceptical smile.

Connor nodded. 'I know it must sound insane, George, but I have this feeling that this woman – if I can find her, will be the *one* that will become my wife. I have never had a feeling like this before. I don't usually go in for all that psychic nonsense, but this is so strange. I feel like a compass needle being drawn towards the North Pole.'

George nodded, even though he did not understand the mission at hand, and he raised his eyebrows and said: 'Well, sir, where do we start? America is a pretty big place.'

The square tip of Connor's index finger slid across the various states that were coloured pink, green and peach-orange. 'We'll start with Kansas,' came the reply, 'something tells me it's Kansas.'

Four-thousand, two-hundred and thirty-eight miles and three days later, Connor and George found themselves in Kansas. George was at the wheel of a hired Cadillac Escalade, and he drove across hundreds of miles of dirt tracks bordering farmland as his employer took alternate glances through his sunshades at the panoramic rural terrain and a detailed map of Kansas state. The Englishmen stopped off for refreshment at countless bars and watering holes, and they spent weeks sleeping in hotels and motels, until one day, Connor decided he'd had enough of the barmy search for his dream girl. The men returned to the Cadillac Escalade and with a resigned sigh in his voice, Connor told George to head back to the hotel near to the airport where the private jet was waiting in a hangar. Then tomorrow they'd fly home. But something strange happened. George apparently took a wrong turning which brought the Cadillac onto Route 169, and Connor told him to pull over so he could consult the map. They had ventured into the outskirts of Garnett, Anderson County, by the looks of it (according to the map). On either side for miles there was nothing but telegraph poles and tillable acres of farmland. And then Connor saw her – a girl in a flowing dress, carrying that white book or pad, and she was wearing boots this time, and the same terrier dog was with her. There was no mistaking her – same long dark brown hair and that angelic, beautiful face. Connor slapped the fascia and George turned to him, startled.

'George, that's her,' Connor said, and he sounded so nervous for a man who was dauntless, iron-willed and remorseless in his business transactions.

'Are you sure?' George mumbled, unsure what to do.

'Yes! Stop the car!' Connor was already removing his seatbelt.

'You can't just go and – '

'Stop the car George!'

The SUV slowed and came to a halt, and Connor got out of the vehicle and walked slowly down the ditch at the side of the road. He then wiped the sweat from his brow and removed his shades as he climbed the slight incline. There wasn't even a wire fence or any sort of barrier at the side of the road, and he found himself walking through the long grass.

The woman and her dog spotted him. She halted and the dog stopped and barked.

'Excuse me!' Connor yelled, and tried to smile, but this felt so wrong. She was clearly the girl he had seen in that dream, but was it all coincidence and wishful thinking? Or was this woman before him the *one* as he felt she was? It was an insane situation.

The girl turned and ran away, followed by the little yapping dark-brown terrier, and she dropped the book as she ran off.

'No, don't run!' Connor shouted after her and he began to run faster. He reached the book and saw that it was, as he had suspected, a drawing book, full of impressive pencil sketches of trees and farmhouses, and portraits of that terrier.

'Sir! Sir!' the faint cries of George, standing at the edge of the field, reached Connor's ears, and he slowed down, stopped, and looked back, frantically beckoned the chauffeur – then ran on.

He came to a farmhouse where a towering giant of a man in denim overalls stood – with a rifle in his hands.

Connor halted, dropped the sketch book and lifted his hands in the air, and the man told him he was trespassing on private land. Connor nodded and saw the girl he'd been chasing peep from behind the rifle-toting giant, and behind her boots, the little scared terrier was also peeping at Connor. Connor gave his full name and told the farmer he was a millionaire from England, and that he had come to Kansas because of a dream he'd had. The man with the rifle was now understandably even more protective of his daughter, and he turned to her and told her to call the police. She ran off with the terrier at her heels.

A police patrol car arrived via Route 169 and the two officers quizzed George and then they took him to his boss, who was being held at the farmhouse at gunpoint. When the police heard the bizarre story about the dream, they smiled and smirked and scratched their heads. They scrutinised the passports of the men from England, but didn't check them out or take it any further. The two men were cautioned, and before they were escorted back to their car, the farmer's daughter – a girl named Casey – suddenly said to Connor: 'I've just recognised you. Do you have a library, and does it have stained-glass windows?'

Everyone present – except the millionaire – had an inane smile on their face when the girl posed this unusual question.

'Yes, I do, and yes it does have those windows,' Connor replied, and he was as intrigued as he was beguiled by the beautiful young lady.

'I have had dreams about *you*,' she suddenly said to Connor, and she blushed and threw nervous glances at her baffled father.

'Get them out of here,' the farmer told the police officers, but Casey intervened and stepped between her father and Connor and George. To the millionaire with some awkwardness in her voice she said: 'I had a dream - that you were looking at the moon through the coloured glass, and you seemed sad and lonely.'

This really struck a chord in Connor's heart, for he had indeed often glanced at the timeless moon through the stained-glass windows of his library on some nights when he was feeling so alone and isolated.

'I'll write to you, Casey,' Connor told the mysterious woman he had travelled four thousand miles to see on a mere strange impulse he could not rationalise.

'You'll do nothing of the sort,' said Casey's father,

'you'll stay well away from her.'

'Stop running my life for me, father,' Casey told her dad, and she shoved past him and gave a telephone number to Connor. The millionaire and his pilot returned to England a few days later, and for the next few weeks Connor had long conversations with Casey via the telephone, and they sent one another pictures by email, and within a few months Casey was making regular trips to Connor's mansion in Somerset. They married in the following year, and they are still married. Everyone who knows the couple says they seem made for one another, and who knows? Perhaps they were.

ALTER EGOS

One Saturday afternoon in 2007 I did a two-hour talk on the subject of the supernatural at the Oxfam shop on Liverpool's Smithdown Road, just around the corner from Penny Lane, and during a tea-break in the talk, a few people waited to have their copies of my books signed. Two girls in their early twenties stood in the line of people at this impromptu book-signing, and I assumed they were twins because they looked identical, but one girl had straight raven-black hair and wore slightly gothic make-up (which included purple lipstick) and the other girl had golden blonde hair wound up in rollers. I asked the girls if they were twins and they said they weren't and the blonde one looked her dark-haired look-alike up and down with a very condescending expression, but then came an astounding – and eerie – revelation: both girls were named Rachel and they both had the same surname, and this second name was very uncommon. The blonde Rachel seemed suspicious of the brunette's claim to have the same surname and she said, 'No way,' but then the dark-haired Rachel produced a credit card and showed her 'dead ringer' the proof of her identity. This could have all been due to coincidence, I thought, but then something made me ask the blonde Rachel where she lived, and she said 'Halewood,' and the other Rachel's jaw dropped. She lived in the Halewood district too, and then the dark-haired Rachel named the road – and the blonde swore and said, 'Shurrup.'

I signed their books and then watched them move away from the table, and other people in the shop who had overheard the uncanny multiple coincidences strained their ears to ascertain if the girls had any further unearthly connections between them – and there were many. They both claimed to live at the same address on that road in Halewood, and the blonde Rachel accused her apparent counterpart of being a liar and a stalker. A young man named Colin, who was into the paranormal, was thinking along the same lines as me, and he calmed the girls down and asked them where they worked. Blonde Rachel worked for Tesco and the brunette Rachel worked in a well-known bookstore in town. Colin asked the girls about their families – and when the brunette Rachel said she had a 15-year-old brother named Niall, the blonde Rachel seemed very shocked, and then she left the shop saying the whole thing was a 'corny hoax'. Colin asked the remaining Rachel for her mobile number and said he'd like to interview her to research what seemed to be a doppelganger case. Rachel never set eyes on her blonde double again, but the encounter really shook her. I don't think the blonde was a doppelganger (a ghostly ominous twin) at all; I have the feeling that the brunette Rachel met her Alter Ego – a version of herself that turned out different. Quantum Physics hints that there are 'worlds beside worlds', lying next to one another like the pages of a book, and in these alternate worlds, there are many versions of you and I with slight differences; you might be richer, or with another partner in the 'world next door' and perhaps under certain conditions, or even during sleep, our minds can temporarily cross over into these parallel worlds where our lives have taken a different course. This theory would explain those commonly reported dreams where people who have died in this version of reality are seen to be still alive and kicking in the 'dream world'. The idea of many universes coexisting – known as a "multiverse" in scientific circles and also "the many worlds interpretation", is taken seriously by many prominent scientists, including the popular physicist and television presenter Professor Brian Cox. In 2014 he was quoted as saying that: 'That there's an infinite number of universes sounds more complicated than there being one, but actually, it's a simpler version of quantum mechanics. It's quantum mechanics without wave function collapse – the idea that by observing something you force a system to make a choice.' Professor Cox also stated that more and more scientists are beginning to accept the view of the multiverse. The many worlds interpretation of quantum physics postulates that, for example, in one universe, President Kennedy survived an assassination attempt at Dallas in the other version of November 1963, and that in another parallel world, the lookouts on the *Titanic* spotted the iceberg in time and the captain of the liner managed to take evasive action, thus arriving at New York on schedule. We just happen to be in the version of reality where President Kennedy was murdered at Dallas in 1963 and the *Titanic* hit the iceberg and went down with over fifteen hundred souls. But, perhaps as the account of the two Rachels in the charity store suggests, two parallel worlds can sometimes overlap. Take the following case, related to me by a retired Liverpool doctor many years ago. In 1965, a 29-year-old Leeds woman named Jean began to act rather strange. She worked in the Schofields department store and to her friends at work, as well as her husband and two daughters, Jean was a very caring person who never had a bad word to say about anyone. And then one morning when she arrived at the department store, Jean's work colleagues were amazed to see that she was wearing a very short skirt, and had had her hair styled and dyed red. She also wore a pair of impractical stiletto heels, whereas she usually wore flat shoes because of the long hours spent on her feet at the store. An elderly customer Jean often served asked her: 'What have you done to your hair?' And Jean swore at the old woman and said, 'You're here to buy things not criticise the staff.'

The old woman gasped at the audacious reply and backed away from Jean's counter. Jean then flirted with a young customer in his early twenties and even asked him if he was 'spoken for' and the young man blushed and made an excuse to leave the store. When a friend Jean had known since their days together at the infants school reminded her that she was married, Jean laughed and said 'So what? Marriage is just a piece of paper, isn't it? These are modern times love, and I want to live a little.'

When Jean got home her husband asked her what she was playing at wearing such a short skirt, and why had she dyed her hair? He also told her to take off the high heels and said she looked like 'a tart'. Jean almost came to blows with him and threatened to leave. The strange thing was that when the husband made enquiries with

Jean's usual hairdresser, Jill, he was told that his wife had not visited the hairdressers recently and no one had dyed her hair red either. A little over a week passed and Jean came home one evening with her hair dyed black – and it had been cut very short in what was then known as the Pixie cut, later popularised by the film star Mia Farrow. Now Jean was very shy and softly spoken, and she wore dowdy black and grey cardigans, slacks and sandals. Jean's husband naturally thought his wife was having a breakdown and tried to get her to see the family doctor but she assured him she was perfectly fine. Again, Jean's husband made enquiries at his wife's hairdressing salon and once again Jill told him she had not seen Jean for weeks. Then Jean arrived in work days after this, and now she had curly blonde hair, and she seemed to be suffering from religious mania. She continually quoted the Bible and accused some of her workmates at Schofields of being sinners and 'fornicators', and Jean's best friend believed Jean had suffered some nervous breakdown and told her to see a doctor but her friend just ranted on about various parables from the New Testament and warned everyone that the Second Coming was imminent.

And then shortly after this, Jean collapsed in her hallway, and her husband and father took her upstairs and put her to bed because she seemed to have a temperature. The doctor who was called out was a locum, and he was originally from Liverpool, and it was he who related this strange tale to me. The doctor – a man named Dennis, went up to see his patient as she lay in her bed, and he felt her forehead and saw she was very warm. He put a mercury thermometer in her mouth and then Jean's husband told him about the strange behavioural problems his wife had been exhibiting. The doctor was no psychiatrist, and although he suspected Jean of having emergent multiple personalities (now categorised as a form of dissociative reaction) he did not offer any psychiatric diagnosis, as he was not at all qualified to do so, but Dennis did suggest that Jean should be taken into hospital. As he said this, Dennis noticed that the husband had a look of amazement on his face as he gazed down at his wife. Dennis looked at Jean and saw something that would remain with him for the rest of his life, and it was something he was unable to explain. A second face appeared at the left side of Jean's head, and this face looked a little like the patient. The right eye of the weird extra face was the left eye of Jean's face. The husband was so afraid at the sight of the second face, he backed away from the bed with an expression of horror. But things were to become even more surreal, because another face appeared, this time at the right side of Jean's head, and its left eye was also Jean's right eye. Dennis was at a loss to explain this unearthly transfiguration and he also moved away from the bed and left the thermometer in the middle mouth of the triple-faced woman. Dennis felt so confused and in his own words, 'I felt a let-down as a doctor, almost abandoning the patient because I had never seen anything like this.'

But then, moments later, the two extra faces vanished as quickly as they had appeared, and the fever also left Jean. She voluntarily had herself evaluated by a psychiatrist who found no evidence of a multiple personality, and there was of course, nothing in any psychiatry text book to explain how Jean had acquired two extra phantom faces. Where modern psychiatry failed to provide a solution to Jean's change in personality, as well as the weird additional faces, the multiverse theory of modern physicists could perhaps throw some light on this strange case. I might be way off the mark, but for all we know, perhaps the versions of how Jean turned out in neighbouring parallel words somehow managed to occupy her mind and body during that period in 1965. In one parallel world alongside this one, Jean turned out as a religious fanatic, whilst in another world she was a fiery-headed nymphomaniac, and so on, and these versions somehow replaced the 'usual' Jean people knew in this world. That would explain why her husband could not find out who styled and dyed her hair – the stylists were in a parallel world too. If this theory is true, perhaps some people who have been diagnosed as having a multiple personality disorder are just people who, like Jean, have been somehow mentally displaced by alter egos from a neighbouring plane of existence.

And finally, I would like to conclude this chapter of speculative thought with a few brief details of two possible alternate world cases I am actively investigating and researching at the moment. In May 1982, Andrew Connolly, a man in his twenties, received a very strange letter at his home in Birkenhead, Wirral. The letter bore a stamp which featured the unmistakable profile of Adolf Hitler. *What a bizarre and distasteful subject for a stamp*, Andrew thought, and he saw that although the franking mark on the stamp and envelope indicated that it had been posted in Liverpool, the franking mark also featured a swastika and a faded word that looked as if it read "Postzustellung" – which, I think, means service by mail in German. The letter in this peculiar envelope was from Mr Connolly's friend across the Mersey in Liverpool, John Hughes, who resided in the Toxteth area. The Letter made no sense at all and it rambled on about 'Island Station One' – apparently the name of the UK in a Nazi-run Britain – and the forced labour of "dissidents" to a Welsh mine where a valuable power-producing ore had been discovered. According to the author of the letter (and the handwriting matched that of John Hughes perfectly) the Liverpudlian thoroughfare of Lime Street had been renamed Goethe Strasse, and there were rumours of resistance groups in Southport being executed by firing squad.

Andrew went over to Liverpool the next day and asked John Hughes what he was playing at, sending such a ridiculous and offensive letter with Hitler on the stamp. John examined the envelope and its contents and said he had nothing to do with it. He asked Andrew what he would possibly gain from dreaming up a hoax like that? And he also asked why the Royal Mail had delivered a letter without attaching a label stating that insufficient postage had been provided by the sender. It did not make sense. The mystery deepened when a philatelist examined the stamp and said it had definitely been printed using a type of ink used in the production of postal stamps; the stamp had not been produced by any computer printer. It was as if the letter which arrived at Andrew Connolly's Birkenhead home that May morning had been sent from a version of Britain that had been occupied by the Nazis after Hitler had won World War Two. This is just one of the cases of possible alternate worlds which I am looking into. I am also researching the scant details behind a case from 1895. That year, a respected bank manager in Burnley named William Bentham was pestered by a man named Roger Symmonds who told the manager's secretary that he was a close friend of Mr Bentham and wished to see him immediately. Bentham told his secretary that he knew no one named Symmonds and the secretary duly tried to send the caller from the bank. Roger Symmonds ran past the secretary and was chased by two clerks at the bank down a corridor, where he gained access to the bank manager's office. Symmonds somehow locked himself in the office with William Bentham and told him an incredible story. Symmonds had been holidaying in Wales with his fiancée Clara, and a week ago they had both sheltered from a downpour under the roof of a Neolithic tomb one and a half miles west of Llanglydwen, Carmarthenshire. This chambered tomb (also known as a Cromlech) was struck by lightning when a violent storm developed. The lightning-strike knocked Symmonds unconscious, and when he had been awakened by a farmer, he asked how Clara was, but the farmer said that he had found no one else in the immediate vicinity. George Symmonds looked everywhere for his fiancée and eventually reported her disappearance to the police, and they launched a search but found not a single trace of Clara. George Symmonds eventually returned to his home in Chester, and discovered to his horror, that no one knew him there, and his house was occupied by two elderly spinsters who claimed to have lived there for fifty years. Symmonds called into the bank where he was employed as a senior clerk but found that a stranger named Jones had his job. The bank manager was a man he had never seen before, and Symmonds was escorted off the premises. With a sense of grim foreboding, Roger Symmonds walked for miles to the house of his beloved Clara, and discovered that no such house existed in that part of Chester, and no one had heard of his fiancée. Symmonds slowly realised that his entire life had somehow been wiped off the face of the earth, and he suspected that the lightning strike on that Stone Age tomb he sheltered under in Wales had something to do with his highly unusual predicament. Roger Symmonds then told William Bentham that he had got him the job at the bank at Chester, but the bank manager shook his head and said, 'That's quite a tale, but I'm afraid I can't help you, because I have never set eyes on you before.'

There were loud thuds on the office door as the clerks and other members of the bank's staff tried to gain access. Roger Symmonds then said, 'William, you must remember me! I can prove I know you!'

The bank manager warned the disturbed man. 'You'll be for it when the police break that door down, now kindly leave!'

Roger Symmonds correctly gave the names of the bank manager's wife, his children and he also correctly told Bentham what his address was. Then came a startling revelation – a piece of information that really seemed to prove that Symmonds had known Bentham in some personal capacity. Symmonds mentioned the name of a married woman that William Bentham had been having an affair with for many years.

'Good Lord, how do you know about her?' he asked Symmonds, 'Is this all down to some scheme to extort money out of me by means of blackmail, eh? Is that what this nonsense is all about?'

'Of course not!' Symmonds cried, and pounded his fist down hard on the suspicious bank manager's desk. 'I am just trying ever so desperately to prove that I am not some ghost! You must know me! How would I know the things I know about you if this were not the case?'

'Now listen here, if you are hoping to blackmail – ' Bentham was saying when the door to the office burst open and in came two of the clerks and a policeman. Roger Symmonds was taken into custody, and then he was heard from no more. The descendants of one of the bank clerks told me this very strange story, and I have since checked the account out and ascertained that there was indeed a William Bentham who was a manager of a well-known bank in Burnley, and that, strangely enough, in November 1897, he attempted to commit suicide by drinking carbolic acid at a railway station waiting room in Burnley. The bank manager received medical treatment in time and survived the attempt, and when he was charged (as suicide was a criminal offence in those days) he was asked why he had tried to end his life. Bentham enigmatically confessed that the suicide attempt had been the result of 'passion' connected to a certain woman. Because the bank manager was so well-connected in Burnley, he was not sentenced, but cautioned and discharged.

If Roger Symmonds was telling the truth, and was not some deranged individual, had the lightning strike on that Neolithic tomb somehow transported him into an alternate world where he had either died at a young age or was never born at all? What became of Roger? Did he somehow return to the world he knew, or did he end his days in some lunatic asylum?

THE OFFER

In the early summer of 1972, Robin Hawdon's play, *The Mating Game*, was being shown at Liverpool's Royal Court, and it starred Terry Scott, Avril Angers, and Ami MacDonald. Any thespian who has played the Royal Court regularly will tell you the place is undoubtedly haunted, and seems to have more than one ghost, several presences and many inexplicable cold spots. Terry Scott found himself locked out of his dressing room at the theatre on the first night of the risqué comedy play, and he and a fan who had just obtained Terry's autograph, listened to a voice behind the dressing room door; it was someone telling jokes, and not ordinary jokes either. Scott had featured in seven *Carry On* films and was one of the most respected actor comedians in the business, but in all of his years he had not heard jokes like this. They were surreal, very much ahead of their time, and this prankster behind the door had Terry and the fan in stitches. 'Who the devil are you?' Terry asked, bemused and he waited for some punchline reply. There was a click from the door lock. He pushed the door open. There was no one in the dressing room. The fan left not long afterwards, being spooked by the phantom comedian. Terry Scott, who had a keen interest in the supernatural, was more intrigued by the ghost. Whenever Terry struggled to do his makeup whilst playing a panto Dame, he had a ritual where he would ask out loud: 'Is there a spirit of a past artist of any kind wishing to take over?' And without fail, the actor would feel someone guiding his hand and he would apply the greasepaint and powder expertly. But the ghost Terry had heard cracking jokes before was different – he sensed something quite unsettling about it. Then about an hour before curtain up he saw a light appear in front of him. A weird head with horns materialised and Terry froze – it looked just how the Devil has always been portrayed; reddish skin, van dyke beard. 'Your star is setting but I can make you the greatest comedian on Earth,' the disembodied head said in a velvet-smooth voice.

'I don't need *your* help, thanks, now kindly leave,' Terry said, standing his ground. 'Here are the people I have helped – look!' said the sinister visitor, and a circle opened up in the air, and in that circle were the faces of past Presidents, famous pop stars, great footballers, well-known actors…

'Beat it! My soul isn't for sale!' Terry cried, and backed away towards the door. The head laughed and said, 'Who said I wanted *that*? I'm doing this for a bet that's all, and you could have the world instead of pathetic panto and silly little plays! Hollywood is calling!'

Terry turned and ran out of the dressing room and saw a well-known Liverpool actor in the corridor. Terry told him what had just happened. 'I heard every word! Is he still there? I'll take his offer!' the actor said, his eyes aglow with a consuming hunger for fame. He rushed into the dressing room but there was no one there.

Terry shook the actor out of his manic desire for world stardom and after the play he tried to tell him about those incredible jokes the Devil had told in the dressing room – but Terry could not remember a word of them.

PARANORMAL POSTAL MYSTERIES

Around ten years ago, one October evening at 7pm, a 30-year-old lady named Joanne left her home on Devonfield Road in Liverpool's Orrell Park district, and went to post an envelope containing her sister's birthday card (which had a £20 note in it). Joanne only walked a short distance to the pillar box on the corner of Thornfield Road, and then she returned home and did the washing up before sitting down to watch the television. At 7.45pm, Joanne's mobile rang, and she was surprised to see her sister Michelle's name on the screen of the phone as she hardly ever called this late. Michelle said, 'Why didn't you come in?'

'What do you mean?' Joanne asked, puzzled, and she muted the TV.

Her sister wanted to know why she had stuck the birthday card in her letterbox without calling in to see her. Michelle lived in Preston – around 25 miles away from Joanne's home. Joanne was baffled; how could a letter she had only posted three quarters of an hour ago arrive at Michelle's home in Preston? Joanne asked her husband Terry if the Royal Mail were now carrying out evening deliveries. 'Not as far as I know,' was Terry's reply. Michelle didn't believe her sister had posted the card in a pillar box – after all, why were there no franking marks stamped on the envelope? Michelle had never heard of a postman doing his rounds at almost eight in the evening, either. Terry vouched for his wife's story, and finally convinced Michelle that he and Joanne had not made some flying visit to her house in Preston just to post a card through the letterbox before driving back to Liverpool. I mentioned this odd postal mystery on a local radio programme and received a welter of accounts from listeners who had also received mystifying mail which seemed to hint at some supernatural delivery service. In 2007 a lady from Neston, Wirral named Margaret was staying at her friend's house in Thetford, Norfolk, and one afternoon she posted an old paperback book she'd bought in a jumble sale to her sister Eleanor in Heswall. Margaret posted the book in the pillar box set into the wall of the Thetford Post Office on King Street. The time was 3pm. At 3.40pm, Eleanor rang Margaret's friend at her home in Thetford and referred to the paperback her sister had mailed to her. When Margaret arrived at her friend's house she heard about the incredibly early arrival of the book and telephoned Eleanor. It was true; the paperback edition of an old book Eleanor had been looking for had been found on her doorstep at 3.30pm – half an hour after Margaret had posted it in Thetford, almost 170 miles distant. Like the card from Liverpool which Michelle received in record time at Preston, the parcel from Thetford bore no postal franking marks. Firms like Amazon have, in recent years, developed remote-control helicopter drones that could carry parcels from their warehouses to the consumer's doorstep within an hour, but this proposed high-speed delivery scheme has too many safety objections to be implemented – at the moment. However, if the many reports I have received about the 'paranormal postal service' (as I term these inexplicable rapid delivery incidents) are true, it would seem something unearthly has already beaten Amazon to the 'delivery under an hour' programme. Perhaps - and this is a large 'maybe' - the person sending the items which rocket through the post somehow unconsciously teleports the parcels and letters to their destination through some psychic faculty. But then, it would seem that the paranormal postal service can sometimes take an inordinate amount of time to deliver an item. In March 2012, a 27-year-old Irish lady named Aislin posted some photographs to her cousin Sophie in Liverpool. Aislin posted the envelope in the green pillar box on Corrib Road, Dublin, when she was on her way to a shop, and the photographs never reached Sophie. Then, exactly two years to the day the snaps were posted, Sophie woke up one morning at her Liverpool home and found an envelope at the bottom of her bed. Her husband had not brought the mail upstairs yet because he was snoring beside her. Sophie saw Aislin's distinctive handwriting on the envelope – but no franking marks on the envelope or the stamps. Sophie opened the envelope and saw pictures of Aislin's new-born baby, who was now aged two. Enquiries were made at the post office, but a post office clerk said the letter had definitely not been through the Irish or British mail system – so how did it travel 168 miles from Dublin – albeit over a duration of two years?

SOME MODERN VAMPIRES

On Caledonia Road in the Gorbals area of Glasgow you will find the grand and gothic gatehouse to the 21-acre Southern Necropolis, the resting place of a quarter of a million people (many of them notable internments). This vast "City of the Dead" was established at the site in 1840, and it has been the scene of many eerie goings-on over the years. In September 1954, something sparked a massive scare among the children living in the vicinity of the Southern Necropolis which has never been explained satisfactorily by sociologists (who initially blamed the panic among the kids on an urban legend that had escalated – via Chinese whispers – wildly out of control), but the general consensus among the boys and girls – ranging in age from four to fourteen – was that a towering vampire with metallic-looking teeth was at large in the sprawling cemetery. The children armed themselves with sharpened sticks to stake the vampire, and some carried knives. Hundreds of these kids gathered in the Southern Necropolis as the sun was setting to confront a 7ft tall vampire with iron teeth which had, according to sinister rumours, recently kidnapped and eaten two local lads. The fear in the faces of the children is still recalled today by some of the policemen who were sent to disperse the little vampire hunters, and the panic even gripped the children's parents - who pleaded with the police and authorities to assure them that there was not some bloodsucking ghoul on the prowl. The scare eventually died down and sociologists blamed the vampire mania on a silly rumour that had become exaggerated, but then the blame was laid at the door of graphic

American comic books like *Tales from the Crypt* and *Vault of Horror* which the children were supposedly reading. 'The imaginations of our children are being corrupted by this bloodthirsty trash in the American comic books,' one moralistic social commentator told the press, and there were calls for the comics to be censored – even though there were no vampire storylines being featured in either of the publications that were blamed for the Gorbals Vampire scare at the time. Some of the children who roamed the cemetery in gangs, hoping to lay the vampire, are now in their seventies, and I have talked to a few of them - and while some of them have told me that, beyond a shadow of a doubt, that they saw nothing sinister in the necropolis, most of the surviving junior Van Helsings have told me that there was something at large in that cemetery, and it looked positively sinister. Ronnie, who, at the time of writing is 74, swears that he and four other lads saw a bona fide vampire one evening in the cemetery at the height of the scare. He describes it as about six and a half feet in height, all in black with a skull-like head. It moved silently and when Ronnie and the boys tried to run from it, the entity would flit past them at a phenomenal speed and block their path. Ronnie's friend screamed to his brother, who was in another section of the cemetery with a gang, and within a minute reinforcements turned up and the lanky menacing figure was suddenly nowhere to be seen. Perhaps this creepy being is the "ankou" which is said to have been seen in the Southern Necropolis long before the alleged vampire sightings of the 1950s – and is *still* allegedly being seen from time to time in the cemetery. An ankou is a 'graveyard watcher' – a figure which guards cemeteries – said to be a person who was accidentally (and sometimes deliberately) interred alive in the first graves of a burial ground. The role of the ankou is to frighten off anyone who might come to disturb the dead. An old superstition says that when a person remarks, with a shudder, that, 'Someone has just walked over my grave,' the thing that is doing the walking is an ankou, preparing the spot where your mortal remains (or ashes if you have plans to be cremated) will lay for all eternity.

In August 1977 there was a report of a 20-year-old woman who had sex with her boyfriend on a certain grave in the Southern Necropolis, and afterwards she developed a strange rash on her left buttock which took on the resemblance of a man's hook-nosed profile. This bizarre simulacrum of a face, made up of pimples, scabs and red crusty patches failed to respond to all sorts of creams prescribed to the girl by her doctor. Dermatologists examined the strange infection and were stunned to see the likeness of a face of almost photographic quality on the unfortunate woman's posterior. The girl's boyfriend deserted her because his mother mentioned an old superstition about long-lasting rashes appearing on the skin of people who walked over the grave of someone who had been evil. This piece of grave lore is widespread in Scotland and Ireland. The woman with the rash resorted to washing her backside with holy water when she began to feel something (which was rather over-endowed) having very rough and violent penetrative sex with her each night, and eventually the rash – and the nocturnal assaults – ceased. A local historian later discovered that a lecherous old miser had been interred in the grave the young woman had disrespectfully laid upon to have intercourse, and when an etched portrait of this man was later found in the course of the historian's researches, it showed that he had a distinctive prominent hook nose – just like the portrait in pustules on the woman's derrière. That woman, I believe, still refuses to set foot inside a cemetery, even to attend a relative's funeral.

Getting back to the Gorbals Vampire; the origins of the vampire hunt are still shrouded in mystery, but south of Scotland, in England and in the rest of the world for that matter, vampiric beings are still being reported. I have collected numerous little-known cases of historical bloodsuckers in my book, *Vampires of Great Britain* in which I cover vampiric beings from centuries ago, right through to Victorian and modern Britain, but here are a couple of more vampires from across the world. I'll start close to home.

In August 1974, Eva, a beautiful 19-year-old foreign exchange student from Hamburg went to live with a family on Fairfield Avenue in Huyton (then in Lancashire but now in the borough of Knowsley) and enrolled at a local college to further her studies in sociology. It wasn't long before Eva began to attract the attention of the local males in the area, and when she went to a pub one night with her college friend Jenny, a notorious biker named Phil from the Dovecot area approached the German beauty and asked her if she'd go out with him. Eva politely declined, saying 'I have a boyfriend back in Germany,' but Phil took the rejection badly. He grabbed her wrist and said, 'No one turns me down, especially a kraut.'

Jenny pushed Phil away but couldn't break his hold on the scared German teenager, so she slapped him hard. He let go of Eva and shook his head as he glared at Jenny. 'You shouldn't have done that, love,' he said in a low almost growling voice.

'Hey, you're barred,' the landlord of the pub told Phil, and the biker said, 'Am I? Oh well,' and suddenly threw a punch into the face of the pub manager which sent him flying across the room, and through drinkers who were knocked aside like skittles. The licensee hit the floor with a thud and seemed to be out cold, and his wife screamed and told people to call the police. Phil produced a 12-inch knife, calmly went to the end of the room, and cut a wire stapled to the wall with the blade. A man who had picked the telephone up to call the police said, 'The line's dead!'

'And you'll be as well if you try and call the fuzz,' Phil promised, and he walked through the crowd of frightened drinkers, most of them young students, and grabbed Eva by the arm again, then dragged her towards the door. Jenny rushed forward but he stepped aside and pushed her. The girl fell and hit her head against the brass foot-rail of the bar and she yelled in agony as blood poured from a gash above her eyebrow. A man in his sixties stepped forward, raising his fists, and said to Phil, 'You're gonna get a hiding now, mate!'

Phil gave a hollow laugh and replied, 'From you, Dad? Go on! Have a go!' And as he yelled this he had Eva in a headlock and the student was crying.

The man challenging the armed thug looked at something behind Phil, and Phil turned to see what he was looking at; perhaps the law had turned up. In an adrenalin rage, Jenny had somehow managed to lift a heavy bar stool, and she brought it crashing down on the biker's head. The seat came off upon impact and hit a mirror, smashing it to pieces, and bits of splintered wood and blood droplets flew everywhere. People cheered when Phil fell to his knees as he let go of Eva, and within minutes the police and ambulances were here. No one would say who brained the trouble-causer with the stool, and the police certainly never suspected the angelic-faced Jenny as the culprit as she was only five feet tall and rather slender. Jenny went to hospital and received three stitches in her forehead gash, and Phil ended up in hospital for weeks suffering from a fractured skull and concussion.

Back at her home on Fairfield Avenue, Jenny saw that Eva had sunk into a terrible depression since the fracas at the pub. 'Don't worry about that idiot,' Jenny reassured the student, 'he won't come after you; he's learned his lesson.'

'It is not that which is worrying me,' Eva told her friend with a grave look. 'I have a friend, his name is Prest, and I have known him since I was a child, and he looks after me.'

Jenny wondered what Eva was getting at.

'He will come because my life was in danger,' Eva said, with tears welling in her eyes, 'he always comes to me when bad things happen.'

'You mean he'll come over from Germany?' Jenny asked her, 'How will he know, Eva? I don't understand.'

'Prest is a vampire,' Eva said, and from the awful look in her blue eyes, Jenny somehow sensed that her friend was telling some ghastly truth.

Eva nodded, and said: 'I have very rare blood – very, very rare, and he takes it from me. He has always taken it from me, but he is gentle when he takes it. Please don't tell anyone Jenny. No one knows about Prest.'

Jenny went cold inside when she heard this. She felt something unnatural was going to arrive at the house soon; a grim foreboding of something that was not of this world. The weeks went by, and at Halloween that year, a full moon rose, and when it did, Eva suddenly told Jenny: 'He's here.'

'What? You mean in the house?' Jenny trembled at the thought, but Eva shook her head. 'He's outside, and he's protecting me from that man, the biker.'

'How do you know?' Jenny queried, gazing out the window at the moonlit street.

'He tells me in my mind,' Eva said, then jumped, startled as something flitted in front of the moon's full disk. It looked like a falling leaf but it fell too straight. Jenny turned off the lamp in the room and gazed out at the moon-silvered nightscape. What she witnessed was terrifying. A motorbike thrummed to a halt down the leafy avenue, and the distinctive stocky silhouette of Phil dismounted the bike. A tall caped figure approached swiftly from the shadows. Phil lunged at the sinister agile stranger and moonlight glinted off the blade. The biker stabbed the figure repeatedly but the cloaked man remained standing. The shadowy form which Eva called Prest put its hands around Phil's throat, then lifted the biker as if he was a doll and threw him into the parked cars. It picked him up again and again, smashed his limbs with its fists – then something flitted upwards. To Jenny it was reminiscent of an after-image on the retina after gazing at a light, the way it floated away. Phil almost died from multiple injuries; a smashed collar bone, comminuted fractures of the femur, and fingers bent fully backwards by something which had terrific strength – and a very sadistic streak. Phil said he had been attacked by someone dressed like a vampire, and the first policeman on the scene said (rather insensitively), 'Well, it *is* Halloween mate.'

Eva announced she was going home to Hamburg not long afterwards, and for years, Jenny kept the secret about Prest until she finally told me about him. I interviewed Jenny on a radio programme about the occult and a retired policeman who remembered the strange violent attack on the biker also got in touch to back up this strange tale. Jenny lost touch with Eva about a year after the strange goings-on of that night in 1975, and it's not known what became of her and whether the alleged vampiric entity of Prest continued to siphon off her rare blood. Such long-lasting vampire relationships – in which the entity attaches itself to its host at an early age - are said to be fairly common and are almost symbiotic, although in the many years I have studies the vampire phenomenon, it would seem that most of these beings seem to draw off energy from the victim rather than their blood, and I documented a very strange case in my book *Haunted Cheshire* in which two girls – 19-year-old Judith and 16-year-old Zara – both residents of Winsford in Cheshire, became the prey to a vampire which attacked them in their beds at night and assaulted them. After the attacks the girls were left feeling as if they had been drained of every ounce of energy, and they exhibited the symptoms of a condition which would later be categorised as ME – myalgic encephalomyelitis – a benign but very debilitating and long-lasting condition which causes chronic fatigue, muscular pain, headaches, weakness and fever. To date, no one can say with any certainty just what causes ME but its as if something – a virus perhaps – attacks the human metabolism and runs down the biological equivalent of the body's battery. In 1970, the girls left with extreme weakness after the nocturnal vampire attacks finally identified a man who looked exactly like the man in black who had assaulted them in their beds, and he was a 23-year-old Hungarian art student, but nothing could be proved. The so-called Winsford Vampire returned to the Cheshire town in the 1990s and several more attacks on females are said to have taken place, and I still get emails from people in Winsford telling me that the entity is still at large, but not a drop of blood appears to be taken by the creature – just the energy of the victim, which always leaves her extremely weak and ill in the morning.

A rather bizarre and frightening modern vampire is said to stalk a rather upmarket area of Los Angeles – and this being's crypt lies in the 62-acre Hollywood Forever Cemetery (formerly known as Hollywood Memorial Park Cemetery) on Santa Monica Boulevard. What makes this case rather strange (even as vampire reports go) is the involvement of a ghost who has warned people of the vampire. In the late 1990s two young female tourists from Indianapolis were having a look around the Hollywood Forever Cemetery when a tall (almost six feet in height) slender man in a white suit appeared from nowhere and jokingly asked one of the ladies, 22-year-old Monica Jones, if she would like their map of the cemetery autographed. Monica was so startled by the sudden appearance of the debonair-looking man, she said, 'Sure, and handed her glossy map to him. 'Oh dear, I don't have a pen,' said the man in white, chuckling, and Monica's friend, Maddie, fished for a biro in her rucksack and handed it to the stranger. He signed the map "Clifton Webb" – and then his face became quite serious as he told the girls. 'Now, ladies, I don't expect you to believe me, but you must not stay here too long because there's a vampire about to come out of his crypt anytime soon.'

The female duo grinned and then looked at one another, and "Clifton" became annoyed at their sceptical attitudes and said, 'Alright, watch this.'

And he vanished right before their eyes.

Monica and Maddie didn't even take time to scream – they turned and ran out of the cemetery, passing several other tourists along the way who they warned about the ghost, but these people mostly smiled in a puzzled manner. The girls later discovered that Clifton Webb was a famous actor (and once a singer and dancer of some repute) who was born in 1889 and died in Beverly Hills, aged 76, in 1966. When the girls Googled the deceased actor they were stunned to see his online photograph, for it bore a very strong resemblance of the man in white, only the ghost had looked a lot younger than a man of 76. This is a common attribute of many ghosts – they often return from the dead and seem to be rejuvenated, almost appearing as they were in prime of their lives. Monica has since sold her autographed graveyard map to a ghost investigator for a thousand dollars. The ghost's signature is said to be identical to known signatures of

Clifton Webb. Many others have seen Clifton's ghost roaming the Hollywood Forever Cemetery and the grounds of his fine stuccoed mansion upon Rexford Drive in Beverly Hills. But who is the vampire Clifton was warning the girls about? Well, there have been rumours circulating for years about a shadowlike figure – long assumed to be one of the handful of 'celebrity ghosts' haunting the Hollywood Forever Cemetery – which has been seen to leave the place of the dead to go on long roaming treks throughout Hollywood – and the district of Los Feliz in particular. One evening in January 2014 this apparition - which resembles the smoky outline of a masculine figure of about six feet in height - was witnessed by several people drifting through the six-foot-high perimeter hedge of the celebrity-laden cemetery onto North Van Ness Avenue. A couple in their twenties followed this striking ghostly figure north for four blocks, until, around 600 yards from the cemetery, the shadowy entity darted down Fountain Avenue. The couple then lost sight of the 'ghost', but later that evening there were reports of an eerie semi-transparent figure, described as a partial silhouette which seemed almost two-dimensional, walking eastwards along Franklin Avenue, the northernmost street in Hollywood, to the north of Hollywood Boulevard. Traffic on Franklin Avenue slowed when night drivers caught sight of the ominous phantom around midnight turning down one oft the longest avenues in Los Angeles – North Normandie Avenue, which is over 22 miles in length. This avenue forks at its northern end to Ambrose Avenue on the right and a gated community on the left where some of Hollywood's most famous and influential stars live. Whatever this entity is, it always passes through a white gate designed to keep the paparazzi out, and some of the hard-line persistent freelance photographers stalking Hollywood's hottest celebrities by camping out all night in Los Feliz have even reported seeing this apparition, which visits this area for some arcane reason. One person who works in the film industry has told me that the spooky silhouette goes to three specific residences, and sometimes lingers under a certain Deodar tree where it seems to materialise into an almost solid person who seems to be dressed in a black suit with a white shirt and black tie. There was a story of a certain woman in this area almost suffering a nervous breakdown several years ago when she kept waking up all hours in the morning in a paralysed state as this ghost stood over her in her bed – even when her husband was present. The chilling bedroom intruder never spoke but gave off a sweet sharp aroma of some cologne, and it would often get on the bed and put its ice-cold lips on the woman's face and breasts. The house was blessed by a Catholic priest and the ghost stopped visiting for a few months, but returned with a vengeance, and the woman claimed that the supernatural visitor was drawing out her "life force". On one occasion the woman somehow broke free of the terrifying paralysis and managed to switch on the bedside lamp, and the menacing visitant shielded its face with its arm, as if it could not bear the light, and melted into a vapour which drifted out of the room via an open window. The visits became so harrowing the couple sold the house in the end. The present occupiers of the house have seen nothing, but the vaporous figure is still said to prowl the grounds of the house. Considering the warning of Clifton Webb's ghost regarding a vampire being at large in Hollywood Forever Cemetery, and the testimony of a female witness in Los Feliz who described the vaporous entity as drawing her life force out of her, is there really a vampiric menace at large? If there is, was this thing once an actor or screenwriter, make-up artist, film-score composer, or a director? Is it possible he was a vampire by night and some heart-throb actor by day? We can but speculate, but perhaps the solution to this strange mystery will come from some film buff with an interest in the paranormal who can perhaps sift through the lives of the many people interred at Hollywood Forever Cemetery and see if the suspect once lived in the Los Feliz area and whether he was some contemporary of Clifton Webb…

THE ORGISHER

Many years ago when I was a child, I heard a strange thumping sound which echoed through the streets of Liverpool one afternoon. This sound was followed by female screams, and I ran to the source of the noises. A man lay on the pavement in a huge stain of blood, his ruptured and smashed internal organs and fat mingled into a ghastly orange mess. His brains and blood had splashed cars that were over fifty feet away because of the high-velocity impact when he had jumped from a high-rise building. He had been deserted by his girlfriend, and as she left the tower block where she had shared a flat with the man, he had shouted down to her from a tenth-storey window, and when she had looked up, he had jumped.

The girl froze as she saw him fall to a certain death, and she was so traumatised by this tragic incident, I believe that for many years she would suddenly roll her eyes up into her forehead in some sort of nervous tic.

As he lay there, smashed into the paving flags, most of his blood had radiated away from the body on impact so that he lay at the centre of long radiating lines of crimson, yet some blood still left in various cavities of the butcher's mess of a body was trickling down the slight gradient of the pavement towards the gutter, where a light brown and black mongrel dog started to lick the flowing blood until it was chased away by a horrified passer-by. They literally had to scrape the body off the sidewalk and somehow they overlooked one of his front teeth that had been left behind, embedded in a crack between the paving flags. And then the strange stories about the suicide began to circulate. The young man who had committed suicide had not been the type to take his own life over his girlfriend walking out on him; he'd been a tough nut – a cold fish, but he had recently spoken about something haunting his flat which had tried to persuade him to jump out the window. The dead man's girlfriend apparently confirmed this, and spoke of waking up in the wee small hours and hearing whispering voices with strange accents in the darkness of the bedroom addressing her boyfriend by his full name and urging him to jump out the window. In the world of the Occult, such a malevolent entity which tries to make people kill themselves is known as the Orgisher. This being is said to be mostly invisible but sometimes manifests itself as something resembling a dark mist which engulfs a person who then becomes suicidal. It is thought that an Orgisher has been active at one of the most infamous suicide spots in England – Beachy Head, an East Sussex 'beauty spot' – where hundreds of people have jumped from a chalk headland cliff top there for centuries. No other cliff in England has such a deadly attraction as Beachy Head, the highest chalk sea cliff in all of Britain with a drop of some 531 feet. There are on average, some twenty suicides per year at Beachy Head, and until the 1950s, the average number of deaths at the cliff were two or three per year. In the 1970s the average suicide rate was twelve per year (with 19 in 1979), with the most 'popular' months for jumpers being June, July and August. There were 108 deaths at the suicide spot in the 1970s, and by the early 1980s a telephone box had been installed on Beachy Head where would-be suicides can call the Samaritans. Today there are around 20 suicides a year at the Head and most of those who take their lives at the cliff come from outside East Sussex. There are records of suicides at Beachy Head stretching back to the 7th century, and for just as long there have been some eerie tales circulating about the supernatural entity which drives people to take their lives on the prehistoric cliff top. An evil influence, described by some as a gaseous dark cloud and others as a reaper-like silhouetted figure in a pointed hood and a long robe, has been seen at Beachy Head and the surrounding area since medieval times. This entity is said to either draw people to the edge of the chalk cliff by some powerful hypnotic influence or forcefully drag them over the edge of the precipice after enveloping them with its dark mist. On Thursday 12 October 1882, a Miss Filby, the 27-year-old daughter of a London shipbroker, took a trip to Beachy Head, a place she often visited to enjoy the majestic views of the seascape from the lofty headland, and upon this day she was known to have been in a very good mood. Miss Filby had taken apartments at an upmarket seaside lodging house in Eastbourne and had given instructions to her landlady as to what she would have for tea. The landlady recalled that Miss Filby had been smiling and in very high spirits. At half-past two that sunny October afternoon, a fisherman spotted a dreadfully disfigured body crumpled on the shore at Beachy Head. It was Miss Filby, and her face had been driven inwards into her skull by the impact, and her scalp had been horrifically severed from the skull for some reason. The spine was completely broken in two and the arms and legs were bent at very unnatural angles. The Times of London (October 16, 1882) reported on the inquest into Miss Filby's death, and detailed the coroner's findings – or, should we say, lack of them? No reason could be found as to how the lady had fallen over the cliff; it was a spot she knew very well and her brother stated that he did not believe it was a suicide, and he also told friends that foul play was a possibility as his sister never ventured too near the edge because she had a type of vertigo. Two local boys playing truant said they saw a man dressed as a monk in a black cowl up on Beachy Head that afternoon, but no one took this claim seriously. There were many more incidents attributed to suicide – some of them in very mysterious circumstances – at Beachy Head after the strange death of Miss Filby. In August 1885, the body of a young woman named Annie Sharpe, of Littlestead, Berkshire, was found smashed on the rocky shore of the Head, and although the death was 'explained' as a suicide in consequence of some differences Annie had with a sweetheart, many of the locals said otherwise. A fisherman said he had spotted a girl up on Beachy Head that day and becoming suspicious of her intentions, he had approached her, but the girl smilingly informed him she had told her boyfriend she'd end her life on Beachy Head unless he married her, and she assured the fisherman she had no intentions of committing suicide. The fisherman left the girl, and when he looked back, he heard screams, and saw that the girl he had spoken to was running from someone – or something, and glancing back as she fled. She was heading towards the edge of the cliff. The girl then seemed to vanish. The fisherman walked to the spot and said he felt the hairs on his arms stand up and had the feeling he was being watched. He felt dizzy as he inched towards the edge of the chalk cliff top and managed to take a few brief glimpses over the edge, and the distant horizon of the sea seemed to tilt, making him think the cliff was tipping over into the sea. The man's heart pounded with fear and he crouched down, closed his eyes, and crawled face-down through the grass till he was some thirty feet from the edge of the cliff. Then a very strange impression came over the fisherman as he clutched the grass, for he now felt as if gravity was working in reverse, and that if he was to let go of the grass, he would somehow fall into the sky. He began to pray out loudly and squeezed his eyes shut as he crawled as far from the cliff edge as possible. He then went home, and days later, heard of the supposed suicide of Annie Sharpe. He never ventured anywhere near Beachy Head after that day.

The suicides continue to this day at Beachy Head, and the stories about the "Monk" who mesmerises and physically throws people off the cliff has passed into urban folklore. Mediums and dabblers in the occult have tried to contact the evil spirit over the years. One wild stormy night in February 1952, a hundred people accompanied a medium (named in some sources as Ray de Vekey) who went to Beachy Head to contact the entity blamed by the locals for the inordinate amount of suicides which had blighted the name of the beauty spot. By the light of a dozen or so torches, the medium appeared to make contact with something. 'Give me a sign, spirit!' the medium called out, looking up into the cold night air. And then all of a sudden the psychic ran from the beams of the torches into the darkness – towards the edge of the cliff. 'There is a bearded man!' the medium shouted as he ran, 'And he is evil; he's calling us blaspheming fools – and he is saying something else. He is saying he'll sweep us all over the cliff!' The alleged clairvoyant then began to laugh hysterically – as if he was possessed. Four or five of the braver ones who had followed the medium to the troubled spot rushed forward before he could totter towards the edge of the cliff, but the psychic seemed to have terrific strength and was apparently hell-bent on running off the edge of Beachy Head. 'He wants revenge!' he cried, still laughing, 'he's just getting his own back! He has waited – lain in wait – for years!'

Somehow the voluntary rescuers subdued the medium and dragged him away from the edge of the cliff as he gazed madly into the abyss below, and the sounds of the Channel's waves crashing against the shore. The psychic went limp and the men dragged him towards the other followers and laid him on his back. The medium seemed to snap out of a trance and said: 'That was the strongest influence I've ever felt in my life. I had this urge – I was impelled by him towards the cliff-edge. All those people he has sent over to their deaths! Victims of sacrifices. He was in chains, and he was a sacrifice, I think.'

About a week after this the medium and a group of fascinated followers assembled at Beachy Head and the medium led them in prayer – and this time the malign entity – whatever it was – failed to appear. The medium believed he had laid the Evil Monk of Beachy Head to rest – but within a few weeks there were more suicides there, and the sightings of the black misty entity continues to be seen. In March 1961 a former food firm chief was found dead on the South Downs near Beachy Head, the same day that several tourists saw a black vaporous object (initially believed to be a swarm of bees) in the area, but this black swarm had two points of crimson light within it which resembled a pair of demonic eyes, and the amorphous shape took on the vague outline of a person of enormous stature (around 7 feet tall) at one point. That same month a couple from Cheshire, Tim and Miranda Knight, moved into a 5-roomed cottage on the South Downs which had its own tennis court set in seven acres. The couple believed they had found their dream house, but one evening towards the end of March 1961, they invited some friends to the cottage, and towards the end of the evening, Miranda and three female friends talked of horoscopes – and the ouija board. Miranda said she had felt a presence in the old cottage, which was hundreds of years old, and so her friends egged her into making an ad hoc ouija board from an upturned wine glass and thirty-six little paper squares cut from a newspaper, with each square featuring the 26 letters of the alphabet and the other ten featuring the numerals zero to nine. Tim was afraid of the supernatural and said the whole thing was a bad idea, but the four girls and two of the men went ahead with what they saw as a harmless bit of fun. 'Will Sharon marry someone called Tony?' Miranda asked the glass. Sharon was a close friend who hoped to marry Tony - one of Tim's many friends - who wasn't present at the time.

The glass slid about in a steady straight line. 'N-O' it spelt.

'Aww, why not?' Miranda asked, noting the glum face on Sharon at the glass's 'reply'.

The glass moved at a fast rate and the sitters could hardly make out what it was spelling out. It spelt out the name 'CATCHPOLE'.

'Who the hell's he?' Sharon asked with a puzzled, but nervous expression.

'Maybe he's a secret admirer,' Miranda suggested in an effort to cheer her friend up.

'Or maybe Catchpole is the name of the spirit,' a guest named Mike suggested, and he asked the glass: 'Are you Mr Catchpole?'

'N-O' the glass indicated.

'Well what *is* your name then?' Sharon asked, and smirked as she looked up at the low beams of the cosy cottage, waiting for the spirit in the glass to reply. She believed the "spirit" was her friends mucking about, pushing the glass around, perhaps even unknowingly, given the amount of wine they had all consumed on this evening.

There was a pause, and all of the sitters smiled at one another, perhaps thinking that one of their friends – or all of them – were shoving the glass about. But then the glass began to trace two words, and no one could make head or tail of the reply.

'G-O D-E-O?' Sharon tried to pronounce the words in a slurred voice.

'What a stupid name – ' Mike was saying when the glass flew off the table and continued in a straight line through the air as if it was sliding along an invisible counter – until it smashed into the open fire, and as it shattered, strange green and blue flares erupted from the coals and log which had been burning merrily with little flickering flames until that moment. Then came something which all of those present would talk about for the rest of their lives. In the green and blue flames there appeared – just for a few seconds – a long hideous face framed by a black hood, and this weird vision was very clear. The eyes of the man were jet black and piercing, and Sharon screamed when she saw the face flash into existence for a moment. Then the face was gone and the flames returned to normal. Everyone continued to gaze at the fire for a while, and then simultaneously, Miranda and Mike gasped: 'What the hell – '

It wasn't long before the guests - spooked by the face of what had looked like a monk, appearing in the fireplace – made their excuses to leave, and that night, as Mike and his wife drove away from the cottage, they saw huge boulders landing in the road in front of and behind their car, as if something with enormous strength was hurtling the rocks at them. The boulder-throwing went on for about a minute and the couple ended up speeding at almost 80 mph to reach their home. Tim and Miranda asked everyone they knew what "Go Deo" meant, and no one seemed to know, but one evening when Tim was talking about the ouija message in his local pub, and old Irishman came over to him and revealed that "Go Deo" was an old Irish Gaelic phrase which meant both "forever" and "a very long time". Had the entity communicating through the inverted glass been stating that it had been around for a very long time? About a year later, Miranda's friend Sharon was on holiday in Italy when she was killed in a head-on collision with a British motorist who had been driving on the wrong side of the road – and his surname was Catchpole. Sharon had been killed before she could marry her long-term lover Tony.

Was the manifestation of what seems to have been a monk in a black hood in the fireplace somehow connected to the legend of the Evil Monk of Beachy Head who supposedly lures people to end their lives on the cliff top? Some folklorists believe a monk from nearby Wilmington Priory is said to have cursed those who snatched the Priory and the land it stood on during the Dissolution of the Monasteries (between 1536 and 1541) in the reign of Henry VIII. I have a feeling that the malevolent presence connected to Beachy Head has more to do with Druidism and a mysterious hillside carving around six miles north of the suicide spot – the Long Man of Wilmington. The Long Man is 227 feet in length from head to foot, and was originally carved out of the slopes of Windover Hill, but now his outline has been "highlighted" by the insertion of white painted breezeblocks in the original shallow trench that formed his body (by the exposure of the underlying chalk common to that area). No one seems to know just how old the Long Man of Wilmington is, and while some experts think he dates back to the Iron Age or Neolithic Period, some archaeologists have recently considered the possibility – from the unearthing of new evidence at the site of the carving – that the Long Man may in fact only date back to the 16th century. Just what the hillside figure symbolises or depicts is also a mystery; he holds a staff in each hand, or perhaps he is opening doors. The locals call the Long Man the "Green Man" and have done so for generations. 'Modern' druids from the 18th century onwards have also claimed the enigmatic figure of Wilmington and in a probability he probably does have some connection to the ancient druidic order. I feel that the hooded figure which haunts Beachy Head may be some ancient druid who went bad for some reason. If the entity at Beach Head is not a renegade druid, then it may be an actual Orgisher which will continually lead people to their deaths unless it can be professionally exorcised.

From 1896 to 1900, something along the lines of the Orgisher was at large at a house in Litherland Road, Bootle (then in Lancashire). In December 1896 a married man named George Roberts had a sudden urge to hang himself as he worked the late shift as a foreman at a bakery on Strand Road, Bootle, and at midnight, he went outside, and using his scarf and a belt, he hanged himself from a pipe in an alleyway. A PC Fisher came upon the scene on his beat that night and cut Roberts down. The baker appeared to be dead but the policeman administered artificial respiration for some twenty minutes and managed to revive Roberts, who later explained how a strange melancholy had overcome him before he decided he'd end his life. He vaguely recalled picking up a pencil, writing on a scrap of paper: "Goodbye, my children" before going to hang himself.

Back at his Bootle home on Litherland Road, Mr Roberts was visited by a cousin a week later, a man named Joe Hunter, a plasterer by trade who was in his early twenties. Just after dinner, Joe went missing, and then the wife of Mr Roberts screamed when she saw him standing halfway up the stairs in the hallway with a noose round his neck. The other end of that rope had been tied to one of the railings on the next floor, and as Mr and Mrs Roberts came to the foot of the stairs, Joe warned them: 'Stay where you are! If you come any nearer I'll end myself!" And as she said this he raised his right leg over the rail, and then brought his second leg over.

'Don't do it man, you have everything to live for!' George Roberts shouted to his young cousin. 'You're getting married soon lad!'

'I don't want to live any more!' Joe yelled back and seemed to have tears in his eyes.

Somehow, Mrs Roberts talked the young plasterer out of hanging himself, and just as he was about to take the noose off, a hand – black, as if it wore a very tight black leather glove – came through the railings and seized the feet of Joe Hunter. It dragged him off the edge of the steps and he fell and made a terrible choking sound, and as he kicked his legs and his face began to turn dark that mysterious hand seemed to vanish. George Roberts flew up the staircase and grabbed hold of the kicking legs. He used all of his might to push Joe upwards, and the plasterer's hands grabbed at the noose and pulled it up, over his head. Joe then fell backwards and landed on his back on the steps, winded, but alive, with a terrible crimson rope-burn on his neck. The door to the coal storage cupboard under the staircase was yanked open, but no one was there, and yet the Roberts had clearly seen that hand appear between the railings of the staircase – so who had tried to kill Joe and where had they gone to?

At Christmas Eve that year, the niece of Mrs Roberts, a little 5-year-old girl named Nellie, came to the house with her mother, and while Mrs Roberts chatted to Nellie's mum, the little girl sneaked upstairs and went to the attic, where the child came upon a weird and frightening sight. A row of dolls, some of them intended to be presents for Nellie from the Roberts, were suspended by what looked like miniature ropes that had been strung from nails knocked into the ceiling. At the other end of the rope there were nooses which the dolls had their heads in so that they appeared to have been hanged in a row. That same night, Mrs Roberts awoke in the darkness of her cold bedroom at around two o'clock, and she heard a faint voice close to her left ear saying: 'End yourself, end yourself,' over and over till she let out a scream and grabbed hold of her sleeping husband. The family later moved from the house and when the new family of six moved in, an uncle who paid a visit at Easter went upstairs to the attic and hanged himself. The man who had committed suicide was known as a very happy-go-lucky individual who had no financial or health worries, and so no one could understand why he had decided to hang himself. Three more people hanged themselves at the house over the four years from the time when the Roberts vacated it, and not one suicide could be put down to depression (known then as "melancholia") or the result of some worry about financial or health matters. It was as if something was constantly making people end their lives in that house. A house on St John's Road, in the Waterloo area just north of Liverpool, has a similar reputation to the aforementioned one in Bootle. In my *Haunted Liverpool* 8 I gave the full story of this sinister house and the "Man in Black" who has haunted it for well over a century now. A Mrs Stephenson, who grew up in the house in question, was always having encounters with the terrifying caped ghost from her childhood to her teens, and years later, in 1987 when she had grown up and had a child of her own she returned to Liverpool from Australia (where she had emigrated to many years before) and out of curiosity, she called upon the present occupiers of the old house on St John's Road. The person living there admitted Mrs Stephenson and took her around the house as she reminisced about old times. During this nostalgic tour, the young daughter of Mrs Stephenson wandered off and went upstairs. For obvious reasons, this girl had never been told about the incidents involving the man in black. When her mother caught up with her, she was trembling. Something had obviously upset her. She told her mother that a man's voice had urged her to pick up a piece of glass which was lying on the floor from a broken window, and *to use it to slash her wrists.* He had then added: "*It won't hurt; you will only feel cold for a short while.*" Mrs Stephenson had heard enough. She grabbed hold of her daughter's hand and pulled her out of the accursed house...

TALES OF THE EVIL EYE

A woman in her early 60s we shall call Fiona Jones divorced her husband in 2004 after discovering he'd been having an affair with a 22-year-old girl. She had been baffled as to why her 57-year-old husband Barry shaved at 10pm and took to wearing rather young tee shirts (bearing the names of various indie bands) before he would vanish into his study on numerous nights, but then she caught him one evening chatting in hushed tones to a girl via a webcam. After the divorce she moved from London to go back to her roots – the leafy Gateacre district of Liverpool - and spent about five years on her own, disillusioned with life – and men in general. Fiona thought that love and loyalty were becoming things of the past, and she never actively sought a partner (although her friends urged her too), but spent most of her energy gardening and improving her semi with her formidable DIY skills. She loved long walks, and since a child she had always felt close to nature. She would make little meals for the urban foxes and leave them at the end of her garden each night, and a few of her friends told her not to do that, but Fiona felt that the fox was just a dog which had been given the cold-shoulder by the human race.

One afternoon she visited her friend Celeste, a lady of 37 who was into astrology, Wicca, alternative medicine and yoga. As usual the topic of the paranormal came up, and Celeste pestered Fiona. 'Let me read your tealeaves,' she asked, and Fiona said she'd have a job as the tea had been made with Tetley tea bags. Well, it turned out that sneaky Celeste had made the tea with loose leaves from torn teabags.

'Go on then,' Fiona sighed. The reason Fiona hadn't wanted her leaves read was simply because Celeste was pretty good at Tasseomancy (the official term for divination by tea-leaf reading), and Fiona felt life was complicated enough at the mundane level without involving the workings of the psychic sphere. Celeste turned the cup and pointed at a clump of leaves. Her mouth became O-shaped. 'I can see a man – a tall man with dark hair –' she said with some excitement.

'You sound like an end-of-the-pier fortune teller,' Fiona rolled her eyes and looked at the clock.

'No, Fiona, I'm serious, I can see you walking sort of past him – '

'And hopefully I keep on walking,' Fiona quipped, and fidgeted with that bare finger – the one she used to wear her wedding and engagement rings on.

'And I can see a weird eye to the left,' Celeste squinted, then rummaged for her reading glasses and took a better look. The clock suddenly stopped ticking and the silence became very noticeable to Fiona. 'I don't like the look of this eye, Fiona – it's really creeping me out.'

'Oh stop it, it's like a Hammer House of Horror movie,' Fiona felt a slight dull pain in her knee – an arthritic pain. She looked back at Celeste. 'Can you tell me *where* this man's looking at me? The opticians maybe – I mean with the eye and that.'

'It looks like that road where the thingy pub is – oh, what's it called now? The one in Woolton? You walk that way when you go on your walkabouts? Acrefield Road.'

'The White Horse?' Fiona put Celeste out her misery.

'Yeah! I can see that pub clear as day and the old terraced houses by it, and he's walking past you there and looking at you, like over his shoulder.'

'Well, if I see a tall man walking past me and a big weird eye floating about I'll let you know,' joked Fiona, and she got up and looked at the time on her mobile. 'I've got a doctor's appointment, so I better get a move on.'

'Nothing serious is it?' Celeste enquired.

Fiona smiled and shook her head. 'Just a bit of arthritis in my clicky kneecap – and no, I don't want any ginger, but thanks love.'

Fiona walked to the doctor's, went home, and thought about the tea-leaf reading, and hoped Celeste would be wrong on this occasion. Fiona then spent the rest of the day watching TV, cooking, and browsing an old Helen Forrester book. The next day, she went on her daily walk, and something very odd took place. She walked up a rainy Acrefield Road, and as she crossed over – by the White Horse pub – a tall, almost gangly dark-haired man turned his head to look at her and he gave a friendly smile as he passed. He looked about forty-eight or fifty perhaps. Fiona never returned the smile, and felt guilty for not doing so, but she really didn't want to get involved with anyone again.

She tripped.

The world tipped over and the impact against the pavement stunned her. That man knelt by her and asked if she was okay. Dazed, she nodded, and he helped her up. 'Thanks,' she said, and looked at her palm – it was cut. The man whipped out a handkerchief and wrapped it round her hand. 'Thankyou,' she said, 'I feel so stupid.'

'Don't,' the man said with a smile. 'When your twelve and you fall over, you sort of bounce up again and recover, but once you get past twenty a fall nearly does you in.'

And he persuaded Fiona to go to the pub – and she couldn't believe that she was actually accepting the invitation. She put it down to shock from the silly fall. The gin and tonic steadied her after that fall and the man – Mike Baker his name was – gave a potted story of his life. Married for nearly 30 years, cheated on by his wife (who had left him for his former best friend), and now he was divorced at 51. Mike, an electrician by trade, was living with his brother in Gateacre for now, and was quite unsure about his future. He felt like a fish out of water being single and free after being married for so long, but he was also reluctant to get involved in a relationship again – or so he thought.

Well, Fiona and Mike got on like the proverbial house on fire, and it was as if they were long-lost friends, but then as the relationship developed, Fiona began to have an inordinate amount of bad luck – accident after accident, including a minor house fire and a crash in a Hackney cab, and even a health scare when her heart wouldn't stop palpitating one night.

'Someone very jealous has the Evil Eye on you,' was Celeste's chilling verdict, and Fiona recalled the eye her friend has seen in the teacup. Mike laughed at the idea at first, but Celeste told him: 'Mike, I feel this person with the evil eye wants you, and I see a red umbrella.'

Fiona's eyes rolled in an arc from Celeste to Mike and she gave him a sort of apologetic smile, as if to say, 'I'm sorry for having a kooky friend.'

'Wait a minute,' Mike said, and he squinted his eyes and gazed up at the ceiling in deep thought for a moment. 'That day when you fell, love, there was a red-haired woman with a *red brolly* down the road, by the pub, watching us.'

'I don't recall her,' Fiona confessed.

'Yes, she was there, honest,' Mike assured Fiona. 'I am almost certain she was in the supermarket the day before I met you.'

'An admirer maybe?' said Fiona gazing at the little sore on her palm, a memento of the fall. 'How old is she?'

'Oh I'm not good at judging ages,' Mike replied, 'maybe in her forties, mid forties, I don't know.'

Slowly, Fiona and Mike realised that the same redhead had been in the vicinity during the house fire and the taxi crash, although she hadn't been present during the other occurrences of bad luck.

'Surely no one can curse someone like that?' Fiona attempted to remain rational. 'We're just joining up all the dots wrongly – surely?'

'I've been on the receiving end of the Evil Eye years ago,' Celeste told her friend. 'At first the doctor said it was chronic fatigue, but it became steadily worse, and my dog died as well, and he was only two. My Nan then told me that she thought someone had the Evil Eye on me.'

'Why is she doing this – the red-head?' Mike asked, shaking his head slightly.

'Oh stop fishing for compliments,' Fiona replied with a lopsided smirk.

'What are you talking about?' Mike asked, in all

innocence.

'She *fancies* you, and she wants me out the way, probably,' Fiona told him with a little levity in her voice, but he could see that underneath the façade of humour, Fiona was quite worried.

'She's probably right, you know?' Celeste told Mike, and she went out the room and into the kitchen. She returned a few minutes later with a bowl of water and a bottle of olive oil. She placed the bowl on the coffee table and poured a little olive oil into it, then, using sewing needles and scissors, she performed a very old Wiccan spell to reflect the malevolence of the Evil Eye – or Malocchio as occultists call it. She began to chant: '*Occhi e contro e perticelli agli occhi, crepa la invida e schiattono gli occhi*,' which means 'Eyes against eyes and the holes of the eyes, envy cracks and eyes burst.'

Celeste dropped the needles on top of the oil and then she sprinkled three pinches of salt into the water. The scissors were jabbed into the water through the oil three times. Celeste then cut the air above the bowl three times, as if she was snipping an imaginary length of string.

'The spell is now broken!' Celeste announced confidently, and the air in the living room felt electric now.

The red-head was taken away by an ambulance that night, suffering from a seizure, according to her neighbours and all of the bad luck afflicting Fiona ceased – and never returned. Fiona later married Mike and at the time of writing they are still together.

The Evil Eye – in which a curse is literally cast by the malevolent eye of an envious person, is a phenomenon which is documented in almost every culture on this earth, and it has been referred to in ancient Babylonian, Chinese, Greek and Roman texts, and even within the Old Testament. It would seem that some envious people – mainly those who have unusually beautiful or peculiar eyes (and sometimes those with a squint) possess an inexplicable power to supernaturally inflict injury to a person by merely gazing at them with hatred in their mind. The envier can harm the person in that instant, but the usual outcome is for the target of the Evil Eye to become jinxed and suffer hours or even days later. Many years ago in the 1970s there was an old bitter woman named Peg who lived on Liverpool's Penny Lane, and she was widely feared throughout the neighbourhood for causing miscarriages, marriage break-ups, automobile accidents, health scares and all sorts of bad luck – allegedly just by staring at those she wanted to jinx, with her left eye, which had a peculiar greyish-green iris. Peg's other eye was sky-blue, and this condition - having different coloured eyes - is known as heterochromia. In 1975 a 20-year-old girl named Christina Campbell became pregnant by a man named Stephen who abandoned her once he heard she was 'in the family way' (an old-fashioned idiom from that era to denote someone who was pregnant). Christina had a tremendous fall out with her mother around this time because her mum said she should have long found someone decent and settled down 'into a normal married life like the rest of the human race'. And so Christina ended up living in the back bedroom of a house on Penny Lane owned by the parents of her best friend – June. Some women sail through pregnancy, whilst others have the worst forms of morning sickness and become very emotional due to hormonal changes. With Christina, the pregnancy had a very strange effect; firstly, at 16 weeks she began to have strange prophetic dreams about things which would come to pass, then Christina would have strange daydreams – visions almost – as she was awake of course, and these strange episodes were very similar to the out of body experience which is commonly reported today by people who have had near-death experiences or been out for the count under general anaesthetic during an operation. The dreams were the precursor to this strange psychic faculty. Christina dreamt that a sobbing woman in a royal blue coat had called at June's house, and three days later, June's Auntie Jill turned up in a royal blue coat, crying her eyes out because her husband had just died of a heart attack. Christina had several of these dreams which came true, and they spooked June a little. Then the strange out-of-body episodes began, and the first one began when Christina was sitting in a chair in her bedroom, reading a magazine as she listened to the radio. She felt light-headed, and found herself floating over Penny Lane. Wherever she willed herself, she would float in that direction. She drifted through a closed window and found herself in the house opposite June's and she could see a grey-haired man in his sixties wallpapering a room and the surroundings were very vivid. Christina knew she wasn't dreaming. She floated up, through the ceiling, through a dark loft, and found herself hovering over the slates of the roof. She then found her consciousness back in her body in her bedroom where she reflexively kicked her leg out with a jolt. On the following day, Christina and June went to the chippy on Penny Lane when Christina saw a familiar grey-haired man standing in the queue there – it was the man she had seen wallpapering during the 'detached consciousness' episode of the day before. 'Excuse me,' Christina tapped the old man on the shoulder, and he turned with a start.

'Yes?' he asked.

'Are you wallpapering your house?' Christina queried as June looked on bemused at her asking such a random question.

'Yes,' the man replied with a perplexed look, 'but how did you know that?'

Christina didn't want to tell the man how she knew, but just smiled and said, 'I saw you carrying rolls of wallpaper into the house the other day.'

'You can't have,' the man - now fully turned to face the pregnant young lady - said with a look of suspicion, 'because I'm using rolls of paper that I've had since the 1950s. So how did you really know?'

'Oh, never mind,' Christina said, and the woman behind the counter asked the old man what he wanted.

'How *did* you know he was decorating?' June wanted to know.

Christina just smiled, and said: 'I'll tell you later.'

Around this time there was a pervert making vulgar anonymous telephone calls to women who answered him in the Allerton and Mossley Hill areas, and June's parents believed the culprit was a particular bachelor in his forties who lived on nearby Heathfield Road for some reason. The pest would ask the lady what she was wearing or utter a shocking line of filth before heavy breathing. During this particular week, two women in Penny Lane had answered the phone and found themselves subjected to this sex pest, and on a Tuesday afternoon around 4.50pm, the telephone rang in June's house, and as no one but Christina was in, she answered. It was the nuisance caller, and straight away he asked Christina what colour her knickers were. She realised with shock that it was the sex pest, and she swore at him, but he phoned back five times until Christina left the phone off the hook. When June came in later that afternoon with her mother, Christina told them about the anonymous caller and June's mother said once again that she thought the culprit was an unmarried man in a nearby street. That evening, Christina was lying on her bed in her room, reading a paperback when she drifted off. About fifteen minutes later, June came into the room and unintentionally woke her friend – and as she apologised for doing so, Christina said, 'June, I know who it is who's making the dirty phone calls.'

'Who?' June asked, all intrigued, then she said: 'How do you know?'

'I've just had a real vivid dream of a man doing something disgusting as he spoke to someone on the telephone, and that person was that fellah who runs that shop on Smithdown Road [which is a major thoroughfare just around the corner of Penny Lane].'

'What shop? Which fellah?' June asked.

Christina told her the name of the shop and described the man she had seen making the obscene phone calls in her 'dream'.

'No, don't be daft, Chrissy,' June told her, 'he's very religious, and he's not that sort. I've known him for years and he's never looked at my legs when I've had a mini skirt on or anything.'

'And I'm telling you it's him,' Christina assured her sceptical friend. 'He has a slight lisp, and I saw him clearly – '

'In a dream, Chrissy – in a dream! The police would laugh if you told them that.'

June told her mother about Christina's bizarre dream and she said the same as June: that the man who ran the shop attended church and was very prim and proper. Christina was determined to prove that the man was the perpetrator of the disgusting anonymous phone calls, and so, she sent an anonymous letter to the shop that the man owned. The letter read: 'Stop making those calls you dirty old bastard – or I will go to the police.'

The sex pest made no more calls after that – but something frightening took place. Christina told June what she had done – and described the contents of the letter. June said it was a mean and irresponsible thing to have done, and then she scared her friend by telling her that the mother of the shopkeeper she had accused was a woman who was greatly feared in the neighbourhood because she had the power of the Evil Eye, and anyone who crossed her path suffered terrible runs of bad luck – or even death, and pregnant women in particular had supposedly miscarried when she had cast her weird-looking eye upon them.

'How will she know I sent the letter?' Christina asked, 'I've only told you. You're not going to tell your mum are you?'

'No, I'm not,' a worried-looking June told her, 'but this woman – Peg's her name – is really weird, and they say she's psychic. She might already know.'

'Oh come on, June, you're acting all paranoid,'

Christina said, and she tried – unsuccessfully – to raise a smile, then gazed at the window at the gathering twilight filtering through the drab curtains.

'I wish you'd think before you did these stupid things, Chrissy,' June said and shook her head, and then she left the room. About two minutes later, June barged back into the room and said to Christina. 'She's outside now! She's looking up at your window!' And the girl turned off the light and crept to the curtains.

'Who's outside?' Christina whispered, going to the curtains and trying to look over June's shoulder.

'Who do you think?' June sounded as if she was talking through gritted teeth. 'Peg!'

Christina managed to peep out through the lace curtains – and she saw a woman who seemed hunched over in the street below. She wore a babushka scarf, tied under her chin, and she was looking up at the window with her head tilted sideways. The old woman's eyes were not visible because the street lamp was creating the impression that the woman's eyes were two black sockets.

'See what you've done?' June whispered in a paradoxically harsh-sounding voice.

'It's just a coincidence June, stop panicking will you?'

'That is *no* coincidence, Chrissy! That old woman knows you sent that letter to her son.'

Old Peg turned and slowly walked up Penny Lane, and she stopped a few times and looked back at the window, as if she knew the girls were watching her.

When she had vanished into the distance, June turned the light in the room back on and Christina asked her: 'Can she really cause miscarriages?' And she felt her slight bulge as she posed this question.

'That's what they say,' June told her friend. 'Maybe you'd be better leaving if you're worried.'

'Where could I go?' Chrissy asked, all tearful at feeling unwanted.

'Your own home – make it up with your mum, Chrissy. You're bound to bump into Peg at some point, and once she casts her eye on you, God knows what will happen.'

'I can't go home, but if you don't want me here, I'll find a place to go,' Christina said, and tears fell from her eyes. 'I'll try the Y.W.C.A.'

June hugged her. 'I don't want you to go, I was just thinking of you and the baby, that's all.'

'I could just stay in, and try to avoid that horrible old woman,' Christina said with her face buried in June's bosom.

'Yeah, you could, so stop crying now, love – stop crying.' June went and fetched a box of paper hankies and told her friend to blow her nose.

Christina stayed indoors for as long as she could, and when she could not take the self-imposed seclusion any more, she would go into the backyard, and sometimes she'd venture down the alleyway for a walk.

Then, about five days later, June took her old Labrador for a walk on Penny Lane – and she literally bumped into Peg by the Church of St Barnabas. The old woman's toothless mouth turned down at the corners and she shot a terrifying hateful look at her. June saw that fear-provoking left eye of Peg's – the left greyish-green one, which looked as dead as a doll's eye. The girl shuddered, and she turned and walked away. As she crossed the road, the dog somehow slipped off its lead, and a bread lorry came around the corner –

and went straight over the poor animal. The dog lay crushed into the road surface, its intestines showing and one of its eyes was protruding from the crushed head on a stalk. Bizarrely, the animal's tail was still wagging, perhaps solely because of some effect of its nervous system as it lay dying – or perhaps the Labrador was in shock. June screamed to the circle of morbid people who gathered around her: 'Help him! Call a vet, please! Help him!'

But a corpulent man dragged June away from the horrific scene and said, 'Come on love, he's good as dead already.'

'He's not!' June cried, and she could hardly see as tears flooded from her eyes. 'They can save him!' She tried to return to her dog but the man held her by the shoulders and tried to calm her down.

The poor Labrador stopped wagging its tail and opened its mouth. It vomited blood and the remains of its last ever meal, then its tongue flopped flat onto the road and it exhaled a last breath.

'It's a goner,' some insensitive bystander announced.

The lorry which had killed the animal had halted about a hundred yards down the road, but now it suddenly moved off.

'Ew, is that its ribs?' A schoolboy asked his mother, who then dragged him away.

June was in a terrible state when she got home, and could hardly talk for crying, and when her mother heard about the death of the family dog she broke down too. Christina could hear the crying downstairs and went to see what was going on. By now, June had told her mother about Christina sending the letter to Peg's son, and incurring her wrath as a result, and June and her mother glared at Christina as she came into the living room and the latter told her she'd have to find lodgings elsewhere. Christina turned and walked in a daze up the stairs to the room, and this time she was determined to leave. She heard a key rattle in the front door and someone heavy-footed came in. It was June's father, back from the pub. When he heard about the dog being knocked down and how it had all been her fault because she had accused the son of a woman with the "Evil Eye" of being the telephone sex pest, he told his wife and daughter they were acting like superstitious peasants from the Middle Ages, and he went upstairs and closed the suitcase Christina had been packing on the bed. He persuaded her to stay, and then he went downstairs and told June not to ever mention all of this rubbish about Evil Eyes and curses ever again. 'Everyone's got that old woman down as some witch,' he told his wife, 'and its mostly through people like you, spreading barmy gossip.'

'But dad, she looked at me and then the dog was knocked down,' June told him, then began to cry again.

Her father raised his voice, angered by this assertion. 'That's because you were probably that terrified of a harmless old woman you didn't look where you were going when you rushed away, and the dog's dead because of all this now! Let's have no more talk about this superstitious rubbish.'

A hard silence then descended on the living room, and June went upstairs and cried in the arms of her friend. In the midst of all the tears, June suddenly pulled herself together and told Christina that perhaps her father was right – maybe the stories about Peg were all nonsense and superstition. 'We *should* go out and let her see us, nothing will happen. We shouldn't let anyone make us prisoners in our own home,' she told Christina with an angry tear-streaked face.

On the following day the girls ventured out and went to a sweetshop on Allerton Road, just a five-minute walk away, because Christina had developed a craving for fried chicken flavoured crisps. The sun had broken through the low grey clouds and when they left the shop, June suggested going to Calderstones Park for a picnic. They walked off towards Penny Lane, intending to pack all kinds in a basket, when Christina saw a tiny fly caught up in her friend's long hair. 'Ew, what is it?' June asked. She hated flies and insects.

'Just a tiny ickle fly,' Christina managed to extricate it from the silky strands of hair and she blew it from between her finger and thumb. She remarked on how lovely and long June's hair was, because Christina's locks were just shoulder-length. June tossed back her head, then flicked her hair from her shoulders with her index finger and smirked, saying, 'Oh well I do use Sunsilk Egg Shampoo you know,' and she told Christina she could brush her hair in the park as they had their picnic.

'Oh thanks,' was Christina's sarcastic reply.

Then they both saw Peg, standing close to the large oaken door of St Barnabas's Church. She was all in black this time, and even the babushka scarf was black too. She almost grinned as the girls looked at her and watched them gazing at her in terror as they crossed the road.

'Don't look at her! Don't look at her!' June bowed her head and looked at the floor as she hurried along, and Christina also averted her gaze, but she could see the black outline of the sinister old woman out the corner of her left eye.

Christina said they should forget the picnic in the park but June got the wicker basket from the top of a cupboard in the kitchen and said, 'No, we said we weren't going to let that woman cast a shadow over us. We're going to the park.'

And June began to make sandwiches and she also appropriated the remaining three quarters of a Sayers sandwich cake from the fridge and a large bottle of her father's cider which he kept hidden in the cellar from June's mum because he had promised he'd stop mixing it with his home-brewed ale.

Well, the girls were soon enjoying the modicum of sunshine in Calderstones Park as well as the cake, sarnies and cider, and yet every now and then they'd look around to make sure old Peg wasn't about. At one point, June rummaged in the picnic basket and produced a hairbrush and smiled broadly as she handed it to a groaning Christina. 'Go on, Chrissy, I know you love doing it.'

'Oh, it wears me out brushing your hair, and we'll have hairs on the food,' Christina complained.

'Are you saying I moult?' June said, and cheekily laid her head down on her friend's lap. 'It really relaxes me when you brush my hair.'

'Well I'll do it if you'll promise to scratch my back tonight then,' Christina stipulated, and the two young ladies laughed.

Christina drew the brush back, and noticed that June's hair was coming out in clumps.

'Oh, why have you stopped?' June asked, looking at

a little patch of blue in the cloudy sky.

'June, don't panic, but er – '

'Don't panic *what*?' June sat in an upright position and turned with a look of worry on her pretty face. 'What's wrong?'

'A big piece of your hair's just come out as I brushed it,' Christine told her.

June's eyes bulged as she saw the long bunch of her hair strands in the bristles of the brush. She put her hand to her hair and grabbed a lock, and gently pulled – and yelped as she felt the roots come away at the scalp with a barely audible tearing sound.

'Oh my God,' Christina recoiled as she saw the small resulting bald patch on her friend's head.

'My hair,' June said, and her face became red and her little petite hands trembled as she ran them through her hair, and this time, fearing more hair would come out, she tugged ever so gently, hoping to heaven that none would come out this time, but even that minor tug brought the hair from her scalp. 'Chrissy, what's wrong with my hair?'

'We better go home and tell your mum, June – maybe its just because you've been upset.'

'It's that old bastard, that Peg who's done this,' June pulled more hair from her head, and then she buried her face in her hands and cried. 'I can't cope with all this, I've had enough,' she sobbed.

Christina said nothing – but she recollected how the old woman had been watching when she had removed the fly from June's hair, and how she had complimented June on having such lovely hair. That woman had obviously overheard them and seen June flicking her hair back in a tongue-in-cheek show-off manner.

June had to go to the chemists wearing her mum's head-scarf and the pharmacist said the condition looked like a form of alopecia, and opined that a lack of sleep and some types of stress could cause the hair-loss. He suggested a coal tar derivative soap and June used it as soon as she got home, but when she washed her hair, it fell off and blocked the plug hole – leaving her bald. The girl also noticed that her eyebrows were also slowly vanishing.

June's mother said she'd had enough, and intended to have it out with Peg, but June begged her not to, saying she feared that the old woman would inflict some fatal condition on her. On the following morning, June's mother was brushing her teeth as she gazed in the mirror, deep in thought about the malicious old crone, when she noticed blood coming from the gum above her right front tooth. She stopped brushing, gargled, spat out, and took a look at that front tooth. She felt it, and it seemed loose. At first she thought it was the fleshy pad of her thumb going in and out, but it wasn't – the front tooth was loose – and felt numb. It broke at the gum-line and she held it in shock. She'd always taken great care of her teeth, brushing and flossing to a Spartan routine, and so this was a big shock. And then she thought of Peg; had this had something to do with her? June's mum felt so embarrassed showing her husband the unsightly gap in her teeth, and she started to cry and said it was definitely Peg who was behind the family's recent medical problems.

Feeling she had brought all this trouble upon June and her mother, Christina packed her suitcase and quietly left that afternoon, unsure where she would go. She wondered if she could make it to her Aunt Una's house down in Crewe, but didn't have enough money for the train fare and she wasn't at all certain that Una still lived in that town. Christina walked up Smithdown Road, and something made her go down a certain quiet avenue. Halfway down this avenue, Peg came around a corner, and again she was all dressed in black, and she stopped dead in front of Christina and shot that look at her.

Christina was so angry at the old woman, she continued to walk towards her and she felt like throwing the suitcase at her. 'Why are you doing all of these horrible things to people? Is it because of me?'

Peg said nothing, but Christina could see that the woman's gaze was now directed upon her abdomen – fixed upon the bulge of the baby!

'You do anything to my baby, and I promise I'll kill you stone dead and happily serve time for doing you in,' Christina's hands covered the bulge.

Peg shook her head and looked up at the girl's distressed face. 'Don't worry,' she said, and her voice sounded deep and masculine. 'That baby can't be harmed, and neither can you as long as you carry it.'

'What?' Christina seemed a bit taken aback by this strange statement.

There was a pause, and then, as the woman turned around to walk in the opposite direction, she said faintly, 'The baby's…'

A car sped down the avenue and drowned out the rest of Peg's words. Christina found herself hurrying after the weird old woman. 'What was that?'

In an annoyed gruff voice, Peg shouted, 'She's got

the eye!'

Christina stood rooted to the spot, trying to take in the meaning of what she had just heard as she saw Peg turn down an alleyway. Peg had referred to the unborn child as 'she' – and in that day an age there were no ultrasound scans or sex testing of the unborn, so Christina didn't know what sex the baby was, and yet she had a feeling it would be a girl. Christinal put her pride aside and she walked back to Smithdown Road, hailed a Hackney cab to her home, and told her mother and father to pay the taxi driver outside. Her parents were glad to see her, and she settled back with them in her old room, and she wrote a long letter to June, saying she was sorry for bringing so much trouble to her door. June's hair slowly grew back and her mother had to pay out a small fortune for a crown at the dentist.

When the baby was born, it was a girl, and when Christina saw the child's eyes for the first time, she recoiled in horror, for they were violet. The nurse told her this was normal in some babies, and that their eyes were often strange shades of blue, but the little girl – named Talitha by her mum – never lost that shade of violet, and as the child got older, Christina realised that "Tali" was not only psychic (for she would predict things quite accurately and tell her mum about the various ghosts who chatted to her at night in her room) it was apparent that she also had the power of the Evil Eye. When children had things she wanted or if they bragged about certain things which Talitha envied, those children would meet with terrible accidents, some of them almost fatal. At the time of writing, Talitha is in her late thirties, and still possesses eyes of a very similar shade to those of the late Liz Taylor's irises, and the woman has a daughter of her own now who also has eyes of a very peculiar but beautiful greenish-blue shade. Be careful who you boast to, for you never know when the Evil Eye will be upon *you*...

A WOMAN OF MANY PARTS

What follows was related to me many years ago, and it's a case I have theorised about a lot, but I still cannot explain. The private detective featured in the account told me the story, and over the years I have developed a talent for knowing when someone is lying, and the man who told me what you are about to read struck me as one of the most honest and down to earth people I have ever met, and other people who have known him over the years have said the same.

Rodney Dougal was a young private detective and part-time roadie to the many bands that had sprung up in 1960s Liverpool in the wake of the Beatles' phenomenal rise to international stardom. His office was a small cramped room over a garage on Duke Street, quite close to the Anglican Cathedral, and he had a small enamel sign bearing the words "R. Dougal Private Investigator" mounted on the crumbling red brick wall next to his window which was now partially obscured with dust and black grime from the car exhausts forever passing and belching on the main road. Dougal's speciality was tracing missing persons, which either meant working for a solicitor seeking a witness to an incident, or finding a person who was someone's old flame from a long time ago. The best case that ever came Dougal's way was a year back in the summer when a wealthy jealous man in his sixties asked him to keep an eye on his 22-year-old mistress on a fortnight-long pleasure cruise to the Canaries. The mistress was seeing no one and spent the whole of the voyage drinking with Dougal. Such dream cases were a rarity – most clients wanted mundane tasks – proving a partner was being unfaithful for divorce cases, and only last week a client had asked Rodney to find out who the older man was who was knocking round with his 16-year-old daughter; it turned out to be her English teacher at school.

Rodney Dougal wanted a change of career. He had applied for the job of a store detective at Harrods down in London but had not yet received any reply, and the GPO were due to cut off his phone any day now. On top of that, the car he used for his line of work – a Ford Prefect – belonged to his brother Ted, and he was getting impatient waiting for its return, as Rodney had said he'd only borrow it till he got his own set of wheels – almost six months ago. In short then, things were not looking well financially for Dougal as he sat in his office, looking out the window onto Duke Street. If he had not been living with his mum, he'd be existing on a quarter of tea, a couple of Woodbine ciggies and a stale portion of chips from last night. Then his luck changed with the arrival of a Brewster green Rolls Royce on Duke Street. A white-haired man looked in at the mechanics who were gawping at him from the garage bay, and then he happened to gaze up to the source of a squeaking sound. It was Rodney Dougal opening the window of his office, hoping the wealthy visitor was looking for his services; he was.

Rodney came down to let him in through a doorway which lay in an easily missed recess in an alleyway. The client was a Mr Woodford, and by the time he had climbed the two steep flights of wooden steps to Rodney's office, he could hardly speak. Rodney sat him in his own leather office chair and poured him a black coffee but Woodford shook his head and waved it away. In a wheezing voice, the man – who seemed to be in his late sixties, or early seventies - asked Rodney about his fee.

'A guinea an hour plus expenses,' Rodney said, and expected some haggling – but Woodford nodded and produced a cheque book and a silver pen.

'I prefer cash, if that's possible Mr Woodford,' he said rather self-consciously, and Woodford rolled his eyes and put the cheque book back in his inside jacket pocket, then fidgeted with the pen. 'Look, Mr Dougal, let's see if you can even help me first,' Woodford said, still sounding breathless from the ascent of the steep steps. 'I want you to find out who my wife is seeing.'

Rodney pulled a rickety old stool to the other side of the desk, and as he sat he said, rather confidently: 'I can do that. I undertake that type of work quite a lot. Do you have a description of the man or a photograph of him?'

'It's a woman actually,' Woodford said from under a pair of heavy half-closed eyelids as he noted the young PI's reaction.

'Oh,' Rodney was taken by surprise, 'well the same procedure applies, erm – '

Woodford gave a little cough and clarified the situation. 'There's nothing romantic – or sexual, but I need to know why she is seeing this woman.'

'I see; well can you tell me a little about your wife and how long she's been seeing the lady concerned?'

Woodford took a deep breath, and then he alternated glances between the desktop and Rodney's intrigued face. He told the private investigator that he was 72 and his wife – his second wife, that is – was thirty-one, and that her name was Connie. He provided for her and she no longer worked as a waitress at a café in the popular Reece's Restaurant in Liverpool city centre. Mr Woodford was retired now but had made a fortune in the scrap metal business over almost fifty years. He had been married to Connie now for three years and he often let her loose with a cheque book to go and shop on Thursdays and Fridays, and on those days she had been seen with a red-haired woman in various pubs and some clubs when she decided to stay out late. When he had asked Connie who this woman was she had become very protective towards her, and had claimed that the woman was named Lili and that she was in her twenties but seemed much older in her ways. She was very well-spoken – and – well, that was all she would say. He had asked her if she was spending any money on this Lili and Connie had been angered by the question and said Lili was not a shallow materialist like him.

Mr Woodford thought there was more to this Lili than meets the eye, and on one occasion he had followed his wife – and Lili - to the Majestic Ballroom on Birkenhead's Conway Street one evening, but she had spotted him and reacted by calling him 'a suspicious old square.'

'That's where you come in', Mr Dougal, said Woodford, 'you can no doubt tail her – whatever you call it - without her knowing. I need you to somehow get close enough to overhear the conversations between Connie and this woman who's leading her astray. Can you do that?'

'Yes, Mr Woodford, I can do that. I'll need to know where she's going to be, if possible, and I will need a photograph of her, if you have one.'

Woodford nodded, and then he delved into his inside jacket pocket and produced a thick bulging brown leather wallet. I'll find one and get someone to drop it off, or you can come round to my place, I live in Woolton Hill.'

He paid twelve guineas up front, and Rodney visited him at his house at 3pm on the following day to obtain the photographs of Connie, and for a briefing as to where she'd be. As Rodney looked around the luxurious lounge, he noticed a few books on the Tarot and the supernatural, and asked if they were Connie's. Woodford nodded and replied, 'Aye, she's a sucker for all that claptrap. She says she's psychey or whatever you call it.'

'Psychic?' Rodney asked, and Woodford nodded and smiled.

The next morning at 11am found Rodney Dougal pretending to read a newspaper as he sat in Reece's Restaurant on Parker Street, off Church Street, in the centre of Liverpool. Before him on his table were the half-eaten remains of bacon on toast and a full cup of black coffee. A woodbine was smouldering in an ashtray and through the twisting wisps of blue smoke from the fag, Rodney was taking sly glances at the two women at a window table just twelve feet away. There was a real irritatingly loud chatterbox of a man seated behind Rodney, and the private detective was trying to filter his noise pollution out as he strained to hear the conversation between Connie and a very attractive red-haired woman in her twenties – possibly the mysterious Lili. Some five minutes into the surveillance, the gabby man behind Rodney suddenly got up and left, and now the dialogue at the table where Connie was seated was much clearer. They were talking about a train journey, but it was hard to get the gist of the conversation. As Rodney eavesdropped, he noted something trivial which struck him as odd but not inexplicable. The cup of tea and the assortment of biscuits which lay before the redhead were not touched by her once. Connie, on the other hand, was eating a plate of sandwiches and went through two cups of tea. In his little dog-eared notebook, Rodney made a rough sketch of the woman seated opposite Connie. She wore her red coppery hair in a sort of beehive reminiscent of Bardot, and although he saw her face mostly in profile, she had very pale skin, a long nose, a full mouth enhanced with cherry-coloured lipstick, black swept-back eyebrows and dark eyes with long curling eyelashes. She wore what looked like a cream-coloured plastic jacket featuring geometric squares, triangles and trapezoids, and this futuristic coat looked like something that the ultra-modern French fashion designer André Courrèges would have created. Below that impressive jacket, the unknown lady wore a yellow mini skirt and dark brown tights. Rodney put the folded broadsheet newspaper on the table and leaned forwards slightly in an attempt to hear the conversation, but the red-head with the beehive suddenly turned to face him and cast a suspicious look at him. She then leaned forward and whispered something into Connie's ear, and Connie also turned to look at the private detective.

Moments later the two women stood up, and

Rodney could see that the woman who was probably Lili, was quite tall – around 5 feet seven perhaps, although he couldn't see if she was wearing heels at this point. The women left the restaurant and Rodney felt they had somehow sussed him out, so he followed them at quite a distance. They walked up Church Street and turned left onto Ranelagh Street, where they crossed the road and went into one of the biggest and most impressive stores in Liverpool – Lewis's. Somehow, Rodney lost them in this store, and so he picked a vantage point outside Lewis's where he could keep watch on the three exits of the store, and this was the steps of the Adelphi Hotel, and after standing there and smoking six and a half cigarettes over the course of forty minutes, Connie emerged from Lewis's – on her own. She hailed a Hackney cab on Renshaw Street and Rodney had to do the same to tail her as the Ford Prefect he ran around town in was parked too far away to use in the pursuit. The taxi driver returned a bemused look via his rear-view mirror when Rodney told him to 'follow that cab'. It was a waste of time and taxi fare because Connie, it transpired, was headed to her home in Woolton Hill.

Rodney returned to his Duke Street office and sat tight, waiting for a call from his client, which came at 6.30pm.

'Well?' Woodford asked in a low voice, as if he was talking quietly because his wife was within earshot.

'I got a little bit of info on this Lili,' Rodney fibbed, 'but just want to check something with you; this Lili *does* have red hair?'

'Yeah,' Woodford said, his voice barely audible. 'I'll call you around eight, if that's alright.'

'Eight in the morning?' Rodney asked with dread, as he was a late riser.

'No, this evening. Can't talk now, know what I mean?' Woodford said, then hung up.

At 8.10pm the phone in the office jangled, startling Rodney from a light sleep. He turned down the music from Radio Caroline on the Dansette radio and answered the call.

'That Mr Dougal?' Woodford asked.

'Yeah,' Rodney replied, and he grabbed a pencil and looked fror a scrap of paper, but couldn't find any, nor could he find his notebook so he tore open an empty Woodbine box and got ready to jot down information.

'Well, what's the gen on Lili?' Woodford wanted to know, and as there was nothing to tell, Rodney cringed and said, 'Well, she has a few bob, the clobber she's wearing indicates that, but I'm in two minds at the moment as to whether she's blackmailing Connie.'

'Blackmail? Over what?' Woodford raised his voice and sounded very alarmed.

'Don't worry, Mr Woodford, that's just a possibility, but listen, I need to know where your wife's going next and when, and I'll bring a camera this time and some specialist gear I have.'

'Like what?' Woodford asked.

'Miniature tape recorders, maybe even a bugging device,' Rodney was on a roll this evening.

'A bugging what?'

'It's a little box, size of a matchbox it is, and it transmits even a whisper to a special radio,' Rodney explained.

'I think you've been watching too many James Bond films – is that necessary? Will that come at an extra cost?'

'No, no, it's still the same fee Mr Woodford,' Rodney assured his client.

'Well, listen, Connie told me she's going to meet an old schoolfriend at a pub in town tomorrow around eight, but she won't tell me which pub. She acted very suspicious when I asked her what boozer she was meeting this old friend at, and when I suggested going with her she threw a tantrum. I sometimes wonder why I'm with her, you know?'

'Well,' said Rodney, 'I'll have to wait in my car up by your place tomorrow evening and follow her. I assume she'll be getting a taxi into town, like?'

'Yeah, and listen mate, make sure she doesn't see you, because if she found out I had people shadowing her she'd go berserk – okay?'

'Don't worry Mr Woodford, she won't suspect a thing – I'm very discreet.'

'We'll have to meet up for a bevy some time, and you can tell me what you've found out and give me all the info on this Lili one.'

'Yes, Mr Woodford, that'd be ace.'

And so, on the following evening at 7.30pm, Rodney sat in his brother's Ford Prefect, about four hundred yards from the house of the Woodfords in leafy Woolton Hill. He was in a disguise. He wore a flat cap, a stubbly-looking moustache (made from rubbing newspaper print into the skin), and he also wore a pair of glasses, and a long mackintosh. At around ten minutes to eight, a Hackney cab pulled up outside the suburban house and Connie came down the path sporting a very short new hairstyle – the pixie cut. She also wore a black sleeveless top, a red mini skirt and knee-length boots. She waved to her husband and then opened the gate and entered the taxi. The cab drove off, and about fifteen seconds later the Ford Prefect's engine rumbled and the car moved off slowly down the road. Rodney could see the lone silhouette of Mr Woodford against the red curtains of his front room as he passed the huge house. The taxi Connie had hired took her to Lime Street Station, and so Rodney quickly parked up in a poorly lit Bolton Street and for a while he lost sight of Connie, and then he spotted her – walking with Lili from the station onto Skelhorne Street, heading in the direction of the city's most famous thoroughfares – Lime Street. Lili had on a stunning outfit and now her hair was not done up in a beehive but down and straight, the embodiment of chic sophistication. Rodney tried to disguise his youthful stride by limping and hunching over, as most people who don a disguise give themselves away by failing to alter their unconscious signature walking style and posture. Rodney followed at a distance of about fifty yards, but all of a sudden, Lili stopped and turned around to face him, and then Connie walked on for a bit, apparently unaware that her friend had stopped, and then she too halted and turned to see why her young friend had stopped.

Lili angled her face sideways but her large dark eyes were fixed on Rodney. He pretended he had no interest in the young lady and tried to walk past but, in a very well-spoken voice devoid of any accent, Lili said to him: 'Why are you following us, eh? What's your game?'

Rodney halted and shot a puzzled look at her, then looked over his left shoulder as if he thought she might be addressing someone behind him – but from the expression on her pallid face he could tell his play-acting was fooling no one.

Connie walked towards her friend and asked what she had just said to him.

'I asked him why he is following us around,' Lili replied. 'Yesterday he was sitting near our table in the café, trying to eavesdrop on our private conversation.

'I don't know what you're talking about,' said Rodney in a put-on voice which was some awful emulation of an indistinctive northern accent which even made him cringe.

'*Are* you folloing us?' Connie asked, squinting as she studied Rodney's face. She could now see that the moustache on the young man's face looked fake and like something that had been applied. Then, getting no answer from the private detective she asked, 'Did my husband hire you to follow us?'

'Oh I think you two have been drinkin',' Rodney said, feeling such a failure at blowing this lucrative job. He walked off.

'You *have* been hired by him, haven't you?' Connie shouted to Rodney's back but he kept on walking and he eventually turned a corner onto London Road, then walked back to his car on Bolton Street, livid at himself for being found out. Woodford would probably sack him now, he thought – and he was right. On the following morning the telephone rang at the Duke Street office and Woodford turned the line blue, calling Rodney an incompetent fool who was too young and inexperienced to be a private detective. He slammed the phone down as Rodney apologised.

'Ah, up yours, you old goat – she was far too young

for you anyway, cradle-snatcher!' Rodney told the telephone receiver as he banged it down onto the cradle. He lit his last cigarette and tilted his chair back against the noisy radiator as he contemplated a change of career for a few moments. He had always wanted to be a songwriter but this dream dissipated as quick as the smoke from his Woodbine.

And now for a rather strange supernatural twist to this story.

A year on, Rodney Dougal still took on cases as a private eye, but that job was now a part-time one, as he earned a more reliable wage from a new occupation, that of a Hackney cab driver. On this windy November night he was parked at the taxi rank outside the Liverpool Playhouse Theatre on Williamson Square (which has long been flagged over and pedestrianised) when two women in their mid-to-late twenties got into the back of the cab and asked to be taken to the Zodiac Club on Duke Street. They had just come from the Playhouse. One of the women, a petite pretty blonde, gave directions, but Rodney told her he knew the club well and added that he worked on that street in his other job.

'What job's that?' asked the blonde.

'Private eye,' Rodney couldn't help himself boasting but the blonde laughed and looked out the window of the cab as if she thought he was just joking.

Rodney, on quick reflection, thought he'd better keep the details of his other job quiet, as he didn't want a reputation as some police nark, and word of mouth via the customers travelled faster than light in this city. So there was the usual small talk from Rodney about the weather, and enquiries as to what teams the girls supported (neither followed football), and whether the play they'd seen at the Playhouse had been any good, etc. About ten minutes later the two ladies were dropped off at 28 Duke Street, location of the Zodiac Club, a place frequented by a clientele of the more sophisticated type than those raucous Cavern-dwellers of Mathew Street.

'Thankyou, bye,' said the blonde, paying the fare.

'Bye Rodney,' said the other girl in a well-spoken voice.

Rodney had not told the girls his name, so how had this other girl known who he was? He hadn't set eyes on her before. He tried to take a look at her from the nearside window but by then the girls were entering the club. It bothered him all night. How had she known his name?

A few months after this, Rodney was again at the taxi rank on Williamson Square one evening, when a girl in her twenties hailed him with a wave. She had just left the theatre, and when she got in the cab she told Rodney to take her to a house near Sefton Park. Her well-spoken voice sounded so familiar to Rodney, and he looked at her face in his rear view mirror and thought those dark eyes reminded him of someone – and then suddenly he realised that the passenger bore some resemblance to Lili, the lady who had seen through his disguise on Lime Street.

'That's right,' she said, and smiled. It was so eerie the way Lili seemed to know what he was thinking.

'Lili, isn't it?' Rodney said, turning to look at her.

'Keep your eye on the roads Rodney,' she advised him, and now the smile had evaporated from her face and she looked at him with a grave expression.

'Who *are* you? And how do you know my name?' Rodney asked her reflection in the rear-view mirror.

'Oh, I'm a woman of many parts,' Lili told him, 'I used to tread the boards long ago.'

Rodney raised his eyebrows. 'You used to act? Must have been when you were a kid then, you only look at about 25 at the most.'

'I'm a lot older than you think,' she said, and gave a smile that did not connect with those serious dark eyes.

'I'm not having that,' Rodney told her, glancing over his shoulder, but once again she told him to keep an eye on the road.

And all of a sudden when Rodney looked in the mirror – he saw that she now had that beehive hairdo he'd seen when he had first seen her at Reece's Restaurant. Seconds ago the girl's hair had bee straight and flat-looking, and so this instant change to another hairstyle really unnerved him. 'How did you do that?'

Now Lili's face changed. She looked like a girl of about fifteen.

Rodney didn't even realise he was stopping the cab. The brakes went on, he lurched forward, having no seatbelt on. He put on the handbrake and turned fully in the seat to get a proper look at this quick-change artist – but the back of the cab was empty. Rodney got out the taxi and looked at the back seats, somehow unsure as to whether the girl had collapsed and fallen on the floor of the vehicle, but there wasn't a trace of her to be seen.

With the stark realisation closing in on him that Lili was some ghost, Rodney literally felt the hairs on the back of his neck stand up. He was so badly shaken by the experience he returned his cab to the taxi company and said he was finished for the evening because he felt ill. He got the bus home to his flat in Wavertree (because his brother had at last claimed back the Ford Prefect), and he had the creepy feeling that Lili had followed him, although nothing spooky happened that night. Rodney's mum said he had been seeing things, and that he had been overworking, and his father tried to explain away the ghost by suggesting that Rodney had had an open-eye dream – he had been so tired he had experienced a type of dream while still awake.

Rodney knew these explanations were ridiculous, but he never went on duty on the Williamson Square taxi rank after that, just in case the ghost hailed him again. He thought of what Lili had said about treading the boards, and wondered if she had been the ghost of some deceased actress. She had certainly seemed too real to be a ghost – at least the ghosts he had imagined, for he had always pictured ghosts as being semi-transparent things in chains. Now it made sense – that time when he had kept watch on her in the restaurant – she had not touched the tea or the biscuits – *ghosts can't eat…*

Some five years after this, Rodney had given up the taxi job, but had remained in the private eye business, and now had a decent office with a typewriter, filing cabinets, telephone and fax machine – and he had a Jag – it was six years old but it looked impressive and had given him no trouble whatsoever, so far. Moreover, the cases he was receiving were becoming quite regular (and actually interesting) and he was even able to put a few bob away for the first time in his life.

Then one sunny morning he received a query from a

Mr Reed, asking Rodney if he had worked in the area of commercial and corporate theft. Without fully comprehending what Mr Reed was asking about, Rodney answered in the affirmative and then added: 'I deal with many aspects of the private investigation business.'

'When can I see you to discuss this matter further?' Reed asked.

Rodney checked his diary and said: 'Tomorrow lunchtime? Say about one?'

'Excellent,' Mr Reed sounded enthusiastic. 'Shall I come to see you or should we meet somewhere less formal and have a spot of lunch perhaps?'

Forever the freeloader, Rodney said: 'That arrangement suits me fine Mr Reed, where shall we meet?'

On the following day Rodney met Mr Reed at Coopers Restaurant on the corner of Paradise Street and Church Street, and the case seemed straightforward enough. Mr Reed was the senior manager of one of Liverpool's largest and most famous retail stores, and someone was removing large sums of cash – over a thousand pound on some occasions – from the company safe. It had to be someone who worked in the higher echelons of management who knew exactly when the weekly takings were deposited in the safe and – of course – knew the combination. Mr Reed kept his suspicions to himself because he had no proof it was someone working on the inside, but there were no signs of any break-ins in the office in the store and no signs of violence upon the safe. Reed was originally going to call in the police immediately but thought he'd try a private detective first. Reed showed Rodney the layout of the office and the position of the safe, and Rodney immediately suggested a way he might catch the culprit red-handed. The robber almost always struck on a Thursday night when a cash deposit from the week was placed in the safe, so Rodney said he would lay in wait in a small cloakroom (which was more of a large cupboard) and listen out all night for the thief's arrival. Rodney arrived at the office on the Wednesday, disguised as a decorator who was supposedly going to paint the skirting boards and doors of the office, and when he stayed on at the office after most had left, it was understood that he would also be leaving about 6pm – but instead, of course, Rodney hid in the cloakroom with a long-lasting Ever Ready lantern torch, a thermos flask of coffee, and a few magazines to read during a possible long stretch of time.

At 7.45pm that night, as Rodney sat on a bench, reading by the light of the lantern in the cloakroom, he clearly heard a noise outside. He peeped out and caught a young man named Charles, an apprentice manager at the store, opening the safe.

'Excuse me,' said Rodney, and the young man spun round with a look of utter horrified surprise upon his face.

'What are you doing here?' Charles said, and a nervous tic played upon his face, 'You're the damned painter – what are you doing in this office this time of night?'

'Mr Reed hired me, mate, and I'm making a citizen's arrest,' Rodney said with great satisfaction.

Charles broke down and started to cry. He said he had met a girl and needed the money for cars, clothes and holidays.

'Save it for the judge, pal,' Rodney told him and he went to the telephone and dialled Mr Reed, but Charles suddenly turned nasty and picked up a chair. He raised the chair, ready to smash it over the private detective's head, but Rodney rushed forward and punched him hard in the solar plexus, winding him. Reed was contacted, and he arrived about twenty minutes later. He told Rodney he wasn't going to press charges or take the matter further, but he did tell Charles if any further thefts took place he'd go straight to the police. Reed explained to Rodney that Charles was 'a good kid and a hard worker' but he wouldn't last a minute in prison. Rodney had the impression that Charles had something on Mr Reed, and that something was the real reason for the insane leniency. Rodney received £500 for his work, and he was also offered a post as the store detective – which he accepted. On his second week at the major store, Rodney was wandering the perfume section on the ground floor when he saw *her* again – Lili, only this time she looked as if she'd had a facelift. She looked younger this time – in her early twenties, and she wore her hair – which was now blonde – in pigtails. Under a black jacket she had on a plain white shirt, and the royal-blue blue pleated dress and white ankle socks made her look like a schoolgirl. Although Rodney was in the midst of so many shoppers and staff he still felt a little afraid of the ghost. She looked so real, so solid, but he did notice that she had not touched anything in the store. She toured the perfume counters and when the woman on the Chanel counter asked her to try a dab of the perfume on her wrist, Lili declined. Rodney his behind a lipstick stand that was being rotated by a young lady who regarded the store detective with suspicious eyes, so he moved away and went around the long counter and took another look at the ghost from this second vantage point. What was her game? He wondered. He watched the entity for about fifteen minutes, and then she was gone. One moment she was standing there, and then - nothing. On three more occasions Rodney saw Lili appear in the store, and on two of those occasions others had seen her too, and on those three times when she had walked the store she had been slightly different – sometimes with her hair blonde and done up in a beehive, or red long and straight, or dark with masses of curls, and yet it was unmistakably Lili. Then the visitations stopped and two years on, Rodney was in a club in town one night. He'd had a little too much to drink – and he took to the dance floor and was rejected by a few of the girls who were a lot younger than him, but one girl danced with him, and it was hard to tell what colour hair she had because she, and most of the dancers, were bathed in red or yellow light. This girl danced so seductively and when Rodney tried to get hold of her she would throw her head back and laugh as she evaded his grasp with amazing agility. Her skirt was the shortest he had ever seen on any girl, even in the Swinging Sixties, and she was quite leggy. After the clubgoers poured out onto the backstreets, Rodney staggered along, singing to himself and blundering into other drunken people heading for home or a party – and he heard a female voice cry out: 'Hey, you!'

He turned and saw it was the incredibly attractive girl he'd danced with earlier. By the light of the lamp posts he could see her hair was a mousy brown and her eyes were big and dark. She was about 5 foot seven, and that was in flat shoes.

'You want to go to a party?' she asked Rodney, and then looked back at a gaggle of young men and girls standing on the corner.

'Yeah, course I friggin' do! As long as you're going too, love,' was Rodney's slurred answer. He couldn't believe his luck, and yet the analytical and streetwise centres of his private detective brain told him through the alcoholic haze that this was too good to be true. He staggered after the girl and asked her what her name was, and the girl said 'Jennifer,' then asked him to hurry up as she turned away and headed towards the group on the corner.

'Jennifer, eh?' Rodney grinned, and the street seemed to be pitching and rolling like the deck of a ship. He began to sing the Donovan song *Jennifer Juniper* as he followed the stunning girl.

And then, out of the depths of his mind came a recollection to sober him up. The face of Lili. He realised with a shudder that the girl leading him towards the gang on the corner was that ghost in her latest incarnation. The dark eyes had given her away. The eyes hadn't changed.

'Arrgh!' Rodney tripped and fell hard, palms down in the middle of the road, and two passing lads cheered. The gang "Jennifer" had been making her away towards came running down the street, and one of them, a man of about 22 years of age with long blond hair and a Sergeant Pepper moustache, said, 'You okay old chap?'

Rodney looked up and saw the gang of about 6 girls

and four young men gathering around him. He tried to warn them.

'She's a ghost!' he said from the gutter, and pointed a sprained finger at a poker-faced Lili.

The group just giggled and looked down at him, but the young man who had come to Rodney's aid crouched by him and said, 'Pardon?'

Rodney slowly hauled himself off the floor. 'She's a ghost! Her, there! Calls herself Jennifer now, but her name's Lili!'

'Why are you so prejudiced about ghosts?' the young man asked with a mischievous smirk, and all of the friends gathered behind him laughed.

'I'm serious you stupid bastard,' Rodney told them. 'She's a ghost! Look, she isn't denying it. You should be in a grave somewhere or in Hell, probably!' He told Lily, and she still didn't react.

'Now now, old chap, there's no need for that,' said the young man, and he beckoned for Lili as he rejoined the gang.

As Rodney looked on, Lili went among the group and they all walked off up the street – and then, they all *faded away* as he watched. Only then did the realisation hit him. They had all been ghosts – the six girls and four lads – all spirits. Rodney found himself running towards Stanley Street, where he hailed a taxi to take him home.

The ghost he calls Lili is still being seen today, in her many guises, and time after time I have heard about her. She has even been seen mixing with the living down in the Liverpool One shopping complex recently, and I have built up an identikit type of picture of her over the years, based on all the descriptions of her. At first, I and many other ghost investigators didn't realise that the many reports of this entity were all one and the same 'person'; we thought that different ghosts haunting different places in the city were responsible for the reports, but gradually I realised Lili was a rarity in the supernatural world – the ghost that gets around - as most ghosts are obsessive compulsive haunters who frequent one place. Who is Lili? Well I have a theory, that she was once an actress – possibly at the Liverpool Playhouse – for she has been seen in this theatre and the square it overlooks – Williamson Square – many times. I dug deep within the records and archives of many theatres and found an old monochrome photograph of one Lilian Braithwaite – a beautiful actress of stage and screen who came into this world in 1873 and exited the stage of life in 1948, but perhaps she has returned from the wings to play other roles. Lilian was tour de force on stage and worked with Noël Coward and even Hitchcock. She was a regular at the Liverpool Playhouse and loved that well-respected venue. I can't help thinking that somehow, she has returned from beyond the grave to take on the mantle of other characters. When I showed the photograph of Lilian to Rodney Dougal he recoiled in fright and stated that, without a doubt, it was the ghost he had encountered several times. That photograph was mixed up with other pictures of actresses of bygone days, yet Rodney singled her out.

Many years ago an elderly man assured me he would return as a ghost after death because each day he performed certain mental exercises – a type of meditation – to strengthen his will, as he was of the opinion that most people, being weak-willed, have a hard time persisting after bodily death; finding they have no physical body, the newly-deceased try to utilise their mind to continue their existence, and find their will sadly lacking - and so they fade away into nothingness. True to his word, that old man, within weeks of his death, was seen haunting his old home. That is *one* of the ways to cheat death – any Christian will tell you that if you truly believe in Jesus Christ, you will inherit Eternal Life - but others have entered into bargains with the Devil for immortality, although I can't see Lilian resorting to something like that. I think her very love of life and drama was so strong, she refused to let the curtain come down when her time in the limelight was done – and now she continues to roam the realm of the living in the ongoing theatre of life, and who knows - perhaps *you* will see her yourself if you haven't done so already!

AN EVIL ROYAL RAPIST

In January 1976, 32-year-old Roy Hargreaves left Liverpool and went to find work down in London. He stayed in the spare room of his cousin Gerry's terraced house in Lambeth, and he wasn't there long when he started to moan about the lack of well-paid jobs. 'No openings for a decent wage,' Roy complained, reading the situations vacant page of the local newspaper, 'just low-skilled work. They want all these A Levels and university qualifications for the big money jobs. I've got experience, but that counts for nowt nowadays – just silly certificates.'

'Just what type of job were you hoping to get, Roy?' Gerry asked, tiring of his cousin's continual pickiness concerning the labour market. Gerry had a full house on his hands, a four-bedroom terraced house with two children and a pregnant wife to look after, and his father was also due to stay over soon because his wife (Gerry's stepmother) was ill in hospital. Roy was going to have to give up the spare room soon and sleep on the sofa – unless he found work and a flat somewhere. Gerry had a word with his neighbour, an Irishman named Dave who worked as a foreman on a building site, and Dave got Roy a start on a site in the city as a labourer, and Roy hated the job at first – the early starts and the fact he had to use his hands and take orders when he thought such work was below him. Eventually though, he put enough of his wages away to start looking for a flat. He perused the Rentals column of *The Times* - which amused his cousin Gerry. 'You really have an over-inflated opinion of yourself Roy,' he said, sitting besides him on the sofa with a can of lager in his hand. 'First you expected to get a job as the bleedin' Chancellor of the Exchequer or something, and now you're probably looking for a town house in Belgravia.'

'I don't belong to your class, Gerry,' Roy said in a very earnest manner, 'I want to rise above all of the working class cradle-to-grave routines we've been brainwashed into since the day we were born. Why shouldn't I live in Belgravia – or Mayfair?'

'Cos you're skint that's why son, so stop dreaming,' Gerry told him, and swigged hard from the can.

Roy went quiet, and Gerry thought he was sulking at first, but then he saw that something had caught his hyper-optimistic cousin's eye.

'There's a flat going here, to share with another person like, and it's in Mayfair, and its eight quid-odd per week,' said Roy.

'Nah, that must be a misprint, matey,' Gerry tried to burst his bubble. 'you couldn't get a flat that cheap in Mayfair without a catch.'

Roy read the ad under the column titled: 'Flat Sharing': 'Mayfair, W1. Superior unfurnished two-bedroom flat, 1 study, modern tiled bathroom, living room with east and west facing windows, modern kitchen. Would suit two professionals, £8.75 pp pw. Contact Charles Abbey-Knight Tel: 01-499…'

'Oh there you go then!' Gerry laughed, and burped.

'Two *professionals* - not labourers. No hod-carriers need apply.'

Roy found a pen and circled the ad. 'Well, I'm applying anyway,' he assured his off-putting cousin, 'and it's got a study – I've always wanted a study. I'll get a writing bureau for it.'

'Listen mate,' Gerry dug his index finger into Roy's forearm, 'if you read between the lines, does the fellah who put that ad in mean two professional *birds*? Because if he does you know what that means don't you?'

'I don't get you?' Roy said, innocently.

'Prostitutes mate, that's what he's looking for. He probably a pimp,' Gerry said, then swigged more lager.

Right there and then, Roy put on his coat and left the house with the newspaper. He went to the nearest public telephone box and called Mr Charles Abbey-Knight. After four rings a well-spoken man who sounded like the actor Terry Thomas answered, and Roy tried to speak in an articulate and affected voice, emphasising the H's and over-pronouncing every 'ing'. 'Hello, I am enquiring about the Mayfair flat that you have advertised.'

'Ah yes, when would you like to view it?' Mr Abbey-Knight asked.

'As soon as possible, really,' Roy told him.

'Tomorrow, say 4.30pm?'

'Yes, where about is it?' Roy knew he'd forgotten something – a scrap of paper and a pen to jot down the address. He'd have to rely on his memory.

Mr Abbey-Knight gave an address just a stone's throw from Montagu Square, Marylebone – not Mayfair as the advert had said, but not being familiar with London, Roy didn't notice this.

'And your name is?'

'Roy. Roy Hargreaves.'

'There's a lady viewing it at the same time tomorrow, and she might be your future flatmate. She's an artist, I believe.'

'Oh, splendid,' Roy said, and cringed at the voice he was putting on.

'Bye Mr Hargreaves.'

Roy arrived at the address ten minutes late, because he'd had to go home and change after knocking off early on the building site in Hammersmith, but luckily, Mr Abbey-Knight turned up at 4.25pm, and a minute later the prospective female tenant – a willowy blonde in her early twenties named Calli (short for Calliope)Bates – arrived on her scooter. Mr Abbey-Knight apologised for being late and blamed a traffic jam, and then he pointed up to the windows of the flat, and one of Calli's eyebrows dipped with scepticism mingled with disappointment. The curtains looked dusty and the window panes looked as if they were caked and blackened with dust. 'Looks like its been empty for some time,' she said, taking off her helmet.

'Yes, it does, doesn't it?' Roy said in his silly affectation of a upper-class voice.

The interior of the flat was dark, cold, cobwebbed and a musky smell pervaded the place. 'This is the study, oak-panelled as you can see,' Abbey-Knight waved his hand in a semi-circle and Roy's heart somersaulted – just the type of study he'd always wanted, but Calli smiled and said: 'Oh, just the place to set my easel up.'

'And through here, you will be pleasantly surprised by the spacious living room. We removed the carpet to reveal the original wooden floor which dates back to the Regency period. And look at the views – '

'What's that?' Calli nodded at the huge rectangular square mirror with the faded golden frame. It was ridiculously large with one end on the floor and the other almost touching the high ceiling.

'A mirror,' Mr Abbey-Knight replied. 'It makes the room seem more spacious.'

'It's absurdly too big,' Calli said, gazing at herself in the oversized looking glass. 'Someone vain must have lived here.'

The bedroom windowsills were dotted with dried dead flies. Calli said she would only take up the residency if the place was cleaned first.

'I'd clean it, Miss,' Roy volunteered, but Calli shook her head and said: 'No, I mean professional cleaners. This place is like a health hazard. No wonder the rent's so low.'

'We'll have it cleaned, don't worry. We wouldn't expect you two to move in with the place like this,' Abbey-Knight said with a forced chuckle. 'So, are you otherwise happy with it?'

Calli and Roy talked for quite a while. She knew nothing about him and he knew nothing about her. She asked him if he was married, had he a criminal record, was he a loud snorer, and she also enquired about his occupation. He told her he was in the construction industry, but neglected to mention he was a labourer. They both signed the tenancy agreement and then Mr Abbey-Knight took a £50 deposit from each of them – and told them the flat would be ready in four days. Calli asked for a loan from her father, a broker in the City, then went to the Portobello Road Market with her friend Suzi and bought a few rugs, a huge old rattan and bamboo peacock chair, a vintage 1950s Grant Barnett automatic umbrella, a lava lamp, a Hamadan Persian carpet, a grandfather clock, an allegedly genuine West African tribal mask, an Indian coffee table and some polka dot patterned beanbags. Roy, meanwhile, bought a cheap double bed and purple polyester bed sheets with orange pillows, and an equally tasteless teak-effect dining table with fold-down flaps, as well as three characterless white dining chairs with an almost plastic finish to them. Calli, being a Bohemian, was not at all impressed with Roy's choice of tacky furniture. She got her brother to string a hammock up in her room and planned to paint a mural of abstract shapes on one of the walls of the living room. She duly claimed the study as her Art Room and when Roy objected she asked him what exactly he wanted a study for anyway and he was lost for an answer.

Calli asked him if he was asthmatic and when Roy said he wasn't she proceeded to light joss sticks in the living room to rid the place of the musky smell that was still hanging in the air. It took about a week for the two tenants to move fully into the Marylebone flat, and Calli's friend, Suzi spent a lot of time there. One evening the two young ladies and Roy shared a bottle of expensive wine, given to Calli by her father. Three glasses into this wine, Calli suddenly told Roy: 'Oh by the way, Roy, I'd never go out with someone like you – you're totally into the Rat Race and normality.'

Suzi went red and didn't know where to look.

'Well, it's a good job I have no intentions of asking you out then, isn't it?' Roy retorted, and he swigged back the wine, pretending not to be hurt by the wine-fuelled remark, clunked the glass down on the Indian coffee table, and went off to his bedroom. He dozed off on the bed reading a Sven Hassel war novel, and awoke around 1.20am. He could hear Calli and Suzi still talking in the living room, but couldn't make out what they were talking about. He reached out and switched off the bedside lamp, then fell fast asleep without even taking off his jeans and tee shirt.

He was then roused from his cherished sleep by someone shaking his forearm. He opened his eyes, rubbed them, and heard Calli's voice.

'Roy! Roy, wake up!'

He opened his bleary film-coated eyes wide then squeezed them shut, then opened one eye and saw Calli's outline silhouetted against the light coming from the landing into his room. She stood at the side of the bed. 'Roy, there's something funny going on in the living room.'

'What time is it?' he turned and looked at the luminous pale green numbers and hands of the bedside clock. It was just after three in the morning and he had to be out for half-past six.

'Roy, come and have a listen,' Calli said with great urgency in her voice, and she walked to the bedroom doorway and looked along the short landing to the living room.

Roy dragged himself out the bed and went to her. 'What? I've got to get up in a few hours.'

'There are really weird voices in the living room, like people singing a hymn,' she whispered.

'Let's have a listen,' he said, heading down the landing. 'Probably someone having a party somewhere.'

'It's like no party I've ever been to,' Calli told him, staying well behind Roy.

And she was right. When they entered the living room, which was lit by a lava lamp. He listened; the echoing sounds of people chanting and singing in what sounded like Latin, could definitely be heard. Roy opened the window and listened. Perhaps the singing was coming from one of the houses over on Montagu Square. But no, the sounds seemed to be coming from within the building the flat was in. 'The two people in the flats below us are in their seventies; can't see them having a shindig at this time in the morning.'

'It started about half-past two, about ten minutes after Suzi went home,' said Calli.

Roy switched on the main light in the room, and curiously, the singing stopped immediately.

'They've stopped,' Calli's eyes suddenly turned towards that large rectangular mirror.

'What are you looking at?' Roy asked; Calli's glances at the looking glass made him nervous. He wasn't normally the type who gave any thought to the supernatural and the unknown, but there seemed to be something weird hanging in the air at this time in the morning.

'Could that be a one-way mirror or whatever you call them?' Calli wondered out loud.

'Eh?' Roy yawned and thought of going back to bed now that the singing had stopped.

'That mirror,' Calli turned now to Roy with suspicion in her eyes. 'Could there be someone behind it watching us?'

Roy lifted his face and looked at the mirror. 'Let's see, behind that mirror would be the hot water boiler, so no, no one could be behind it.'

'I'm almost certain those voices came from that mirror,' Calli said in almost a whispering voice.

'I'm going to bed, I'm knackered,' Roy announced, and he walked out the living room and down the landing.

'Roy,' Calli hurried after him. 'Can I sleep with you tonight?'

'I thought you said I wasn't your type?'

'I just mean sleep as in get shut-eye, not sleep in the slang sense,' she told him, matter-of-factly.

'Calli, you're not a kid, and there are no such things as ghosts,' Roy told her, disappointed deep down that she didn't want to sleep with him in the sense he imagined.

'You won't even know I'm there,' she promised. 'This has really scared me, I'll never get to sleep in my hammock.'

'Alright, go and make yourself comfortable, I'm just going the toilet,' he said, and then as he walked off he hesitated and asked: 'Unless you'd like to come with me?'

'Hurry up!' said Calli, impatiently, and she went into his bedroom and switched on the bedside lamp. She never undressed, but slept in a white tee shirt and a pair of jeans she'd cut into shorts.

Roy appeared a few minutes later – in his Y-fronts, but before he even reached the bed, Calli said: 'Get your jeans back on.' Just her face was visible over the edge of the blanket.

'This is ridiculous,' Roy went back into the bathroom and grabbed the jeans he'd left on the door hook.

It was strange having a female beside him in the bed – not cuddling, but laying beside him, and when he took a sly glance, he could see Calli's face in a silhouetted profile, and her eyelashes were flickering, because her eyes were wide open and Roy could guess that she was listening out for the spooky singers.

'Go to sleep. Night.' Roy turned away from her so he faced the window, and closed his eyes.

'I will soon. Night.' Calli exhaled and closed her eyes.

When she woke, Roy was gone, and she sat up in bed and saw that it was just getting light. She went into the living room and opened the curtains, then switched on the main light and the lava lamp. And then she clicked on an old transistor radio for company. An hour later a letter landed on the doormat. It was from a primary school where she had applied for the post as an art teacher; the headmaster wanted to interview her next week. This promise of a job alleviated her nervousness and by 11am, sunlight was shining into the room, exorcising all of the fears the night had brought.

Calli called on Suzi and they went window shopping and stopped off at a café and Calli told her friend about the weird singers she'd heard. Suzi offered the usual explanation about sound playing strange tricks at night when the acoustical properties of the world change, and even the ticking of two clocks can merge and conspire to create an auditory hallucination. But Calli said the voices she and Roy had heard had not been hallucinations, but apparently something from the sphere of the supernatural. Calli didn't dare admit to sleeping with Roy because she'd been scared, or Suzi would have fallen off her chair laughing.

At 11pm that night, Calli cooked Roy a curry supper, which he really seemed to enjoy, and afterwards he enjoyed some delicious ice-cold and potent German beer served to him in a huge ornamental ceramic tankard with a lid that Calli had bought as a souvenir in Stratford-upon-Avon.

'That's custy beer,' Roy savoured the taste with closed eyes as it ran down his throat. 'Who makes it?'

'Krombacher,' Calli grinned at the orgasmic expression on her flatmate's face as he drank the beverage. 'Got it from my dad's cellar. He has crates of the stuff.'

Calli had a few glasses of Cabernet Sauvignon and sat watching the new colour telly Roy had brought home, but mindful of the elderly neighbours in the flats below, the volume on the set was turned down low.

'One of the things I like about you is that you don't pry,' Calli suddenly said to Roy, who was now tearing into the garlic bread.

'Oh,' was all he managed to react with.

Calli smiled, noting how he was more interested in his food and drink. She liked that caveman honesty somehow. 'You've never asked me if I had a boyfriend or if I had a girlfriend for that matter, or asked me to give you a potted history about my life.'

'Well, it's the way I was brought up in Liverpool. Manners, like.' Roy mopped the dish up with the garlic bread. 'That was really nice and very, very hot. What's it called?'

'Vindaloo of course, with a few variations. Glad you

liked it.'

'You're a good cook,' Roy complimented her and gulped down some more Krombacher from the tankard.

She talked about the job interview at the school and he talked about his ambition to get away from building sites to do something more 'cerebral' with his life, and Calli giggled at that choice of word.

Next thing the grandfather clock she had bought at the Portobello market was striking the hour of one, and Roy said he was feeling really tired.

'So, you going to bed now?' she asked, and took the plates into the kitchen.

'Yeah, leave them – I'll wash up tomorrow,' Roy told her, taking the plates out of her hand and putting them back on the kitsch teak-effect dining table. 'Are you sleeping in your own bed tonight?'

'Yeah, I think I'll be okay,' Calli said, gazing up into his eyes. 'Let's not even talk about the things we heard last night.'

'Well, Calli,' Roy said, and she grinned when she saw that he was swaying. The Krombacher beer had gone to his head.

'Yeah?' she had to bite her lip slightly to stop herself laughing.

'I really enjoyed our supper tonight and that beer – '
'Oh thanks – Roy.'
'And I was thinking, maybe one night soon I could repay you by taking you to the pictures, and then maybe to a restaurant – '

She couldn't help herself, and had to bury her face in her palms as she stifled a grin.

'I'm serious, and erm, I'm – '

'Drunk, Roy; go to bed.'

Roy closed his sleepy, heavy lids and nodded as he smiled, then went to the toilet as Calli picked up the plates again. She washed them to take her mind off the possibility of a repeat performance by the unearthly singers.

Roy had strange dreams of being on a ship during a storm, and he awoke with the blazing light of a full moon in his eyes, shining through the net curtains, It was ten minutes past three in the morning, and the entire room was ever so slowly tilting to the right. 'That German beer!' he cursed into his pillow as he pressed his face down. He burped and tasted the hydrochloric burn on the back of his tongue mingled with pork vindaloo. He got up and the room really spun for a moment. He went to the toilet and almost fell asleep as he sat there. He got to his feet, pulled the chain, and as he dozily washed his hands he thought he heard something. He turned off the tap and rubbed his hands silently in the towel. There was definitely a strange noise, and it was coming from the living room – as if Calli had the telly on – but there were no TV broadcasts this time in the morning.

He walked along the landing and pushed open the living room door. The curtains were wide open and the silvered light of the full moon was lighting up the living room. There was something whitish to his left, and he turned to see what it was.

Calli was standing there, naked – before the mirror, and the unearthly chanting Roy had heard the night before assailed his ears now that he was in the living room. Calli had her eyes open but seemed to be in some trance.

'Calli?' Roy moved forward, wondering what on earth was going on – when suddenly, he happened to glance into the mirror. There was a group of men – about seven was Roy's initial quick estimate, and most of them were wearing curly white wigs and dark green silky long coats with white stockings to the knees and buckled shoes – but in the middle of these outdated figures, there stood a naked man with a huge erect phallus which looked as if it belonged to some animal rather than a human, such was its size and thickness. This nude man had on a magnificent gold crown topped with an orb and cross pattée with fleur-de-lis around a base that was also spangled with fiery precious stones of ruby and emerald. Within the crown there was a cap of dark, possibly purple velvet, and beneath this an ermine border rested on a mass of black curly hair that went down to the man's chest. This vulgar figure also wore a voluminous scarlet cloak edged with white ermine. The face of the weird crowned pervert was partially hidden behind a black mask of the type Roy associated with the Lone Ranger. The stranger also sported a thin black moustache.

'Calli!' Roy seized the shoulders of the naked girl, but she felt as immovable as a statue. The naked man in the crown thrust out his arms and his hands actually emerged from the mirror - reaching towards Calli. All of a sudden, the chanting became quite loud, and Roy could see that the six men behind the bizarre nude now had their mouths wide open and were singing at the top of their voices. It sounded like some Latin hymn. One of those singing men looked exactly like the landlord who had rented the flat to Roy and Calli – Mr Abbey-Knight, only he had a long curly white wig on of the type you'd associate with judges in this day and age. The whole thing was like a bad nightmare, and Roy kept hoping that it would all turn out be a dream which would end at any moment. He seized Calli again by the shoulders, and this time he gritted his teeth and dragged her away from the reach of the naked apparition coming out of the mirror, and she fell, limp into his arms. He ran out of the room with her and accidentally caught her head on the doorframe as he did. 'Oh!' he said, when he heard the noise of her head striking the frame, and he took her to his bed, laid her down and covered her naked body with a blanket. He went back down the landing, and although he was afraid, he wondered if the naked crowned fiend had somehow left that mirror in the living room. It had, and the nude regal-looking deviant looked terrifying now. His eyeballs had turned black, and a long black tongue shot out of his mouth and writhed like a tortured snake. The six men in outdated clothes appeared behind him and their faces were twisted with fury, as if they were incensed at Roy taking their prey away from them. Roy swore out of nerves and he looked about for something to strike out with. He noticed the vintage automatic umbrella lying in a corner of the landing, and well, they say a drowning man will clutch a straw in a fruitless bid to save himself; Roy had nothing else to protect himself with, so he swiftly picked up the umbrella and lunged forward with its point, expecting the obscene and inhuman thing before him to step back, but instead the entity hissed as the reptilian tongue whipped about and lengthened. Roy swore - again, out of electrified fear, and he thrust the brolly's pointed tip as if it was a bayonet, and he felt its seven-inch metal tip penetrate the chest of the evil-looking man, who now let out a wheezing sound. From the deep wound near to the left nipple of the bizarre-looking man, fluid which looked like black ink trickled down his chest and torso to his groin, where it dripped from his testicles.

'Bastard!' Roy lunged forward again, and this time he felt some bone break as the point went through the skin and muscle of the chest. More dark inky liquid issued forth, and this time the naked figure backed into the six figures and its eyelids flickered over the ebony eyeballs.

There was an ear-piercing scream behind Roy, and he turned quickly to see Calli standing in the doorway of his bedroom with a blanket around her. She was looking at the surreal and frightening scene with bulging eyes.

'Get out of here!' Roy warned her and looked at the door leading to the stairs of the house, and Calli did as he said, and left the door open. Roy hurled the umbrella at the supernatural visitor and then turned and ran after Calli.

They made it into the street, where two policemen in a patrol car picked them up and asked them what they were doing. In nothing but his y-fronts, Roy told them about the crowned would-be rapist from the mirror, then realised how far-fetched it would seem to the officers, and he became quiet. 'He's telling the truth!'

Calli told the highly-sceptical policemen and kept looking up at the window of the flat.

'Look, if you Loony Tunes don't go back to where you came from right now, I'll nick the two of you,' one of the policemen warned with a stern look.

'Okay sir, understood,' Roy said and tried to pull Calli along with him as he went back to the door of the house. 'There's a thing up there – ' Calli struggled to label the men from the mirror, but Roy shouted: 'Calli! Come on!'

She reluctantly walked with him to the door and the patrol car continued on its way. In the hallway, Roy noticed the four bruises on Calli's shoulders where he had tried to pull her from the mirror. The girl bruised easily. She started to cry and begged him not to go up the stairs. They waited and waited, both of them sitting on the stairs, listening, dreading the approach of the demonic man and his cohorts, but it was deadly silent up there. As Calli cried and pleaded for him to come back, Roy went upstairs to the flat and looked around. There wasn't a soul about. He returned to tell Calli the coast was clear, and she quickly got dressed and swore she was going to leave at first light. She went out with Roy to a telephone box and called her father and told him to come and pick her and Roy up. Calli and Roy then lived together in their father's Chelsea flat for a while, until they could get enough money to get a flat of their own, and this they finally did six months later. They became a couple, and although they never married, they had three children and now live in Bath. Roy contacted the landlord of the flat and told him what happened, and how one of the 'ghosts' in the mirror had strongly resembled him, but Mr Abbey-Knight merely said, 'How peculiar. Someone must have spiked you with LSD.'

I have been to the flat in Marylebone, and it appears that the large rectangular mirror has been removed. What became of it is not known, and there have been no further paranormal incidents at the place. I appealed for information about the previous occupiers of the flat and was told that, in the 1960s, there were rumours that several people – including MPs and even members of the aristocracy – had held orgies in that flat, when London – and the rest of Western civilization for that matter - was in the grip of a supernatural renaissance thanks to the rise of the drugs and occult-fuelled counterculture. There was even a claim that rock legend Jim Morrison of the doors visited the flat to see the strange mirror in September 1968 after his band The Doors had ended their European tour. Morrison, undoubtedly a shaman and a man with an insatiable appetite of all things metaphysical, was said to have met John Lennon around this time while The Beatles were at Abbey Road recording the so-called 'White Album'.

And who was the man in the mirror? Well, from the description of the crown, the ermine robes, and the long black curly hair, it's possible that it was the unholy ghost of King Charles II. Again and again I have heard of a very similar figure appearing at Black Masses held in certain venues in London – some of them in houses in the most affluent up-market areas of the City, and a few credible occultists have told me that occasionally, the infernal form of Charles II appears during a Black Mass. Charles II was a man who had dabbled in Satanic orgies that began as masked balls, had fathered 13 bastards from countless mistresses (besides the most well-known one Nell Gwyn), and not only did he have a voracious sexual appetite, he was said to have been incredibly endowed and after holding many Black Masses, his penis underwent a strange transformation whereby it grew and became scaly, and after the monarch died unexpectedly (some say from a witch's curse) he was entombed in Westminster Abbey with a strange graven idol hidden among his shroud. The little statue was thought to be Priapos, an ancient Greek god of fertility, because it featured an oversized penis, but this figurine sported horns, and is thought to have represented Baal – one of the seven princes of Hell…

CPSIA information can be obtained
at www.ICGtesting.com
Printed in the USA
LVOW04s1928301116
515174LV00018B/598/P